LAZY BASTARDISM

LAZY BASTARDISM

ESSAYS & REVIEWS ON
CONTEMPORARY POETRY

Carmine Starnino

GASPEREAU PRESS LIMITED
Kentville, Nova Scotia
MMXII

IN MEMORY OF MY FATHER
GIOVANNI STARNINO
WHOSE CHOICEST WORDS
FOR ME WHEN GROWING
UP GAVE THIS BOOK
ITS TITLE

PROLOGUE

PATRICK WARNER: A lot of poets out there don't seem to respond to criticism. In fact, I've talked to quite a few who just despise any kind of criticism. I was wondering if any of you have any idea of why that is? Carmine?

CARMINE STARNINO: People believe you have this thing called *movements*, *schools*, *controversies* and *debates*. Then you have this whole other thing called *the poem*. The small, perfect lyric. And the poem defeats that other thing. It always trumps that mess of opinions – that foment of intellectualizing and disagreement. The problem is that this humble lyric would never exist without all that intellectualizing and disagreement. To despise criticism, in other words, is to despise one of the forces that makes poetry possible. Poems, after all, emerge out of our ideas about poems. And where do we get those ideas? From other poets, other poems, from the tradition, from the quarrels we have with each other about what poetry should be doing, as well as from our public clashes over what's good and what's bad. Criticism, moreover, is hard-wired into our own pleasure-principles. Not all poems I end up loving I start loving. Not all poems I begin to love I finish up loving. You grow with poems, poems grow with you, poets grow with you. Certain poets you stop reading because your threshold for pleasure has changed and you find yourself looking around for something else. One day you sit down for a beer with a buddy and you say, 'you know what? I can't read *x* anymore', and he says, 'why?' and you say, 'this is why'. *That* is the seed of criticism. That's where it starts. And the tradition would not exist – poetry itself would not exist – if those conversations did not happen, and if poets did not take the time to turn those conversations into well-written, well-argued prose.

Drawn from 'A Passel of Poets / A Snicker of Critics', The New Quarterly, *Winter 2008, based on a panel discussion with Mark Callanan, Amanda Jernigan, George Murray and Carmine Starnino, moderated by Patrick Warner, which took place in St. John's, Newfoundland, on Friday September 28, 2007.*

I

LAZY BASTARDISM
A NOTEBOOK

I'VE NEVER HAD a good feeling about writing poetry. Unease set in early, when I was about seventeen, and, after two decades, the deed still doesn't sit quite right. I'm a victim, I tell myself, of the southern Italian distrust of books. For the immigrants who docked in North America mid-century, education was something to be encouraged, but only as a means to a better-paying end (labourers wanted to sire lawyers, not artsy-fartsy layabouts). My parents were more tolerant than most, but there was obvious alarm that all my reading would leave me 'mixed up'.

Then there was the language. Like most of the little Fonzies bred in Montreal north, I was raised almost entirely in Italian. This had an interesting effect on my English. In high school, for example, 'skinned' was what you said if you came in close contact with something ('that car nearly skinned me'). If you had just stuffed your face, you used 'shkoff' ('shkoffed a sangwich'). The weird sentences I spoke ensured that much of my university life would be spent in disguise. Hanging around silver-tongued creative writing students, I watched what I said and how I said it. I worked hard to suppress the accent in my voice, to better play the fit-to-be-in-literary-company part.

Today the verse hook is planted deep. And with it, the wound: that one of the central activities of my life is tinged with the sense of being dissolute, escapist, fey. Even at those rare moments when, fresh off a new poem, I feel the artisanal high of every word fitting flush, the crash comes swiftly: depression and anxiety at having gotten away with something slightly preposterous. I'm in it now for better or worse, but I'm always on the lookout for some clue that can help explain the emergence of the poet who bears my name.

My first contact with poetry was the 'Our Father' and 'Hail Mary.' Yes, they're prayers, but they're also packets of linguistic energy. Not enough is made of their epic-accented statements ('lead us not into temptation, but deliver us from evil'), the wonderfully archaic usages ('forgive us our trespasses'), the tone nibbed with rhapsodic oddities ('blessed is the fruit of thy womb'). At the time – the only literature in my house was the daily tabloid *Le Journal de Montréal* – this was otherworldly speech. I found lots of other prayers I liked (St. Francis's 'The Canticle of All Creatures' was a favourite) but none that introduced me to such fresh noises and suggestions. Other prayers were loaded with religiosity, but uninterestingly flat. 'Hallowed be thy name' filled my mouth with sound (modernization has scrubbed the prayer clean of out-of-date fillips: 'Holy is your name' is what kids now recite). Nothing in my life matched that language and I rejoiced in its acoustic plushness. Linguistically speaking, I suppose I saw myself as upwardly mobile. These prayers fixed in place my core criteria for a good poem: memorizable, talismanically glamorous and endlessly repeated to stave off setbacks, fears, sins.

It occurs to me that some might interpret that last paragraph to mean that I believe in some equivalency between prayer and poetry. I don't. The distance between prayer, which Thomas Merton called 'a raid on the unspeakable', and poetry, which T.S. Eliot called a 'raid on the inarticulate', is further apart than many might otherwise think.

Writing poetry is not, in itself, a prayerful activity. That's because prayer is not a craft; it is the opposite of a craft. It is a focused devotional feelingfulness, a self-aware, non-naming amplification of faith, a mind tuned to the frequency of the unsayable (Simone Weil described it as 'paying attention to God'). Setting this mystical alertness down as poetry – dressing it in stanzas, line lengths and rhythm – requires the unmystical means of prosody. Poetry can speak about God, it can even speak to God, but poetry is, at bottom, a secular art: its artistry predicated precisely on facing down any threat to its clear-headedness.

In fact, regarded a certain way, poetry might even be said to be a menace to religious belief. This is because poetry, to work, needs to strip religious belief of its theological privilege (poetry, said Valéry, is literature 'purged of idols of every sort'). Put into poetic form, that belief therefore becomes something else: a patient, precise, purposeful, adhesively held-together succession of sounds. Unlike prayer, poems live entirely inside their linguistic devices and designs. Indeed, the poet is someone for whom language is so important it gets the whole of his or her attention – for whom language is more important than God.

Now, I don't want to suggest that one has to be a heretic to write good poetry. (And indeed nothing stops us from enlarging the notion of worship to include poetry's secularists. Sometimes what seem the most superstition-free acts of description are the stirrings of a deeper devoutness: A.R. Ammons's nature poetry fits here, maybe even Ted Hughes'.) My point is that it seems to me impossible to offer up your poem as a kind of worship without recognizing the paradox inherent in the act. The best religious verse – George Herbert comes quickest to mind, Geoffrey Hill too – flirts with faithlessness. There is a Flaubertian attention to style that suggests the poet understands he or she cannot praise God without also, and simultaneously, turning attention away from him and toward language (which doesn't happen during prayer). The utter devotion to crafting a poem, the selfishness it requires, traps one in competing priorities. A good religious poem, like Donne's 'Holy Sonnets', can lock the two struggles together, but one priority is more important than the other. Delete it, and you get mush.

Can critical faculties show signs of wear and tear? Eliot thought so.

'As one gets older', he said in his 1959 *Paris Review* interview, when he was seventy-one, 'one is not quite confident in one's own ability to distinguish new genius among younger men. You're always afraid that you are going as you have seen your elders go'. Helen Vendler admitted as much in her 2006 *New York Times* profile. Then seventy-three, Vendler said she avoided poets under fifty, citing new 'frames of reference' that baffled her. 'They're writing about the television cartoons they saw when they were growing up. And that's fine. It's as good a resource of imagery as orchards', she said. 'Only I've seen orchards and I didn't watch these cartoons ... So I don't feel I'm the best reader for most of the young ones'.

I'm nearly forty, and, while I don't think I'm altogether out of it, I already feel younger Canadian poets are writing poetry that is faster, more sophisticated and smarter than what my generation grew up writing – poetry whose margins of success I struggle to measure, engendering flashes of hostility. Feeling myself touch the edge of philistinism puts me on notice. 'I shouldn't like to feel that I was resisting', said Eliot in the same interview, 'as my work was resisted when it was new, by people who thought that it was imposture of some kind or other'. Joseph Epstein, at seventy-two, is still a very nimble essayist, but now enjoys nothing more than digging in his heels and watching history sweep past him; not 'getting it' has become a matter of pride. Although fifty-eight, fogeyism has begun to catch up to William Logan, who continues to blow the whistle on rapidly rising poets (Cathy Park Hong, Kevin Young), but no longer brokers good new voices (he was one of Gjertrud Schnackenberg's earliest and best defenders). Logan also shows other late-style aspects of the badly aging critic: the one note. Staying on message is a vital part of what makes firebrand critics effective, but they then become so adept at capturing a certain kind of tone – toughened, ornery – they allow themselves no space for surprise. There is something automatic about their relentless disappointment in contemporary poetry, a pre-prepped regret too quickly acceded to.

For a sense of fair play, or an honest attempt at it, you'd have to turn to someone like Stephen Burt or David Orr, two youngish poets (both are under forty) who are performing exceptionally good quality control. Both believe in the merit of their own taste, but their verdicts also exemplify what Richard Blackmur called 'a mind full of provisional faiths'. They never forget that, when it comes to poetry, what we hold as intrinsic is merely one of many persuasive speculations. ('It appears', wrote Howard Nemerov, 'that poems are held together by people's opinions of what holds poems together'.)

In contrast to these critic-explorers, Adam Kirsch might be said to lead the critic-conquerors: fixed upon victory, such critics swarm their subject, seeking to subdue it. But in his excellent online *Contemporary Poetry Review* series 'Young Poets Calling' (where he's introduced readers to the work of David Yezzi, Joe Osterhaus, Joshua Mehigan, A.E. Stallings, Thom Satterlee and Rachel Wetzsteon), even Kirsch seems eager to play his part in welcoming the sea changes Tom Paulin describes in his essay collection *Writing to the Moment*: 'So old styles sink away or are put reverently in museum cabinets, while new contemporary dangerous styles walk the streets and begin to be recognized'.

I finish a poem, and immediately forget how I was able to do it. Of course, I know very well how I did it: the hard way. Twenty drafts to realize number nine was actually the way in (and then backtracking and lighting out again in full knowledge I've probably ducked down another blind alley). Or thirty drafts – endless late-night stitching and unstitching – to figure out 'no, this is stupid, give it up'. Except I don't. I stick with it, frantically trying to keep things alive until something, anything, catches fire and the language takes over, surging ahead of me. Knock on wood, I hope I never lose the knack for inviting such dumb luck into my life. Yet there is nothing remotely nurturing or dopamine-inducing about the creative process. Unlike W.S. Graham, I don't 'feel most alive' when flailing about blindly for the right word, and Ashbery's uncontrollable productivity – where his own writerly difficulties and doubts are swept away in graphomaniacal deluges – leaves me in scandalized awe. Faced with a blank page, my mind is a house divided: deeply at odds with itself, paralyzed and dysfunctional, unwilling to undertake any effort that threatens the privileges of idleness, and, like some evil twin, laying down false trails. It's so easy to lose heart.

Still, there is a great deal of method in it. The multiplication of bottlenecks, always pushing things close to chaos and failure, creates an extraordinary number of points where pressure builds and – just when all hope is abandoned – triggers that release Yeats described as the 'blood, imagination, intellect all running together'. This can also be more plainly described as a good run of words. By what right do I take credit? Stephen Burt has a wonderful line about how poets 'accept on purpose what they have created by accident', and you have to wonder how many of the 'perfect' poems we use as touchstones of excellence – poems academics take apart, analyze, diagram and reassemble – were shotgunned into existence.

Complaints that poetry has lost the ordinary reader stick in my craw. No question, our market share is at an all-time low (a historical situation James Wood recently blamed on 'the big fat greedy monster of the novel, which sucks all the vital nutrition away for itself'). And no doubt, more can be done to persuade intellectually curious folks to take an interest. But the news that poetry's 'diminished stature', to borrow Dana Gioia's term, betrays some crack-up in poetry itself is now so overpromoted as to become viciously self-harming. It's all well and good to be upset with our @##% condition, but it doesn't make a ton of sense to do what a lot of us are unable to stop doing: blaming the poets.

Everything would be different if our stuff wasn't so difficult, or obscure, or highbrow, or introverted, or solipsistic, or autobiographical, or experimental, or academic, or postmodern. Some of these charges may be justified, but as far as the public is concerned, we're wasting our breath. There is no once-popular style and subject that, if brought back, will stop poetry's sliding poll numbers. There is no traditional link between poetry and the public that, if repaired, will turn things around. That's because re-establishing the public's trust in poetry would be like re-establishing the public's trust in Latin. Is it crazy to believe that Latin – once the lingua franca of government, church and cultural circles – has a chance in the age of English? Of course it is. Most people would be gobsmacked to learn the language is spoken at all. Similarly, I'd bet many general readers have absolutely no idea that: 1) New poems are still being written; 2) since the turn of the twentieth century, the public has been tangled up in a lover's spat with the art form, playing the long-suffering Judy to the poet's self-absorbed Punch; and 3) after a series of good-faith attempts at reconciliation, modernism was the last straw – cold-shouldered, readers moved on for good.

This is the perfect example of a story that's kidding itself. The high-stakes drama is all in our heads, though you can see why such a delusion – with poets cringing guiltily – would take hold. As long as we're responsible for our predicament, we're in control of our destiny. But solving one's escalating irrelevancy is hard enough without being reminded of all the more interesting things winning the reader's attention: 'roses and locomotives (not to mention acrobats Spring electricity Coney Island the 4th of July the eyes of mice and Niagara Falls)'. So said E.E. Cummings in 1917.

If grown-ups don't read poetry, it's not because they have a bone to pick with poets. The truth is even more intolerable: they prefer not to. How often do we need to get Bartlebyed before we finally admit to ourselves that those Clancy-thumbing dentists and Grisham-toting lawyers aren't confused or afraid of commitment? They're just not that into us.

Lately it seems no book of Canadian poetry can be put to bed without an epigraph to tuck it in, whether by Susan Sontag or Günter Grass or Nietzsche or Freud or Jeanette Winterson or Homer. It's hard to know what to blame for this. Until Eliot and Pound, epigraphs were rarely associated with poetry. One of its earliest Canadian appearances, as far as I can tell, was in Ralph Gustafson's 1960 *Rivers Among Rocks* ('Canst thou draw out leviathan with an hook?' from the Book of Job). Two of our major poets – Al Purdy and Irving Layton – used them sparingly. Michael Ondaatje, in contrast, has shown himself to be a quirky epigraphophile: the epigraph for *Rat Jelly* (1973) is pulled from a wine description in a magazine.

Whatever the reason for its popularity, the epigraph's spell has never been stronger. Poets use them to seed sub-rosa themes, to create theoretical contexts, or to nudge readers toward moods around which their collection has been structured. As an editor, I've seen poets drive themselves crazy in their search for the 'perfect' epigraph. The device is regarded as the nub of the matter, the absolute condensation of a book's intellectual and emotional intent.

The truth, as is often the case, is a little less dramatic. Epigraphs are the poetry world's emoticons: quick-fix inflections. Poets overestimate their necessity and significance. What they think is a tiny profundity engine is nothing more than a curio, a found object charged with private associations. This is why so many epigraphs appear undigested and attention-begging. ('Names are only the guests of reality'. This thought, lifted from Hsü Yu, would seem to channel some shaman spirit into Don Domanski's *All Our Wonder Unavenged* (2007). To me, it sits right on the edge of flim-flam.)

Epigraphs emphasize poetry-making as a thing of touchstones. They solve our anxiety of influence by flattering it. But poets are getting carried away, like Borgesian scribes compiling an infinite commonplace book. Not to say gems aren't being unearthed (Pascal: 'All human evil comes from a single cause, man's inability to sit still in a room'). But these are exceptions. As a rule, our collective well-readness is withering away into name-dropping.

I'm not calling for an outright ban, just a little more judiciousness. Like any choice quote, a good epigraph whets the appetite of readers by sharpening their curiosity. Simple and unpreening, it brandishes a let's-cut-through-the-cant suavity. Toronto's Kevin Connolly understands this. He opens his recent collection *Revolver* (2008) with these lines by Bill Knott: 'I wish to be misunderstood; / that is, / to be understood from your perspective'. Snap!

I'm a soft sell for the unlucky in fame. Send word of someone overlooked, underappreciated, on the margin, and, like Pavlov's dog, my mouth waters. I treasure not only first-tier loners (John Clare, Edward Thomas), but second-tier (Charlotte Mew, Louise Bogan) and third (Rosemary Tonks, Bernard Spencer). I see myself, deep down, as 'the designated mourner', from the title of the Wallace Shawn play, that person 'assigned to grieve, to wail, and light the public ritual fire' when the last of the tribe passes away. It's a job, I'm happy to say, that keeps me quite busy in Canada. Charles Bruce, A.G. Bailey and Kenneth Leslie are three of more than a dozen exceptional poets who, during their lifetime, never needed to adjust their psychology to a world in which what they wrote was seen as a valuable asset. There was nothing ingratiating about their attitude and they never truckled for attention. Their reputations were like stalled start-ups untouched by any speculative mania. It would be easy to think of Canadian poetry without, say, R.G. Everson, Dorothy Roberts, Anne Wilkinson. The nuances of their style – the precision, the intense musicality, the canny line-making – would never be sensed as missing elements. Regarded as minor, they have been rendered stodgy and inoffensive. All of which means they appear too dull to deserve a second look, much less close scrutiny. They are, to use John Freeman's term, 'the less received' of our poetic past. But to me these figures represent nothing less than the future of poetry: a future sympathetic to singularity and strangeness and the free-range quirks of the individual imagination.

Poetic revolutions are revolutions in diction. That's why the troublemakers responsible for such linguistic shakeups – Wordsworth, Whitman, Lowell – base them on a return to ordinary speech. In every case, however, renewing contact with the 'real language of men' didn't stop poets from composing poems that spoke over the heads of those men. Getting back to basics, in other words, had nothing to do with making poems accessible. It was an intervention: an idiom battling a decadence addiction was rescued before it was too late. The 'breakthrough into life' that produced *Life Studies* (1959), after all, was a solution to a technical problem ('I felt my old poems hid what they were really about', Lowell explained in a letter).

The point here is that aesthetic change is an elite activity, done out of professional boredom. Poets who say different, who claim to heed the wishes of the common reader out of populist duty, are lazy bastards. Lazy bastardism kowtows to the convenience of see-Jane-run simple-mindedness because, by gosh, that's what most people want from their poetry. Lazy bastardism is the only way to explain the existence of phrases like, 'the roaring juggernaut of time' or 'the once gurgling fountain of creativity' (both plucked from Billy Collins's *The Trouble with Poetry*). Lazy bastardism will never come clean and tell you that poetry is an acquired taste, that the pleasure of reading it is assembled over years from smaller, slow-to-learn skills. Lazy bastardism will never insist that you should read a lot of poems, old and new, and try to keep them in your head to help train and trust your ear. And lazy bastardism will certainly never stress that you need to love poetry's artificial and formal aspects.

It is, of course, trivial to think that 'amateurs' don't have the taste for this. Those who protect the common reader from difficult poetry – promoting plain-speaking and conversational directness as having greater relation to real things and real problems – have an odd idea of who this reader is. Accessibility is far more complex, and readers far wiser, than our current theories are willing to accept. The audience-wisdom that helped establish the worth of certain key poets in our tradition – Shakespeare, Whitman, Dickinson, Frost – did so precisely because of the loveliness of their writing, and not just its meaning. But readers can be lazy bastards as well. Faced with a poet who has taken the pains, some would rather not take the trouble. They don't have to, of course. And as far as I'm concerned, better they don't. But let's not let the many who don't sell short the few who do.

'Everything I am writing at present bores me and leaves me indifferent', wrote Chekhov, 'but everything that is still only in my head interests me, moves me, and excites me'. I would go even further, and say that boredom is the highest state of creativity. It is the mind at its best: unable to accept compromises with intention, and unable to lie about it. Hopkins's famous *cri de coeur* – 'Do you know, a horrible thing has happened to me. I have begun to doubt Tennyson' – also reminds us that sudden indifference to any special pleading on behalf of the 'originality' of a celebrated career is, ultimately, what keeps our art honest and goads us to speak in newfangled, untypical ways. We find that we have built up a tolerance to the stimulant of our own idiosyncrasies, or that tedium has inoculated us against the virulent contagiousness of the already-done-well. This can be taken too far: the contemporary avant-garde has merchandised its boredom into life cycles of rapid self-obsolescence (Brodsky called this the 'need for an alternative coming to match a drug addict's daily fix'). But what else is tradition if not a story of poets running hot and cold on each other? This is why I've never fantasized about having what Auden called a 'dream reader' or put much stock in the idea of someone giving themselves over to my poems. I want those who come to my poetry to be both listeners and interrogators, participants in a sincere, half-skeptical conversation. I know the psychoaesthetic tug-of-war I have with poems I encounter, even those I already admire – the withholding and surrender of my affections, the hardening and melting of my tolerances. Why should my work be treated any differently? Indeed, coming on strong while gripped by fear a stranger may not (or worse, may no longer) buy what I'm selling is, for me, the delicious tension of publishing a poem, the dare of it. Forget dream readers, give me real readers: readers who criticize what they once cherished, cherish what they once criticized, and sometimes would rather watch grass grow.

Not the money (at $100,000 Canadian, it's one of the world's richest literary award purses), or the mandate (to divvy up the dough between two English-language poets, one from Canada and one from away), or the motive (to reverse how 'poetry has slipped from the mainstream of our cultural lives', in the words of its sponsor): instead, looking back across the last eight years, the most emblematic detail of the Griffin Poetry Prize remains Toronto comedian Scott Thompson's performance at the inaugural gala in 2001.

Acting as emcee, Thompson launched into an outrageous, dildo-waving routine that got him promptly yanked from the stage. The awards gala – which has since become an annual fixture on Toronto's social scene – was a piece of carefully planned theatre: three hundred guests sitting in a vast room of banner-festooned walls, triumphal arches and red-carpet entranceways. Such a moment called for gaiety, not grotesquery. After all, it's not every day that a private citizen decides to single-handedly reintroduce poetry to the 'public imagination'. Founded and aggressively funded by auto parts millionaire Scott Griffin, the award was touted as a rising tide that would lift all bardic boats. But it's hard not to see Thompson's sex toy blunder as a warning. It not only reminded us of the unpleasant surprises that even the best intentions can bring, but was itself an apt metaphor for the limits of Griffin's optimism: when it comes to prizes, somebody always gets, um, screwed.

On the surface, bad news is hard to find. The Griffin trust has by now handed out a total of $600,000 to fourteen lucky ducks; deserved reputations have been minted (Karen Solie), fine poets honoured (Margaret Avison) and oddities given comfort (Christian Bök). Moreover, the prize's international aspect has helped raise the profile of exciting talents (Durs Grünbein, Les Murray, Charles Simic and Michael Longley) in a poetry culture that has often been too isolationist to notice outside currents. That those outside currents have overlooked us as well is a plight that Griffin, to great expense, has also tried to redress. Every year his outfit runs lavish attention-getting ads in the *Times Literary Supplement* and the *London Review of Books*, and flies the growing family of Griffin beneficiaries – shortlisted and winners – to celebrity appearances at major international festivals. The annual expenditure for administration, promotion and publicity likely exceeds the value of the prize several times over.

Then again, bigness is the Griffin Prize in a nutshell. To get the public to pay attention, Griffin sought a sum 'of sufficient size to make a statement', as he said in a speech at the launch of the prize. Judging by the national hoo-ha around the event, the investment has paid off handsomely. More than a good deed, the prize is designed to grapple with something large: the place of poetry in the world. And according to Griffin, the best way to cue the world about poetry's value is to repackage it as something people can't dismiss as negligible. The problem, however, is that the payday becomes the point. You can bet that when the victors are announced the press will do little to explain how their poetry, in Griffin's words, 'speaks to the soul of a nation and its people'.

The Griffin Prize has been credited with vast health-giving powers. It establishes literary standards, lauds laudable work and enlarges the art's audience by bringing it to wider public notice. In truth, the prize merely feeds the belief that a poet who bags $50,000 is better than one who doesn't. It may be one of poetry's ultimate windfalls, but the Griffin is a vision of meritocracy based on publicity. Which is also the reason no one turns one down. To be a winner, after all, is to be a cut above the rest. Better yet, it is to be cut out from the rest. Which immediately leads us to one of the most nagging ironies of the Griffin Prize. Namely, that an award meant to rescue poetry from anonymity has led to the creation of a compelling new villain around whom poets can construct another narrative of neglect. Unless, of course, we win. And the lure of such honour-mongering is why we are always so slow to realize the catch in the ideal. Scott Griffin is surely a rare good heart in a noble fight, yet nothing proves the neglect of our art as much as the fact that we need prizes to help maintain the myth that we matter. But then, it's beside the point, and bad sport, to protest – might as well wag a rubber donger at it.

II

MARGARET ATWOOD

IF THERE'S A Canadian poem readers know by heart, chances are it's Margaret Atwood's four-liner 'You Fit into Me'. A quick start: 'You fit into me/like a hook into an eye'. A quicker ending: 'A fish hook/an open eye'. As short lyrics go, it's flawless: perfectly judged and perfectly ruthless.

'You Fit into Me' was published in 1971, and its sting is a fair example of Atwood's method at the time. She lures us in with the lovey-dovey associations of hooks and eyes, then draws blood. In brief, she baits us. But you really have to go back to the late sixties and mid-seventies – when her fish hooks were at their sharpest – to understand why she caused such a stir when she came on the scene. *The Circle Game* appeared in 1964 looking more or less like any other slim mid-century debut. But the differences were important. Daughter of an entomologist and student of Northrop Frye, Atwood fronted a poetry whose soundings of female consciousness were forensic and archetype-obsessed. She was, at heart, a young poet with a knack for writing striking descriptions of extreme emotional states. Some of it recalled Anne Wilkinson, who also overhauled romantic emblems and came to conclusions that, for their time, were just as unflinching ('I'd love this body more/If graved in rigid wood/It could not move'). But while Wilkinson's poems simmered without boiling over, Atwood remade her anger into a series of attacks with no retreat.

'Our stories', she wrote in her nationalistic handbook *Survival* (1972), 'are likely to be tales not of those who made it but of those who made it back'. True to form, her poetry foreshadowed the breakthroughs that were to arrive when female poets learned to play through their pain. *Survival*'s vision of a young country toughing it out 'in the face of "hostile" elements' – namely colonialization – is still taken seriously as a theory about Canada's cultural identity. But the book is better understood as a metaphor for a young Anglo-Canadian poet awake to her own colonial cringe. And what Atwood did with this 'cringe' was essentially reboot Canadian poetry's available modes, an achievement she clinched with a series of collections that came in rapid succession, among them *The Animals in That Country* (1968), *The Journals of Susanna Moodie* (1970) and *Power Politics* (1971). In these books, female tropes sifted out of legend and literature are rebuilt from scratch using entirely new ingredients. Atwood created revisionist conjectures – witty revenge fantasies, salty post-Freudian satires – on gender inequalities, the oppressiveness of marriage and the historical anonymity of women. Some of it was overkill, and not infrequently two-dimensional, but it was hard not to be knocked out by poems like 'They Eat Out', 'Speeches for Doctor Frankenstein' or 'Marrying the Hangman'. With expectations still lingering in the fauxpatrician formalist Fifties, readers seemed unprepared for Atwood's rationality and rage, her left-handed moves and wicked deadpan.

Tying a major theme ('the survivor has no triumph or victory but the fact of his survival') to an aesthetic (poetry is 'where precision takes place') helped Atwood win early fame. When she found a way, starting with *Surfacing* (1971), to translate that thinking into fiction, she became more than a culture-hero lauded on school curricula: she became spectacularly bankable. Today, as the best-known English-language novelist of contemporary sexual politics, Atwood enjoys global acclaim (her books exist in twenty languages), graphomaniacal creativity (her fiction alone tips the scales at twenty-two books) and the privilege of being Canada's only legitimate Nobel contender (our last two hopefuls were Irving Layton and Gaston Miron). Not surprisingly, a star-struck literary-industrial complex has sprung up around her. Whether or not you believe she is a major writer, there's no doubt her anthologies, criticism and cultural activism have turned 'Peggy' into a walking manifesto, an all-purpose muse for native sensibilities. For her part, Atwood has accepted the CanLit crown and, with increasing confidence, turned it into an easy rhetorical platform, a good place to start a story ('Recently, I was on a TV show in

Mexico. By this time I was famous ...' is how she opens a personal essay from 2004).

We see that role – or, more specifically, her sense of it as marker of instant authority – on display in *The Door*, Atwood's thirteenth book of poetry. Workaholic tendencies, merchandising savvy, nagging status anxiety: whatever her reasons for publishing a new collection, Atwood's expectation of a large audience has caused her voice to move far up into her head. Her words have become imperial, complacent and vacant – so that, when she needs to describe something, flicked-off nouns and verbs impatiently gesture in the general vicinity of the idea or object. 'The city's old,/but new to me, and therefore/strange, and therefore fresh'. Such a sum-up of an unnamed European city – unsubtle to the point of crudeness – is the sound of a poet who feels she no longer needs to catch our attention.

Some of this can be traced back to the kind of generalizing Atwood has always practised. From the start her poems have been closer to bony soliloquies than fleshed-out confessions – stark asides delivered in the midst of some major, off-stage drama of consciousness. We see this clearly in the 1970 classic 'Death of a Young Son by Drowning', where Atwood ventriloquizes a mother's loss in a generalized setting ('the land I floated on/but could not touch to claim'). Such early poems, restricting themselves to a stark surface, staked everything on their psychologically charged subtexts ('the sun kept shining, the new grass/leapt to solidity;/my hands glistened with details').

Given what's on view when *The Door* finally swings open – curt descriptiveness, sharp-cut diction, in extremis narratives – it would be easy to think we're in store for the usual Atwoodian magic. Some passages carry the old bite ('My mother dwindles and dwindles/and lives and lives'), but too often the heart of the matter turns out to be some tough-sounding boiler plate. One poem's penultimate line, 'Drunks in the gutter' is corrected to 'Drunks in the gutter singing – /I forgot to add that'. But in fact she never forgets the singing drunks. In 'Dutiful', the speaker probes her tendency to blame herself for everything. It's a promising idea – especially coming from a poet as progressive as Atwood – but no matter how severely she dresses her lines, the sentimentality is conspicuous: 'why do I feel so responsible/for the wailing from shattered houses,/for birth defects and unjust wars,/and the soft, unbearable sadness/filtering down from distant stars?' Why indeed. Maybe Atwood believes that star-drizzle of 'soft, unbearable' sorrow lays bare the drama of her guilt-ridden self, but the image is too easy, eager to claim the pain it should be evoking. Again and again, poems that address complex feelings end up feeling like they were written very fast, full of sloppy reiterations ('She looks old,/older than anything'). At best, we get imprecision. At worst, doggerel:

> Despite my singed feathers
> and this tattered scroll I haul around,
> I'm not an angel.
> I'm only a shadow,
> the shadow of your desires.

Atwood has become someone who knows what she's known for, and overindulges expectations even at the price of having nothing interesting to say. As a result, some poems barely improve on their generic titles: 'A Poor Woman Learns to Write', 'The Hurt Child'. What do you get when you add few formal surprises to a feminist thesis stuck on one setting? A voice that has outlived its ability to respond to the felt needs of its subject. The message runs on after the music for it has fallen away. A quick stacking of flat statements ('They are all bald/they are all naked,/they all have wide shoulders') is all we get in the anti-torture poem 'They Give Evidence'. Elsewhere, Atwood struggles to ignite the ominous note that was once the standard operating mood of her allegories ('Go to the mouth of a cave/dig a trench, slit the throat/of an animal, pour out the blood') but the spark is dead. The lesson is clear: writing good poems requires more than the memory of what used to work. Atwood can still find arresting word choices (she says about gasoline: 'I loved the smell:/so alien, a whiff/of starstuff') and craft unusual images ('torn plastic/bags like ectoplasmic birds flitter and stream') but nothing lingers in the mind past a first reading, and sometimes even a first reading is a chore.

Plodding and laxly lyrical, Atwood's present abilities are hard to square with her past feats. The 'girl with the gorgon touch' who, in her first chapbook, *Double Persephone*, hunted through a garden for 'a living wrist and arm', is now the poet who declares: 'I walk along,/looking at everything equally'. The word 'equally' seems to encode a kind of non-attention, a permission not to look too hard. How else to explain why a vegetable 'bursts into song', or clouds are 'downy as pillows' or a 'catlike' cat? (Cats in fact, make a couple of cameos from the grave. It's sad to see our psyche-in-crisis laureate doting on pet deaths.) The irony is that Atwood now seems to model her poetry on the didactic plainspokenness her devotees helped popularise throughout the 1980s. Loss of energy in aging, famous poets is something no one likes to talk about. Creativity, however, is not a renewable resource. There will be fallow periods, and *The Door* proves it.

The book isn't all dud. 'Year of the Hen' is a jaunty poem about parsing out losses by sorting through a houseful of 'junk' that belonged to 'once indelible days'. Atwood's feral self comes alive again in 'Disturbed Earth', a sensuous, barbed, tender meditation that claims the titular image as an emblem of creativity. Both are tightly built and remind us that Atwood always had a good ear for short lines, knowing how to keep them sprung and taut. We see this especially well in the final stanzas of 'Reindeer Moss on Granite':

> In the rain they go leathery,
> then sly, like rubber.
> They send up their little mouths
> on stems, red-lipped and round,
>
> each one pronouncing the same syllable,
> o,o,o, like the dumbfounded
> eyes of minnows.
> Thousands of spores, of rumours
>
> infiltrating the fissures,
> moving unnoticed into
> the ponderous *is* of the boulder,
> breaking down rock.

Atwood finds a matching sound of hard, plain words for the moss, with internal rhymes that try on the compressed phrases for size and find a fit, creating a clarity comprised of satisfying aural textures. As good as these lines are, however, they are nowhere near her finest work. But then, the earlier, better poems never dealt with what Atwood deals with in this book: the angst of old age, omens of mortality and, possibly the central drama driving it all, the handing on of vital instructions to the next generation ('Time for lessons', snaps Atwood) – an act that, of course, comes with its own foretaste of oblivion. *The Door*, you might then say, is a primer: the constant use of 'you', the broad strokes, the unstinting pedantry. The style has been devised as if for highly distractible readers, and with it Atwood addresses – one can only assume – a nascent poet, initiating her into sect secrets. This catechizing strategy can be seen quite explicitly in 'Another Visit to the Oracle' where, in long, exhortatory verse-paragraphs Atwood presents herself as witness, prophet, seer. 'What I do: I see/in darkness. I see/darkness. I see you'.

Frankly this reveals more about Atwood's heroic self-conception than any truth about her poetry or the art itself. 'All I have to do', she says, 'is be present in my head,/which contains your head'. Maybe Atwood is demonstrating her typical sarcasm by mocking the assumptions attached to the poetic office she holds. But then it needs to be said that one of the things Atwood's new book is eager to remind us about (even if sarcastically) is her beyond-all-argument eminence. As hinted by the jacket cover, which features a photo of the poet as a young girl, Atwood takes centre-stage. She began her career by creating the angriest and eeriest parables of political invisibility ('I hiding in the long grass with my two dead cousins/the membrane grown already/across their throats') but now seeks avatars to feed her diva-like addiction for self-dramatization. She is Joan of Arc, a heretic at the stake, one of the ill-fated musicians on the *Titanic*. What do these verse-personas share? Each enshrines a different aspect of Atwood's tortured vanity. *The Door* – a book into whose smallest details Atwood has writ herself large – depicts poetry as a high-risk activity, a demon-ridden pursuit that ultimately leaves one damaged goods. Atwood may not recognize this as the melodramatic dicta that it is, but even for those of us who want to give her the benefit of the doubt, it's hard to stave off disappointment. A poet born with one of the best bullshit-detectors in the business turns shill for the industry's worst cliché.

Saying things too touchy for polite conversation helped make Atwood a polarizing figure. But like one of the avenging Furies transformed into the benign Eumenides, she seems to have forgotten how to strike a nerve. Early books like *You are Happy* (1974) and *Two-Headed Poems* (1978) were often upfront about their social and political resentments, but they never espoused 'causes'. Instead, the poems were lit by a trickster-like mean streak. Spiky humour lanced pretensions; satire confused expectations. The younger Atwood looked for, and sometimes found, exciting and unpredictable ways to turn blasphemy into art. Being a feminist leader, however, seems to have made her job a lot easier: she can simply vent. And why not? Having battled for her ism, she will forever be on the right side of any debate. So if she wants to remind readers that war is a bad thing, she'll just draw a cartoon like 'Nobody Cares Who Wins' and dismiss the medals worn by veterans as 'A hoard of buttons cut from corpses/as souvenirs'. One can admire her willingness to speak her mind, but there's no getting around the ick-factor of poetry that goes about its business with such a clear sense of good and evil. It's the bug all well-feted change-agents eventually catch: insufferable high-mindedness. In Atwood's case, she hijacks every *petits faits vrais* for political gain. White cotton T-shirts call up 'wary impoverished faces,/the grins filled with blackened teeth'. Crickets are 'hordes of the starved dead'.

Hard to believe a poet who once described herself disappearing into 'the stellar/fluorescent-lighted/wastes of geology' is responsible for language so glib, unwinning, so de-energized. These, however, are simply examples of a poet's self-importance exceeding the reader's patience. More disturbing is when that self-importance exceeds good taste. That is, when hanging tough becomes crisis-chasing: the great poet calling attention to calamities that only she has the stomach to behold. Behold 'War Photo':

> The dead woman thrown down on the dusty road
> is very beautiful.

One leg extended, the other flexed, foot pointed
towards the knee, the arm flung overheard, the hand
relaxed into a lovely gesture
a dancer might well study for years
and never attain.
Her purple robe is shaped
as if it's fluttering;
her head is turned away.

One of the oddities of our free-verse precepts is that we are willing to consider bad prose good poetry. Here are ten lines that exist in a state of permanent place-holding for all the better words Atwood never came up with. But there's something even fishier about Atwood's language: it's utterly insincere. The poker 'tell' is the over-puppeteered crumple of limbs, the showily gestural phrasing. Unlike her previous personas, all taken either from history (Susanna Moodie) or myth (Circe), this 'dead woman' is borrowed from stock footage. Constructed out of cant, she exists only in Atwood's poem. Bearing witness to extreme events that you have not experienced is, of course, an enormous moral and aesthetic challenge. Yet such poems have become a feminist genre complete with their own conventions (viz. Adrienne Rich's *Your Native Land, Your Life* and Sharon Old's *The Gold Cell*). Would that Atwood were fooling us here: turning the worst of such pieces on their heads by debunking their drawn-from-cliché provocativeness.

Alas, she isn't. The scene Atwood sets up feels very much like a set-up. The woman is 'beautiful' because the word is attached to the heart-rending effect Atwood seeks – but it's precisely because she needs to be 'beautiful' that the word bears no relation to reality. That such women are murdered and dumped on streets is a vile fact, but Atwood isn't really writing about those women. If she were, it wouldn't be so easy for her to concoct such tragic treacle. (In the next stanza she describes, in an odious image, 'other dead people scattered around/like trees blown over'.) No, Atwood's true subject is herself.

O dead beautiful woman, if anyone
had the power to wrench me through despair
and arid helplessness
into the heart of prayer,
it would be you –

Instead I'll make for you
the only thing I can:
although I'll never know your name,
I won't ever forget you.
Look: on the dusty ground
under my hand, on this cheap grey paper,
I'm placing a small stone, here:
o

You have to admire the gall. Atwood is scaring herself with an horrific image and congratulates herself for confronting it. What is actually scary, and a little sickening, is the icy virtuousness of the whole exercise. Atwood appropriates these women simply to create a saintly-in-her-own-eyes speaker: their reality banalized to fit her sense of invincible goodness. (There is a response-poem that immediately follows called 'War Photo 2' where the emotional vampirism continues anew: 'You are right to be suspicious of me/I can't speak your absence for you'.) I don't know by what authority Atwood feels she can writes so facilely about such things and then have this poem, this tasteless exhibit of fellow-feeling, function as an insistent reminder that we note her compassion. She gets the last, pat word – 'although I'll never know your name,/I won't ever forget you' – and gives us a new metaphor for the fall-flat bluntness that has replaced the razor-edge that once hooked into readers. That 'small stone' also represents another kind of ending: it sets the seal on a book undone by waning vision and waxing vanity.

MARGARET AVISON

WHEN Margaret Avison died in 2007 at the age of 89, she was a major poet, a national treasure and, by all accounts, a sweet old woman. But throughout her reign as a literary doyenne there was a fact about her few admirers liked to talk about. Was she a violent drunk? Had she penned racist, foul-mouthed letters? Did she suffer from severe manic-depressive breakdowns? No, nothing as scandalous as that; and yet Avison's secret was troubling enough to sway critical attention toward less wince-inducing aspects of her originality. It's one of the reasons, for example, she is best known for a sonnet called 'Snow'. First published in her 1960 debut *Winter Sun*, this much-anthologized poem – in which the 'optic heart' is urged to 'venture' past reality's surface – helped cement Avison's reputation as a modern-day metaphysical, who combined abstraction with brilliant metaphor. Of course, there's nothing unusual about slimming down a challenging career, for the purposes of either consolidation or convenience, to the fame of a single work. Yet it's hard not to suspect that the enduring consensus around 'Snow' was set in motion by readers eager to change the subject. When Avison's strangeness was served to them hot, in other words, they blew on the spoon to make the truth less scalding.

And what is this great unmentionable? Early one morning in 1963, Avison was paid a visit by Jesus Christ. 'It was not visual', she later wrote, 'but not a mere feeling – that Person was impingingly present, before me'. The gale-force collision of the encounter upended Avison's life and transformed her poetry. The two books that follow this conversion, *Dumbfounding* (1966) and *sunblue* (1978), burn with unclassifiable properties. Hardly a phrase fails to do something beyond the normal, hardly a line happens you can't help scrutinizing for its peculiarities. The thinking is by turns elliptical, elegant, blunt and urgent. Sometimes it is all these simultaneously. Cracking a unique style, however, is hard enough. What do you do when those tics and quirks track a sincere, non-ironical conversation with 'the living Christ'? Our love of newness no longer leaves room for poetry that is also seen to be a mouthpiece for religious ideas (Hopkins was the last poet to get away with it). One reason is our dislike of writing we feel has 'a palpable design upon us', as Keats wrote. Another is our belief that organized worship is anathema to the poetic act ('The wages of faith', wrote one skeptical reviewer of *sunblue*, 'are intellectual and linguistic diminution'). Unable to square Avison's trailblazing with her evangelism, critics had only one option left: decouple the two parts of Avison's breakthrough. That is, credit her uncommon voice, but put some distance between that voice and its born-again origins. Hence, 'Snow': a poem whose easy-to-describe sense of the numinous becomes a sensible stand-in for a body of Christian work that exists almost entirely outside current categories, both avant-garde and mainstream.

Avison's post-conversion poems, to be sure, have never been taken lightly; indeed they steal the lion's share of scholarly curiosity. My point, however, isn't that we've misconstrued these poems (academics like David Kent have, in fact, been exemplary promoters of their felicities) but that our praise has sapped them of their authentic oddity. In order to drive away the devil of her religious awakening, we've secularized her into a patron saint of contemporary poetry's most cherished truism: the imagination as a force for self-invention and transcendence – or, as 'Snow' famously puts it, 'jail-break/And recreation'. To put it another way, in order to build a stronger case for Avison's genius, we felt it necessary to tune out the very thing that makes her genius so disquieting: namely, how her swift, sharp, impacted style ('The elms, black-worked on green,/rich in the rich old day/signal wordlessness/plumed along the Dark's way') is borne directly out of her belief in Christ's resurrection. We might flatter such poems with church-going terms like 'redemption' or 'grace', but this, at best, is a stopgap reaction: it nervously admits to the poem's theological bona fides while masking our confusion at what to make of them.

What Avison's poems encounter, in short, is the obstacle of secularism's tin ear. Christianity, however, did more than just flavour her poetry with unfashionable surmises: it revolutionized it. There's no point calling her, as George Bowering does, 'the founder of excellence' without grasping that her genius was fulfilled chiefly – indeed, flourished entirely – in the climate of her conversion. Avison's terrifying experience of being reborn, in other words, isn't merely a biographical fact: method is also at stake. Her 'dumbfounding' is the very psychological drama we see enacted in her poetry's rhythm, diction and logic. The terms of that drama – the thunderclap of clarity, the sweeping away of resistance – put constant pressure on the form, yet so discreetly is the ordinary world defamiliarized it's often hard to say just where, and how, Avison's words start to sink into something unpredictable, giddy, wild. In the closing stanzas of 'Released Flow', for example, Avison ends her depiction of a sugar bush (where 'runnels shine and down-rush / through burning snow and thicket-slope') by synchronizing her consonants with a reined-in restlessness, a near-subliminal instability of vast perception and excited language:

> The extraordinary beyond the hill
> breathes and is imperturbable.
> Near the gashed bough the hornets fur
> in paperpalace-keep and -choir.
>
> Across the snowmush and sunstriped maples
> honeyed woodsmoke curls and scrolls.
> Sunblue and bud and shoot wait to unlatch
> all lookings-forth, at the implicit touch.

This is an exceptionally deft and discreet ending, and it is made fascinating by the beautifully destructive precision of 'gashed' as well as Avison's determination to compress the language into fierce oddities, an ambition that enables her to capture the lovely 'paperpalace-keep and -choir' of hornets. This compression can also be seen in the syntactic surprise of 'all lookings-forth' and how it briefly confuses the sentence-sense of the previous line. It is a light-footed, spontaneous moment of disjunct that coincides perfectly with the caesura-generated hesitation of 'at the implicit touch' that itself completes the poem's shift from visual noticing to a very different kind of seeing.

The scriptural frequency to which these effects are tuned may seem low, but it's in the ear of such a style – austere, impulsive, surprising, judicious – that one can hear Avison's message of communion: communion with God, with nature, and, of course, with language. To read Avision seriously is to take seriously the possibility of a poetry whose various successes of image, line, word choice and breath are not just the lean achievements of a disciplined and gifted poet but the fuller achievements of a worshiping Christian. To appreciate what this means, it's important to first recognize that, for Avison, poetry is basically a troubleshooting art: daily mishandling jars language, and poems recalibrate it. I am reminded here chiefly of how, in a review of A.M. Klein, Avison observed that 'everybody's speech is defective' and insisted that poets need to 'discipline speech into clarity'. Christianity thus compelled Avison to move more probingly toward the vernacular character of English, extending a revitalizing hand to its neglected possibilities. If God so loved the world that he gave up, for its redemption, his only Son, then poetry – and its ability to 'resurrect' language from the pallid simulacrum that daily use reduces it to – became for Avison the quintessential form to preserve the concept of this love. Especially significant is how, for Avison, this insight isn't something one rubs on language, but is a natural essence of language. To be a poet who works in the service of God is to believe that words have buried fecundities – asleep until activated by faith. God is the implicit touch, as it were, that unlatches a poem's power:

> He from elsewhere
> speaks; he breathes impasse-
> crumpled hope even
> in us:
> that near.

This chip of dazzling concision only looks simple. Christ is being addressed, but Avison is a poet who lets herself be led by sounds, so that her assertions, however devout, are always authenticated by her ear: 'impasse-/crumpled hope' is spectacular, as is the way the sentence comes to rest in the echo of 'elsewhere' in 'near'. These four lines, composed of the scrimps and economies of language, highlight the complex games with grammar that made books like *sunblue* and *No Time* (1990) so stylistically pioneering. They also remind us that Avison's Christianity does not strip her poems of their aesthetic authority. Her belief in Christ is poetically useful insofar as it lights out in interesting and energizing melodic directions, as it goads new kinds of lines. Avison successfully closes the distance between her tenets as a Christian and her freedoms as poet, encoding her devotion in distinctive and compelling language. One recalls Dun Scotus's theology of the Incarnation which explained Christ's birth – the Word made flesh – as God coming into time and body. In the same way, Avison's unremitting inventiveness – her superb alliteration, her quick wordplay with its fertile interlinking of Latinate and Anglo-Saxon vocabulary, her animating verbs, her specifying adjectives, her gift for compound phrases – represents a tireless search for the form most fit to recall the passion of Christ.

No Canadian poet has pushed to such an extreme the relationship of form to content, where the experimental freshness of the idiom is intended to confirm an idea that for many is as preposterous as table-rapping. In other words, most striking – and virtually unique in our literature – is how Avison's doctrinal sense of the sacred is wrapped up entirely in richly gnarled adverbial routings like 'woodenly they bulk/leafless where all the air is flower-frilled'. She spreads the word by focusing the concentrated hush of the reader's attention on her complex verbal effects and thus on the potency of the precepts that sponsor those effects. She has spiritualized syntax; reading her poems leaves our relationship with language re-angled, giving us a taste of how her conversion topsy-turvied her life ('I hadn't had my senses so vivid for years'). We see this again in lines like:

> A tree its twigs up-ending
> November had bared:
> drenched in height, brisk with

constellar seed-sprigs, thrusting
its ancient ranginess towards
the cold, the burning, spared
of leaf, sealed in, unbending.

The excellence of 'twigs up-ending' and 'drenched in height' underscores Avison's gift for making clapped-out diction potent again. But other pleasures inhere in this passage: how the enjambment sharpens Avison's thinking into a series of deft pauses and releases, the occasional ring of buried rhyme ('November'/'constellar') or the rhyme left to casually linger at line end ('bared'/'spared'), ('up-ending'/'unbending'). Also interesting is the way the lines thrive on minimal gestures yet the outcome never seems starved. Musically, the voice darts about in slantwise ways; again and again one pauses at the staggering of a sentence, the jumpy rhythm of a thought. Her syntax abhors the idea of rest.

These shifts, be they impressionistic and abrupt ('Misty summer/sidetracks years/to disused loading sheds sweet with the/sun on worn boards') or subtle and suggestive ('In the steeped evening/deer stand'), make the best case I know for Paul Valéry's definition of poetry as a 'prolonged hesitation between sound and sense'. Adroit use of this 'hesitation' is why her lines are so quirky and sensuous, seemingly responsive to every nuance of attitude and feeling, and Avison's obvious skill should be enough to discourage the notion that, post-conversion, her poems became creed-driven and cathedral-quieted. Of course, presenting these poems as objects that solicit and reward such technical analysis is largely my aim here. Avison doesn't think inside doctrine, she thinks inside style. But her style is all tricky, shifty business, so describing it is no easy task. Often, it's only after careful study that any coherent arrangement – sonic, prosodic, metonymic, thematic – becomes evident. Even then one may translate Avison's feats correctly and still fail to convey their lustre. So fully do her best poems embody her intuitions, so improvised are their shapes, that her most pleasing lines fly beyond accountability:

Grey by water   fathering fallen
      gold by evening   or morning

gritty by cinder   or grass broken
      greasy by sliding   and sloping

singing by combers   silting slacking
sizzling by horseless   plastic and chrome

acrid by acres   at canal level
oakleaf smoky   at late sunlevel

sour at stoneboat   marsh-lily stalk
            AND
sweet by wicker   or water.

Called, aptly enough, 'Making Senses' this unusual poem is constructed out of elided speech-clusters that Avison seems to have adapted from the alliterative pattern of Anglo-Saxon verse. In terms of what's being 'said', the poem is profoundly periphrastic, using the centre of the line to deflect or redirect expectations. Harder to describe are the 'under-ear activities', to use Heaney's phrase, that comprise the poem's fabric of effects: how the concretizing diction, the concise details, the teetering rhythm and sound-patterns invoke a powerful air of implication that isn't compromised by the scarcity of surface-meaning. We feel an intuition floating in an open-end relation to the form, giving the occasional meaningful nudge. When I read 'water' I can't help think of Christ speaking of being born again 'of water and of spirit', with that lovely image serving as an example of language's helpless metaphoricity before a mystery. Avison's riddling poem seems partly a call-and-response to that gospel moment, a contemporary rewriting of Christ's phrase to describe her own helplessness before the unfathomableness of her rebirth.

The pressure of such subtexts splits Avison's voice into a multiplicity of meanings and intents, ensuring that her poetry will always mean more than she could choose to control. We can see this subtext-pressure again in the exquisite series called 'Sketches' but also in poems like 'Two Mayday Selves', 'Words', 'Urban Tree', 'Psalm 19', 'The Store Seeds', 'Once', 'Natural/Unnatural', 'Hid life', 'Let Be', 'Oughtness Ousted', 'In the Hour', 'Future', 'The Fix' and 'Corporate Obsolescence'. As we discuss the details of this style, it seems important to remind ourselves of the details of the old style she set aside. Avison's poems in *Winter Sun* savoured the sound of words with a visceral relish. This sensuous immediacy, which the early poems worked so skillfully and generously to achieve, is less casually regarded in the Christian work, where Avison's aim is to render not so much the weight as the weightlessness of what she describes. The distance travelled from 'optic heart' to the 'de-/ciphering heart' arrives at an aesthetic that, in its attempt to approximate the discovery of God on the level of words, always preserves what resists verbalization:

The tethered dory thuds
in its lonely sarabande
after the speedboat's passing.
Thuds on the dock, as gradually
criss-crossing wavelets
scallop the weathered piles.
Thud. Then bump. Then nudge.

Wood shaped to shel-
ter even the clumsiest oarsman,
shaped to cumber
the sundanced waters or
the still angora mists of dawn.
Wood of the dock, wet fibring
wood piles solid on rock
fixed in cement – knee-deep
in a dry autumn, hip-deep and standing steady
when March forments the slush to gnaw
and no one sees or listens.

Wood, tied to wood,
but not by wood and
only in waiting intervals;
each mostly on its own.

This poem, called 'Family Members', gives us another marvellous ending, one that provides the subtlest amplification of the poem's argument. The delicately enjambed lines expose the poem's rhythmic nerve-endings and their quivering sensitivity to Avison's emotional and spiritual temperature. Not everyone can do this: rewire verbs and nouns so that readers see a theme – in this case, connection and disconnection – freshly. Sometimes, it's true, her poems set new standards of encryption. Yet this is the result of Avison taking the English language on journeys many of us no longer travel, so that encountering these poems means encountering, down to the micro level, a lost world of devotional thinking. Such intent has led to the blazing oddity of her voice, the live current of its music.

It's ironic to see such unprecedented effects from someone who hardly saw her poetry as 'contemporary'. Her conversion seems to have pushed her voice – already sunk deeply in twentieth-century influences – into a unique time zone, one Avison described as, 'The ancient, the new,/confused in speech'. In a sense, her poems invite us into a space where God's presence is mediated through the poem's exemplary language, which he allows to yield its own unique character and eccentric perfection. God works ministerially through the agency of Avison's modern ear. The balance that's struck makes Avison a marvellous reconciliation of opposites. Theologically she's a straight shooter. Her religious sentiments are not original (but neither, it should be said, were the religious sentiments of Donne or Hopkins). Poetically, though, her breaking of form is often assaultive, alarming. Artifice is a prayerful disruption, a daredevil adventure.

Avison has stretched our recognition of what a poem can be and do. But the lazy confidence with which we misread Christian ideas as anti-experimental might cause us to overlook this. The suggestion that Christianity can be a trigger for innovation has fallen out of favour. It isn't dismissed outright, but something about the way we teach and learn makes it naïve to take such an idea too seriously. Milton, George Herbert, Donne, Hopkins and Eliot – poets who put their faith to work, sometimes on a grand scale – have now had their achievements so secularly parsed that we often forget how, for them, God was where the action was, where the nature of the poetic medium was most at stake. Belief in God and belief in poetry flourished together. Of course, it would be easy to write Christian poems that, by the standards of art, are dreadful; dogmatic, pedestrian, pat. But Avison's poems – which pare away the clutter of conventional expression, revealing not only a thrilling mystery, but a new aesthetic – are not those poems.

EARLE BIRNEY

'We are becoming posterity' is how Louis Dudek, as a reviewer, described the experience of watching a once-proud literary career posthumously fight for his attention. Fifteen years after Earle Birney's death in 1995, and nineteen years after the last major selection of Birney's poetry, comes *One Muddy Hand*, edited by Sam Solecki. We are now that unknown audience that Birney, at his writing desk, wondered about.

But the posterity he has emerged into is sobering. As one of the great mid-century Canadian poets, his legacy seems secure. But it is secure in large part because he is a figure students are likely to write about. His poems are taught, studied, tested – in effect, Birney has been nationalized. What is missing, however, is precisely what claimed our attention in the first place, but what anthologies, seminars and exam questions can't quite recapture: visceral delight; the frolic-in-words Birney called 'a holiday from the prose of life'.

Birney no longer has his hooks in us, that much is clear. It isn't part of Solecki's brief, and certainly beyond his powers, to change that, but *One Muddy Hand* imparts a whole new vibe to the poems. In fact, Birney turns out to be something rather different than the grandee poet we've always had in mind – and a lot more than we bargained for.

To begin, the size of the book startles. *One Muddy Hand* is fatter than Birney's 1977 selected *Ghost in the Wheels* – nearly twenty-five percent bigger (86 poems have ballooned to 124). One would assume that the distance of thirty years would have brought some much-needed hindsight and severity. *One Muddy Hand* would be a more vital book if there were less in it. And yet, surprisingly, *One Muddy Hand* doesn't disappoint. It is everything you want in a Birney selected, as well as everything you didn't know you wanted.

Born in 1904, Birney was a late starter. He published his debut, *David*, in 1942 (which brought him his first Governor General's award) and his follow-up, *Now is Time,* in 1945 (which won him his second). Twenty more books (not including two novels) followed over the next thirty-eight years, among them four selecteds and a collected. The achievement, properly sifted, is not only a baker's dozen of dazzling anthology pieces ('Vancouver Lights', ' 'Anglosaxon Street', 'Caribbean Kingdoms', 'El Greco: Espolio', 'The Bear on the Delhi Road', 'Can. Lit.') but 'Bushed', which apart from being his best poem, is also one of the most remarkable English-language poems of the twentieth century.

The career-defining 'David' was his biggest crowd-pleaser (so much so he eventually claimed to regret he ever wrote it). It's a first-person account of a young mountain surveyor named Bobbie who watches his friend, David, plummet to the ledge of a cliff. Paralyzed, David begs Bobbie to push him off to his death. The poem led to anxious questions about its veracity, and this was fifteen years before the term 'confessional' even entered popular use. But *One Muddy Hand* confirms two things: that 'David' has always tugged our perception of Birney in the wrong direction, and it's the poem he tried his entire career to defeat.

Solecki's goal seems to present Birney's achievement as a 'maker', a word Birney himself preferred over 'poet', mostly for its pretentious-free odour (Solecki's decision to publish some of Birney's lucid critical pronouncements is an excellent attempt to take a fuller measure of the man). And a high-spirited constructedness is indeed one of the signatures of Birney's poetry, whether it was the concrete verse (hand-drawn or typewritten) that increasingly obsessed him, or the DIY formalism that lead to his greatest successes.

Magisterial and hyperactive, ungainsayably well-made but rutted with glitches, Birney language is unique and got into trouble (or, to use a Birney neologism, was more 'pervertible') in ways that were sometimes beyond even Irving Layton's powers. Birney was also astonishing prescient. Not only a sort of proto-Purdy nationalist (he had Canada on the brain long before Purdy's breakthrough collection *The Cariboo Horses* appeared in 1965), he also practised the sort of creative bilocation (being in two places at once) plainly visible in the themes of so many of our younger poets. A seasoned traveller, he drew inspiration from yonder regions of the world with an 'ism-less' fervour.

What makes the question of posterity so fascinating, therefore, is that he seems the verse elder best suited to our era. What may have stymied early readers about his work – Birney's anti-pastoral tone with its *fin-de-siècle* air – is now the basic twenty-first-century cadence. *One Muddy Hand* anticipates the characteristic triumph of current Canadian poetry: its collision of linguistic registers, its nonconformist energy, its shifting, plural wordplay. (Ken Babstock can be seen as part of the Birneyesque bequest.)

There are spectacular failures (tedious formal workouts like 'Sestina for the Ladies of Tehuantepec', shaggy-dog historical fables, 'Charité, Espérance et Foi') but very little here flickers weakly. Solecki's selection also confirms, more broadly, that the most innovative work in our literature is found in poetry. Little in Canadian fiction (with the possible exception of Leonard Cohen) can compare with Birney's startlingly visceral phrasing. His sound has been repurposed from Anglo-Saxon and set loose on the modern world:

> Flowers live here as easily as air
> They hang from power lines they grow on light
> A scalloped leaflet lying on a stair
> will puff pink buds and root itself in stone –

Birney's poems are difficult to quote from because it's difficult to convey, in quotation, the fear of insufficiency that makes its mark on every page; the impossible-to-absorb-tumult of insight and incident. That Birney was himself swayed by his fecundity is suggested by his infamously relentless revisions (scarcely any of his poems escaped changes, often major, of some sort). George Woodcock put it best when he described Birney's distinctiveness as the 'sense that the future is always open, that nothing written is ever quite finished while the author is alive'. The author is not, but his poems most assuredly are.

J.D. BLACK

THE POEMS IN *Black Velvet Elvis* (2006) surprise twice. First by their distinctiveness, then by how they leave you unprepared for what comes next. To go from a gory workplace accident ('Incident on the Plant Floor') to a sly satire on fashionistas ('Labels') is to experience the invigorating diversity of J.D. Black's first book.

Such chameleonic unpredictability is by no means the least of Black's gifts. There is his wit ('So keep revisions up to date: / You're working in a long tradition. / For final thoughts you must await / the posthumous edition'), his precise image-making (a bat swooping down on a moth is a 'dark-gloved hand closing') and his near-Byronic love of rhyme ('Vanished like a jinn, / From tail-tip in, / Past his chin, / To thin / Grin'). And then, of course, the way so much of his work rises to quotable passages:

> Phlegmatic plants, these rhododendrons:
> This small one, hibernation-dour,
> Its fanned leaves layered in alexandrines,
> Has never yet exclaimed a flower.

This stanza, taken from 'March Rhododendrons', is an example of how tiny touches ('Phlegmatic', 'hibernation-dour', 'exclaimed') can create a believable mood. No surprise, then, that Black excels in little dramas. He hits his note – and his stride – with a quartet of plain-spoken sonnets about a ne'er-do-well named Len. Ultra-nimble, flecked with colloquialisms ('I was some heavy on the gas / Pedal then: didn't give a good God-damn') and carefully rationed details, the voice in these 'vignettes' gives no sense of being laboured over. Whatever artifice is there is lightly worn, the structure invisible but entirely felt.

All this puts into perspective how, as a book, *Black Velvet Elvis* isn't the product of streamlined standards and quick turnarounds. Long hours have been put into these poems, toil that again and again breaks through into playful, liberated writing. Not to mention mischief. In a very fine piece called 'Signatures' the poet dwells on the 'large aggressive scrawls' made by 'rampant egos'. He isn't impressed:

> But none of these, or any that I know
> Can match the immunity from forgery,
> The glad, ornate, baroque virtuosity
> In cool effrontery's flagrant-yellow flow,
> Which my dog can sign a bank of snow.

This is writing to make one stand and cheer. Black's perfect ear for diction ('forgery' is a lovely choice) and attractive coinings ('flagrant-yellow flow') show him to be an exceptional judge of tone and register. What I love most about the poem (surely worthy of anthologizing) is its shrewdness in using mock-formality to underwrite an insult to decorum. Hard not to read the poem as a coded message to the 'curlicues and flourishes' of his poet peers.

The capstone of the book is perhaps the title poem. Set in a back-country Quebec gas station (or a 'gas bar de la nuit'), it stars 'the benignant presence' of a grinning Elvis who, from his perch above the register, is given to 'blessing villagers and passing travellers / through cracked, grime-mottled, grease-streaked glass'. Black uses the kitsch cult-figure to recreate both an intriguing portrait of a nondescript rural community (with its 'small swarms of boys in tight jeans') and the lost religiosity of a Catholic culture (for which the church is now merely an 'ornate immensity').

The poem's mix of wry comedy, social observation and understated pathos is exceptionally well-done, entirely characteristic, and only one of many successes to enumerate in this standout debut.

JAMES DENOON

IN THE SUMMER of 1860, the eighteen-year-old Prince of Wales was on a steamship headed for Newfoundland. It would be weeks before he would begin his five-month, whistle-stop tour of Canada and the United States, but the young monarch was already a media sensation. His name was being used to peddle waterproof coats, his portrait peeked up from memento plates, and a special cookie – the 'Prince of Wales Biscuit' – had been released. Journalists swung into action as well, describing the frenzy of beautification, complete with the 'terrific din of hammering and sawing', that engulfed the country ('Arches seemed to spring up everywhere the Prince would, could, or might pass' ran one report).

The poem 'Canada's Welcome to the Prince of Wales', published in *The Quebec Gazette*, captured the spirit of this anticipation. A sprightly salute to 'the son of our Sovereign Lady' cast in fifteen rhyming quatrains, it reads at times like a chummy field report. 'We are a plain sort of people in these distant parts/Unused to the fashions of splendour' is how one stanza starts; and another: 'We possess all the blessings which freemen enjoy/In a land that is fertile & healthy'. This theme of fertility and health is also extended to reassuring the soon-to-arrive prince that Britishness was in full flower; that while colonists lived a life pared to the stark essentials, their days brimmed with pride in royalty. 'Canada's Welcome to the Prince of Wales' also summed up a belief held by many of the tour's supporters: that beyond cementing colonial ties to the crown, the imperial stopover would give the wider world, watching through the international press, a look at the young country's progress. For all of its oaths to the Queen, the poem was essentially a love letter to Canada, a place it called 'Land of the lake and the river/Where nature's proud forests in majesty wave/ And her cataracts thunder forever!'

The man who set those lines down was a 58-year-old officer of the Royal Artillery named James Denoon. Born in Scotland in 1802, the exact date of his arrival in Canada is unclear, but we know he was stationed here as early as 1833. At the time, British soldiers were an everyday sight in this country, seemingly on perpetual parade. This was when British garrisons were used to guarantee a colonial *fiat lex* across Upper and Lower Canada. The Royal Artillery, with major batteries in Kingston and Quebec, provided the army with the firepower it needed. True to its motto – *Ubique* (everywhere) – there was scarcely a campaign fought by British troops where the Royal Artillery were not front and centre.

Denoon, in other words, did the job of empire. And in his only existing photograph, he certainly looks the part: sitting bolt upright in full regalia, bearded, with receding hair, caught in a cheerless gaze. It's the physiognomic embodiment of an age famous for its civic conservatism; as well as a visual marker of a time when setting up 18-pounder batteries (a fast-moving contingent of men, artillery and wagons) was the cutting edge in warfare.

But Denoon had another dimension: he was a closet poet. In truth, it was a pretty big closet, with room enough for thousands like him whose industry insured that the overweening rhetoric of 'Canada's Welcome to the Prince of Wales' would be taken for granted by nineteenth-century readers. Newspaper verse was at its heyday, with choice examples like Denoon's appearing prominently on front pages. No topic too trivial, no form too tricky, the contributions – which included ballads, epigrams, sonnets, odes, squibs, elegies and nursery rhymes – comprise a fascinating, if slightly fussified, airing of opinions on the varied concerns of the time. Like every other local daily, *The Quebec Gazette* played a part in this vox-pop boom. Its editorial policy was for 'such Originals, both in Prose and Verse, as may at once please the Fancy and instruct the Judgement'. Needless to say, Denoon's welcome to the prince fit the bill. The poem rings awkwardly in our contemporary ear, but it's not hard to see why it would have struck many early Canadians – who likely clipped it out and slipped it into their family Bibles – as inspiring.

Written by a man in the thick of military duty, deep into middle age and living on the imperial margins, 'Canada's Welcome to the Prince of Wales' introduces us to a time when versifying was the workaday rite of people too busy to give it a sacred air. One of the outcomes of a culture where huge chunks of poetry were learned by heart was that a knack for prosody became part of the skill set of most educated figures. American presidents were dab hands at rhyming (Lincoln and John Quincy Adams) as were Canadian prime-ministers (Darcy McGee) and scores of public figures: diplomats, ambassadors, mayors, judges and priests. As a dabbler, there was no reason for Denoon to harbour dreams of being sanctified by some calling, or of possessing an uncommon gift, or about 'Canada's Welcome to the Prince of Wales' deserving a fame beyond friends or family. Twenty years after its publication, Denoon recopied the poem by hand onto sheets of lined foolscap, sewed them together, and bestowed the pamphlet, as keepsake, on his granddaughter. The keepsake not only outlived its author (Denoon died in 1901), but went on to survive another 105 years in the afterlife often reserved for such ephemera: a dusty bookshelf. When it finally materialized last year in Montreal's Lower Westmount, it was accompanied by another forty homemade pamphlets. Mostly bootleg editions of his newspaper poems, each is carefully dated, all in excellent nick.

The discovery of this corpus offers nothing that would force us to redraw our poetic landscape. Yet the objects are mesmerizing for the unabashed way they bear – down to the thumping beat of their verse-lines – the marks of their maker. At first glance, you would anticipate the poems to bristle with that sense of might and right one imagines as the *sine qua non* of soldierly scrivening. On closer inspection, however, the clichés that cluster around *Pax Britannica* derring-do seem to cohere poorly in the person of Denoon. We get no imperialistic cant about the joys of being a redcoat, nor any heroic ditty from the front lines. There is one 'impromptu' composed on the occasion of the 79th Cameron Highlanders shipping out from Quebec in 1835, but the result is nowhere near the brutal Kiplingesque pep-talk one might have hoped to see. (Kipling: 'If your officer's dead and the sergeants look white,/Remember it's ruin to run from a fight'. Denoon: 'They are now on the wave, the gallant & brave,/And safe be their ride o'er the deep'.)

If Denoon ever led a crew of husky menfolk into combat, he kept it to himself. Instead, his poems are armed to the teeth with nineteenth-century poeticisms. Morning breezes are 'a balmy breath', cheeks are wet with 'tears of joy' and the dead rest their heads 'on earth's lovely pillow'. Everything is mawkish, cloying, sub-Keatsian ('How chaste the Lily's snowy vest/Emblem of all that's fine & fair'). The 'rural muse' is feelingfully invoked ('Instruct me while attempting to rehearse/Our country's grandeur in thy flowing verse'), and elsewhere we find a brace of sentimental 'paraphrases' on various points of scripture (the 90th psalm – that great prayer on life's 'dust to dust' transitoriness – was a big favourite). To be fair, there are pieces that do take the temperature of his political sensibilities, like 'Queen's Visit to Canada' or 'Lines on the Death of the Prince Consort'. But even here Denoon bestirs himself into sententiousness, never jingoism. In short, he emerges from these poems an oversensitive man's man. Faithful servant of the empire, but knuckled under. Uncomplaining and dutiful, but sans backbone.

These florid canticles are the part-time poems of a man who spent his days being full-time at something else. And the details of that 'something else' conjure up interesting visions to set against images like 'the opening Rose/Besprinkled with the tears of night'. Meting out punishment, for example, was probably one of Denoon's most important duties. The British army demanded absolute discipline, and soldiers found guilty of the slightest lapse were mercilessly flogged. ('There were few Saturdays', wrote the ninteenth-century French Canadian writer Philippe Aubert de Gaspé, 'on which those who went to the market in Upper Town in Quebec City were not saddened to hear cries of pain emanating from the barracks yard'.) As well, artillery combat was gruelling, and afforded no margin for mistake. Denoon and his gunners would have been required, at frantic pace, to judge the elevation, lay the gun, and correct the fall of shot.

The experience of fighting in a battery position must have been both frightening and thrilling (and dangerous, as not a few one-armed gunners in those days could confirm). Think of it: the ear-splitting explosion, the thick smoke, then the cursing of gunners already hustling to ready another round, faces blackened by powder. Imagine the rush of standing in the middle of such live firing – the bright flash of sight, sound and smell. Surely it was, in itself, a kind of poetry in motion: back-breaking, relentless and perfectly timed.

Yet it was also a regimental existence that – especially in colonies as becalmed as Canada – could be beset by boredom and restlessness, where each day was divided from the next by the isolating hierarchy of rank. Poetry might have become, for Denoon, a way of speaking freely. Off-duty hours in which he could lark. As it is, some of our information about him is drawn from the sundry coda he added to his compositions – comments, reminiscences, explanations, all jotted down during his last years in Three-Rivers. This colour commentary often hints at an ambivalence toward active service. For all its hardships, the Royal Artillery offered young men the prospect of adventure, as well as a salary. Part job, part calling, it acted as a magnet for certain personalities. Given the warm and non-confrontational simplicity of his 'sweet and harmonious' poetry, however, we're left to wonder if Denoon really had it in him. An intriguing poem called 'The Convict' is set on a prisoner transport ship where one of the convicts – 'the peasant whose crime was shooting a hare' – tells a sad tale of being torn from his life. The poem, we learn, was drawn from experiences during Denoon's 1825 command of the 'convict guard' at the Norwich garrison in England, the place these very prisoners where headed. In his afterward, Denoon expresses sympathy for the prisoners who were transported there, and the 'cruel treatment' administered to 'these erring children of Adam'. One can't help but wonder if his unhappiness with his work was decaying into guilt.

Am I pushing these poems to say more than they deserve to say? More to the point, do you care? The story of a wallflower Victorian soldier burning the midnight oil might satisfy the odd fetish for the bygone, but will leave most others cold. Yet it's worth recalling that Denoon's literary kin are very much alive today. By which I mean the taxi drivers, accountants, mechanics, dentists, elementary schoolteachers – everyone who scribbles greeting-card accounts of their sadnesses and joys without ever entertaining the hope of an acceptance letter from *The New Yorker*. In the ongoing debate about whether poetry has lost some central place in our culture, it's ironic that we overlook this faction, these poets laureate of community weeklies and Christian newsletters, who are surely the sole surviving vestige of an era when poetry fell within eyeshot (and earshot) of a wide readership.

It also bears recalling, in the ongoing debate about *why* poetry lost its central place in our culture, that newspaper verse's popularity likely had a great deal to do with the core behaviours it embraced: to rhyme, to scan, to make sense. The strictness of these codes helped to more efficiently transmit a temper of thought, a style of humour, a sensibility specific to the day. One might even argue that the assumption – shared by reader and poet – that longstanding literary conventions could carry the weight of lived experience was precisely what gave newspaper verse its range and unpredictability. It was doggerel, yes, but what else is doggerel if not antiquarianism in action, guilt-free and perennially fertile? Today these poems are placed behind the museum glass of special anthologies, which is not at all how they were intended to be consumed. The poems were what the French called *bruits publics* (or 'public noises'). They were part of everyone's literary diet: scanned while hurrying down the street, or snickered at while sitting in a tavern or declaimed to family after dinner. They were not, were never meant to be, 'good'. At least not as we understand the term. Readers sought them out for their tartness, wit, topicality, moral guidance – whatever it took to 'please the Fancy and instruct the Judgement'.

Denoon wasn't unsophisticated: he clearly had some sense of the ins and outs of the larger literary scene, as evidenced by his 1832 elegy 'On the Death of Sir Walter Scott'. Yet a salutary side-effect of the newspaper verse phenomenon was that it brought about a great deal of psychological clarity and good sense. Since poetry wasn't a specialist pursuit, occasional verse-writers could accept the truth of a higher range of ability without feeling judged by it – just as, today, the existence of the NHL doesn't negate one's enthusiasm for a game of shinny. When Denoon wrote 'Canada's Welcome to the Prince of Wales' the Charles threesome – Heavysege, Mair and Sangster – were the dominating Canadian poets of the day (the post-Confederation grandees – Bliss Carman, Archibald Lampman and Duncan Campbell Scott – were not yet born). I'm left wondering if Denoon ever knew about these poets; and whether, in an unguarded moment, he thought of himself as being, in his way, one of them. More likely he knew his place.

But then there are the pamphlets whose existence speaks of an eye firmly on posterity. The asides – always rich in background detail, always fascinating – suggest a self-consciousness about his activities, a curiosity about how they might be perceived. In one example, worth quoting in full, Denoon describes how he submitted his first poem:

> 'The Young Soldier's Dream' was one of the first essays I had ventured to offer to the newspaper press for insertion. I had sent a copy of the piece by one of our gunners to the Kingston *Chronicle* office with the request that if the lines appeared to the editor to possess sufficient merit, if it was convenient that he would give them a place in the *Chronicle*. It was subscribed A Scotchman & A Soldier. In the next issue of the paper it appeared with the following kindly notice. 'The Young Soldier's Dream' which appears on our first page reflects credit to its author, and we assure our gallant contributor who ever he may be, that so long as he continues to possess the feelings indicated by his sweet and harmonious verses he need never blush to subscribe himself 'A Scotchman & A Soldier'.

He was both more and less than Scotchman and soldier, though: simply a man, one faced with personal tragedies. In the pamphlets we learn that his son 'little Jamie' died in 1834, followed by his first wife, Bethia Scott, one year later. With regards to the youngster, Denoon writes that 'sickness came with withering breath' and it should be remembered that cholera was a big killer then, with an epidemic that raged in Upper Canada between 1832 and 1866. (The mortality rate for the disease in Montreal alone was given as 95 percent.) The elegies, even with their artificial diction, sting. 'Lines on the Death of

Little Jamie, Aged 7 months' is far and away his most moving piece. His lyricism, to poignant effect, stops just short of overripeness: 'Pale is thy form, dear faded flower,/Thou tender blossom of an hour'. You get a hint of out-sized grief tucked away inside tidy metaphors ('Thy lovely eyes now sealed in sleep/Shall never know the way to weep'), and, more faintly still, a reminder of those far-off days when people believed it took this sort of art to make life bearable.

Afterward we pan to 1841, and 'The Farewell Visit'. Written after attending the graves of his wife and child a day before embarking on an England-bound troopship, the poem is filled with the sort of lines ('Farewell my sainted wife and darling boy,/the parting kiss of love I may not give') surely only permanent and irresolvable bewilderment could make possible. It is hard to imagine a scene more emblematic of Denoon's character than that final goodbye in that windy cemetery. The next day he climbs aboard, a storm-tossed man.

This is the power of occasional verse. It offers up the meagrest of aesthetic satisfactions but is worth a thousand facts. Denoon's poems represent the countless counter-currents and backflows of literature – all the rookie minstrelsy that fights, futilely, art's tidal push toward originality. But these poems, precisely because of their collusion with cliché, seem to embody an intuitive sense of the world, of something 'felt in the blood'. And in reading Denoon I can't seem to shake the isolating aura of a man alone in his skin. An intensely sublimated melancholy filters through to us. The tactful, comfort-giving, meditational terms of his poetry suggest someone on the run from a private bogey. Words are so optimistically chosen ('How pure the joy, how sweet the peace') they disclose an opposing darkness. We are liable to reckon that his quieter moments must sometimes have been decidedly unhappy to produce such recycled scriptural wisdom.

Hard to say what this unhappiness might have been, though the verse holds some clues. Exile, for example, was Denoon's most consistent theme. 'The Young Soldier's Dream' is about a depressed overseas recruit pining for home. And the peasant-prisoner in 'The Convict' begins his story with a cry of leave-taking: 'The home of my childhood, the land of my birth/And all that is sacred and dear upon earth/Must I bid farewell'. Indeed, Denoon's most relentless inspiration was the highland countryside he roamed as a child. We can see this especially with a late-appearing series called 'Scenes in the Settlement' which rounds off a lifelong yearning for the *temps perdu*. Embedded deep in this rural memory-theatre are 'The Old Parish School' and 'The Forest-Church', two symbols of the pastoral ideal Denoon glommed onto during his idle hours. There is something poignant about the agent of a superpower yearning for a sleepy, bosky alternate realm. You're left to ponder the basic unreality of the attitude until you realize, with a shock, Denoon's nostalgia had transformed Canada into a version of what he had been helplessly coveting. A 'cloudless & fine' landscape whose prosperity is abundant and near at hand is, after all, the very Edenic vision he sought to convey to his 'honoured Prince'. So overriding were Denoon's tristful channels of thought they converted everything into the childhood memories he cherished, and single-mindedly elegized, in his final years. 'Scenes in the Settlement' comes close to being his most private confession.

This is not a search for the 'real' Denoon. He can't be found. All we can do is carve a character out of a few treacly images and the belief in poetry as a social grace. The grandfatherly gift Denoon ultimately made of his poems would, perforce, suggest how lightly he regarded his efforts. On reflection, however, the opposite is just as likely. The very lightness of the act implies someone for whom time weighed heavy in his hands. When you read the formality of the dedication – 'Offered for the acceptance of my beloved granddaughter Bertha with the affectionate regards of her grandfather in the eighty-eighth year of his age ' – what lowers over these slender artifacts is the mood of a man in whom the world is no longer interested. In an 1885 poem called 'The Changes of Home' the homesick young soldier returns to find everything altered ('the rude hand of innovation/Almost at ev'ry spot'). The subject is painful, evoking *fin-de-siècle* anxieties and the feeling that the speaker has somehow walked on his own grave. Denoon died six years later.

Verse – or rather versifying as a public pastime – disappears from the pages of newspapers during the 1920s. Blame the Great War, which changed people's ideas about the sort of bromides Denoon summoned into his verse. Blame T.S. Eliot, whose ideas encouraged poets to sign an exclusivity contract and restrict themselves to a specific branch of categorization. In 1836, such a sea-change was nearly a century away. That year, Denoon stopped at Niagara to watch the waterfalls. He reached into himself, inspected his feelings, and used them to write this: 'The tremendous cauldron/That's boiling down below/And wreathing in its agony/With sweat as white as snow'. That vivid image – at once mixed and fustian and fervent – belongs to an age before poets became their own class and caste. It also belongs to a Scotchman and a soldier whose poems waited, *samizdat*-like, for their day to surface and open his life to us.

JOHN GLASSCO

I love John Glassco's book about Paris but I don't really identify with it ... Partly because he comes from the 'other Montreal' I suppose.
GAIL SCOTT

UNSMILING AND SEIGNEURIAL, John Glassco stares out from the back of his 1971 *Selected Poems*. He is sixty-one. His mustache is trimmed, his ascot crisp; a pampered air attends his expression. 'A very Edwardian-looking gentleman' – this, from Louis Dudek, nicely sums up the sophistication in that face: the face of aplomb, of a man who knows his worth.

Glassco – Buffy, to friends – was at the height of his prestige not only as a poet (*Selected Poems* would go on to win the Governor General's award for poetry) but a diversely gifted man of letters. *Memoirs of Montparnasse*, a sparkling evocation of expatriate Paris during the 1920s, had been published to wide acclaim the previous year. *The New York Times Book Review* called it 'a delightful, on-the-spot report of the days when it was still possible to be very young, very hip and very happy'. It was joined by *The Poetry of French Canada in Translation*, a landmark anthology in which nearly half the contributions were done by his own hand. Adding to these achievements were critical essays, book reviews, short-stories, even pornographic novels. ('We never knew', Robin Skelton later recalled, 'what he would write next, what he would renew by translation, what he would say'.) A first-rate stylist, Glassco deemed writing a challenge best overcome by panache. No matter the genre, he was always garbed in a well-cut form. He ran with a pack of Montreal poets, among them A.J.M. Smith, F.R. Scott and Ralph Gustafson, who brought something courtly and dashing to Canadian letters. Together this 'Montreal Group' embodied a set of ideals – in Glassco's own words: 'mastery of line, cadence, perfection of ear' – that were, in their day, the epitome of cool. And, as the photo proves, even in a group with a well-known punctilio for jackets and ties, Glassco stood apart.

Yet his gaze gives pause. Lidded eyes sit on heavy bags, drained and disillusioned. It reminds us that, besides the suave Glassco readers know (made famous by all the merry-making and skirt-chasing in *Memoirs*), there's another rarely talked about – the self-loather, the lamenter, the loner. The Glassco who, in a late letter, counted himself among 'the tired generation, the finished men'. The Glassco who, according to biographer Brian Busby, dreaded three things: 'His birthday, Christmas and New Year's Eve'. The Glassco who critic Philip Lanthier claims was 'wracked by the terrors of having lost his way in life'. As it happens, this fellow is fairly easy to find: his poems give him away.

Glassco was one of the first Canadian poets to show a sincere interest in decay. Decades of residence in Quebec's relic-strewn Eastern Townships sharpened his eye for emblems of decline: dilapidated farmhouses, barns and sheds. His tendency to dote on debris, often emphasizing its grungier aspects like 'mouldering walls' or 'tarpaper hanging in tatters', was sometimes seen as evidence of a bathetic bent. (In a 1964 letter, Al Purdy warned Glassco about the risks of swooning over 'ruined things'.) Yet Glassco's poems contrast sharply with the soft-headed rusticity that afflicted Canadian poets at the time, including his Montreal group. 'It snows on this place', goes one of Gustafson's typically tranquil lines, 'And a gentleness obtains'. Glassco saw nothing gentle about it. The pastoral, for him, was a postmortem on its own prettiness. Nature spawned weeds, scarecrows, cow-piss puddles, concrete cubes, barbed-wire and 'graveyards minding their own business'. Weather was hostile ('sun and rain / Score harshly') and countrysides teemed with malign verbs: choke, crumble, drag, dump, grind, rut, scour, spew. To Northrop Frye, who believed the Canadian imagination was at its best when pitted against 'a huge, unthinking, menacing, and formidable setting', Glassco's reply was: don't bother. Our defeat is a *fait accompli*. Indeed, grouped a certain way, his poems even lend themselves to being read as a semi-dystopian narrative, starting with 'A House in the Country' with its suggestion of huddled survivors ('when the rains come on we'll set/Pans in the attic to catch the drip') to 'Deserted Building Under Shefford Mountain' with its image of a post-human world ('Dark houses that are void of man'), to 'The Entailed Farm', where a deserted farm evokes the rewilding of structures left behind after man vanishes:

> Where the stone wall is a haven for snake and squirrel,
> The steepled dovecote for phoebe and willow-wren,
> And the falling field-gates, trigged by an earthen swell,
> Open on a wild where nothing is raised or penned

Glassco was acutely aware of his rubble-gawking ('Why do I love you, ragged things?'), and, in some of his best poems, tries to probe it. 'The Burden of Junk', which appeared in his first book *The Deficit Made Flesh* (1958), finds the poet dropping by a scrap dealer named Corby and his 'Yardful of rusty and broken machinery'. Corby's delight over a recent acquisition – 'Swapped the old three-teated cow for a genuine walnut harmonium!/Look, ain't a scratch or a brack on it anywhere – pedals and stopples/Work just as good a fellow could ask for!' – causes Glassco to reflect on what he can offer in 'trade':

> Mine is a burden of lumber that ought to be left with him also:
> This is where it belongs, with the wheels and the beds and the organ,
> With all the personal trash that the spirit acquires and abandons

Nothing quite like this exists in Canadian poetry before Glassco. Even Atwood's most twisted psychodramas at the height of her 'survivalist' stage fall short of a 48-year-old man comparing himself to a 'burden of lumber' fit to be tossed on a rubbish heap. Glassco's sense of unsuitability was, in part, linked to worries about wasted literary effort. As poets often do, Glassco brooded on his career until fear of neglect mixed indistinguishably with fear of death. This comes into ironic play in the above lines, which grapple with the idea of oblivion in dactylic hexameter (a staple of epic poetry). The lines are also a warning that Glassco's well-groomed bon vivantism can only take us so far when assessing poems one critic called 'splinters from a damaged sensibility'.

'The Burden of Junk', then, shows signs of a breakthrough. Compared to poems by his contemporaries, it carried a different, more mordant, slightly unhealthier idea of what a person was, or could be. Eating away at Glassco was the hard-to-shake sense of being damaged goods. Some of his peers (Dudek, say) thought Glassco's gift for staging desolate tableaux owed something to the over-hatted *fin-de-siècle* Decadents. In the passing years, however, poems like 'The Burden of Junk' have revealed themselves to be stranger, more disturbed, more genuine. Far from striking a pose, Glassco feels the unease within his own skin. His best poems are an account of how things – including humans – fall apart. The world for him comes alive only from the bottom down; and even then, only to the extent to which it carries the clarity of its ruin. We can see this in the excellent ending to 'The Burden of Junk'. Fusing earnestness and unsentimentality, the poem draws on memories of Glassco's salad days to evoke 'the loves that a dreary process of dumping/Leaves at last on a hillside to rot away with the seasons'. The slippery ambiguity released by that closing line-break, making 'leaves' both noun and verb, both deed and symbol, masterfully embodies Glassco's dead 'loves'. The effect – heaviness of heart synced up with the unbeautiful – puts 'The Burden of Junk' within shouting distance of other works that explore the impact of discarded matter on identity: Stevens's 'The Man on the Dump', Ammons's *Garbage* and DeLillo's *Underworld*.

Glassco was saddled with the Midas curse: the compulsion to turn pain into art. He was a dab hand at sonnets and could turn a rhyme on a dime. He also had a taste for syntactically daring stanzaic experiments ('Gentleman's Farm' is a three-page poem constructed out of three long sentences). Into these Fabergé forms, he poured acid. An inveterate phrase-jeweller, Glassco was extraordinarily deft at conveying varieties of hard luck: missed chance and failed opportunity, rural lives reduced to 'rotten fencepost and old mortgages'. He gives us gallows wit (his 'coffined farmer' simultaneously captures two kinds of death), woebegone maxims ('Hope battered into habit, and a habit/

Running to weariness') and chisel-struck formulations ('troubled joy that's half despair').

The result, in poem after poem, is a music unfazed by its bleak content. Alternately, you might say Glassco turned gloom into ear candy. Few poets possessed of so much anti-charm have worked harder to win over readers. He gives us striking images of entrapment ('watch the struggles soft moths make / Fast bound within the spider's web'), entombment ('the closed / enclosing house') and decomposition ('papery corpses crumbling'). One poem addresses a mother holding a screaming baby and calls her child a 'growth of a moment's infection dredged from your loins'. The shock of that line, set off by its cool crispness, illustrates what Eli Mandel identified as the 'Satanic Glassco and the Wordsworthian one'. With their excellent table manners, Glassco's poems mount their upmarket appeal on the illusion of speaking for Wordsworthian nostalgia ('You natural scenes to whose eternity / My transient vision and my life are bound, / teach me to see'). But searing through his sparkling stanzas and rhymes is something darker: despair at the futility of human life, at how man 'is destined for slaughter in the course of things'. And because Glassco had no goal above that of writing well, it is despair on display, despair that seeks to seduce, with violent images wrapped in plush tones.

> I am a homestead in a hundred acres:
> I draw them around me and devour them.
> I eat the farmer's flesh and his children
> – Who but I hollaed the sweating team –
> Their hands were worn away in my service,
> Sold my acres one by one to strangers.
> Ere I was done the dying farmer cursed me,
> Crying within the strangling noose of hope.
> I am the grave of the husbandman's hope.

These lines, from 'The White Mansion', are spoken by a century-old house who boasts of using her feminine wiles to ensnare unsuspecting proprietors and drive them to the point of obsession, exhaustion and ruin: 'Within and without, he dressed me in splendour. / Ere

I was done, I stripped him naked,/Sent him away weeping, to beg for money'. The house becomes an avatar for the universe's mean streak, its utter hostility to human happiness: 'I am the death of man and of his dream'. Glassco based his poem on the spacious, manor-like home he moved into in 1936, located on a farm on the outskirts of Knowlton, Quebec. He lived there for over a decade, enjoying an idyllic, semi-reclusive country existence until – as we learn from Busby's biography – woman troubles turned the place into a living hell. With its filigreed English, disquieting images ('Swan-white I float among bare crusted maples./Grey hills behind me, black water at my feet') and careful application of theatricality to conjure an atmosphere of Gothic noir, the poem is a gorgeous demonstration of Glassco's biases. He seemed ready to use any pretext – and every bell and whistle – to indulge his appetite for doom.

Biography played a part in this as well. The grim phantasmagoria of Glassco's poetry had roots in an astonishingly brutal upbringing. Glassco, as he revealed in 'Autobiographical Sketch', was raised by a 'sadist' father who beat him savagely during his childhood, a humiliation that triggered years of 'cruel and unremitting nightmares' (the outlines of their relationship can be seen in 'The Whole Hog'). In this sense, Glassco's taste for the macabre was bred in the bone. It seems fitting therefore that he used masks ('masks that misery has put on') to vent his feelings. Along with the pseudonyms he adopted for his erotic novels, Glassco also turned to historical figures whose lives, he felt, held moments of crisis that mirrored his own. These include medieval religious writer Thomas à Kempis ('I think we are/Coals ever cooling, blown at times by God') and the half-mad French painter Utrillo ('Colours of crucifixion, dying graces,/Spatter and cling upon these sorrowful places'). Translation afforded yet another mask. He found his greatest affinity with Quebecois poet Saint-Denys-Garneau, whose anguish-ridden journals and poems ('Oh into what wilderness we must go/To die quietly by ourselves') moved him deeply.

By these repeated bifurcations, Glassco not only assembled a Greek chorus of doppelgängers, but revealed a key truth about himself: his civilized tendencies were the reverse side of a horrified self-knowledge, one too hot to handle directly. His disguises freed him to speak. His most memorable alter-ego in this regard was iconic fashion plate Beau Brummell. Nineteenth century's 'it' boy, and the inventor of dandyism, Brummell was celebrated for his razor wit and sense of style until a poorly judged insult (he called the Prince of Wales 'fat') got him booted from high society. Gambling debts then forced him to flee to the French city of Calais. He later died in an asylum, penniless and syphilitic. In one of his finest and most revealing poems, Glassco tries on Brummell's demise for size. 'Brummell at Calais' is a portrait of 'a foolish useless man' done in by narcissism and who posterity further punishes by remembering him precisely for his superficiality. The poem ends on what Glassco calls the 'The triumph of his veritable art':

> An art of being, nothing but being, the grace
> Of perfect self-assertion based on nothing,
> As in our vanity's cause against the void
> He strikes his elegant blow, the solemn report of those
> Who have done nothing and will never die.

Those familiar with Glassco's chronic doubts about himself ('I have turned out a failure in everything I have tried to do', he wrote in an early letter) may find it hard to read these lines, published in his second book *A Point of Sky* (1964), as anything other than a stinging self-indictment. Glassco, after all, was Canada's dandy-poet, the literary *arbiter elegantiarum* of his day. It was a role he publicly relished (George Fetherling tells a story of paying Glassco an early morning visit and finding him already in a silk smoking jacket and cravat, sipping breakfast champagne). But if his author photograph is any hint, fears he had fallen prey to Brummellian vanity were maybe starting to take hold. This was a misery in which he had company. The sun setting on Glassco was also setting, as he knew all too well, on his friends. Indeed, 'Brummell at Calais' is especially interesting if read as a kind of high formalist *Howl*, a lament for the best minds of a Montreal generation who had produced the most peacocking artifacts in Canadian poetry: dazzling, begemmed with verbal bling, ringing with emptiness. What Glassco's face betrays, in other words, is a poet coming to terms with the possibility of his own ridiculousness.

If one wanted to trace the beginnings of that expression, as well as its insights into Glassco's career, *Memoirs of Montparnasse* is a good place to start. The gone-to-seed decadence of the photograph – dewlap and sagging jowls against impeccable attire – stands in stark comparison with the fresh-faced university dropout ('just beginning acquaintance with the razor', according to Leon Edel) who decamped for Paris in 1928. The city's bohemian heyday of Hemingway and Stein ended almost a decade earlier, but Montparnasse was still every bit the street that inspired Cole Porter's song 'Let's Misbehave'. Like many young writers in flight from North America, Glassco was desperate for a piece of the Lost Generation myth. He got his wish. Adopted by a troupe of literary ex-pats soon after making landfall, he began to document their gin-soaked escapades along with his own makeover into a bed-hopping *dolce vita* operator 'sunk in greed, sloth and sensuality'. Published nearly four decades later – allegedly in its original state – the book is more than a memoir. It's a love letter to a vanished era of excess.

But for all its tales of youthful rakishness, *Memoirs of Montparnasse* also specializes in candid depictions of old age. Glassco's Paris was filled with legendary editors and novelists such as Frank Harris, Ford Madox Ford and George Moore. The nineteen-year-old Glassco is clearly smitten with these men (he calls Moore 'my literary god'), but they emerge from his narrative as sad figures, condemned to the reputational afterlife of lesser literary lights. Their fate serves as a poignant counterpoint to the nonstop frivolity. Glassco revels in the brat-pack antics, but keeping such fast company comes with an unexpected cost: he feels time running out. His developing fascination with what he calls 'the inexorable progression of my own body to decay and death' is forewarned in explicit fashion early on, when his travel companion, Graeme Taylor, dreams of him 'as an old man with whiskers, writing'. The ensuing portraits of Harris and Ford reprise that basic image. Especially Moore's: 'the sloping shoulders, the beautiful drooping moustache, the exquisite chinless face, the heavy-lidded eyes'. This turns out to be an uncanny description of the older man Glassco would one day become.

Of course, that's because Glassco *was* an older man when he wrote it. Whisked to Montreal in 1931 after being diagnosed with tuberculosis, Glassco insisted that *Memoirs of Montparnasse* was completed in a hospital bed and then shelved for thirty-five years, a claim that became part of the book's creation myth. Glassco's archives, however, revealed that he didn't begin work on the book until 1963 – seven years before it was published. What's more, much of his eyewitness testimony was discovered to be largely fabricated. As a work of fiction filtered through actual memories, *Memoirs of Montparnasse* was, critics argued, closer to being a *roman-a-clef*. But Glassco's fib in fact underscored a book that, in one respect, was deeply confessional. Not only did he appear to have recast the physical appearances of Harris, Ford and Moore in his own image, the younger Buffy's sympathy for those fast-faded reputations was the projection of a greyer self who, like them, had outlasted the social order in which his life made sense. Glassco had thus doctored his reminiscences to more effectively remind readers – but especially himself – that a literary scene was no country for old men.

And he would know. When Glassco – the real Glassco – returned from Paris, Montreal had become a poetry boomtown. During the 1940s, no better place in Canada existed to serve one's literary apprenticeship. There are a few reasons for this. First, the city was exhilarating. It was, as William Weintraub writes in *City Unique* (1998), 'bilingual, cosmopolitan, exceedingly handsome and wonderfully odd'. Next, the rivalry between little magazines *First Statement* and *Preview* (which later merged into *Northern Review*) kept the upstart quotient unusually high: John Sutherland, Patrick Anderson, Louis Dudek and Irving Layton were all in close quarters, bristling with agendas. But what really drew ambitious newcomers like P.K. Page were a cadre of painstaking technicians who could not have flourished in any other Canadian city. Lead by A.J.M. Smith, this group railed against a clapped-out nineteenth-century poetic tradition that, as they saw it, persisted into the twentieth century as a zombie canon. These 'undead' ideals were represented, and imitated, by members of the much-reviled Canadian Authors' Association ('Expansive puppets percolate self-unction' begins Frank Scott's infamous verse take-down of a CAA meeting). While there are lots of fun ways to describe these Young Turks – shit-disturbers, giant-killers, exposers of false gods – they were basically conservative experimentalists: they composed poems that married and modified traditional forms and devices with an eye to what critic Leon Edel described as 'the modern idiom, the use of words as this year's language shorn of old accretions of meaning'. By doing so, poets like Smith, Scott, Leo Kennedy and A.M. Klein introduced a dizzying range of new effects into Canadian poetry, from the colloquially offhand to the tightly epigrammatic. It should be said, however, that while these 'angry young men' were internationalists and innovators, they had no truck with the unfriendlier reaches of modernism. They choose euphony over dissonance. They were after the singing line.

Glassco – who was something of a slow learner, and didn't publish his first book *The Deficit Made Flesh* until he was nearly fifty – sided with these control freaks, and in the 1950s often visited Montreal to spend time in their company. Like them, he assembled poems with a deep pleasure in their constructedness (he once defined good poems as having 'a beginning, a middle and an end'). The pleasure wasn't unwarranted. Metrical fluency was still, in many circles, the ne-plus-ultra. True, those circles were rapidly shrinking, but rhyme and meter remained part of the larger frame of reference. It was a period that welcomed experiments (Birney's typographically wild 'Appeal to a Lady With a Diaper') but didn't relieve poets of the duty to satisfy expectations of form and meaning. It was a period that hankered after thrilling oddness (Avison's jaggedly energetic 'The Butterfly') but stayed loyal to poetry as beautiful language. Alas, ideas of good poetry, and the reputations they buoy, are always vulnerable to changes in taste – trend-shifts that can drain those ideas of their authority and leave careers high and dry.

Which is exactly what happened. By the time Glassco's photo was snapped, the larky, natty youth had become, in his own words, 'a new-made ghost'. We can read it plainly on his face. In newspaper profiles he could still play the 'elegantly tailored' cad who spent his afternoons 'thinking, reading, and fortifying himself with martinis'. But the anachronism of the role had been remorselessly exposed by an emerging generation that targeted him in their political-cultural dissent. 'All of John Glassco's works', wrote the 34-year-old poet-critic Frank Davey in 1974, 'have been eccentric achievements, more attached to the values and fashions of the past than to those of post-war Canada'. The reason Davey could write such a sentence, and feel serene doing so, was because the national aesthetic had shifted from the mid-Atlantic voice (Anglo-American in diction, Canadian in content) popularized by the Montreal Group. Thanks in large part to Tish, Vancouver became the new beachhead. Founded in 1961 as a poetry newsletter (its name is an anagram of 'shit'), it regarded itself as a reset button on Canadian poetry's colonial hang-up. It was Tish, of which Davey was a founding member, that first raised alarms about the 'Eurocentrism' of poets like Glassco. A cocktail of counter-cultural fedupness, mud-slinging and political anxieties, Tish successfully tapped into a rising exhaustion for high culture. Anything too revised or technically confident, anything that chimed and rhymed, was square. Or worse, frivolous: cocooned inside an anti-world of style.

In such an environment, a poet like Glassco was easy to mock. In his review of Glassco's second book, *A Point of Sky* (1964), bill bissett was characteristically scathing: 'They all look like bad trips to me'. Those sorts of hipster sentences – and Tish had a gift for trash talk – did mortal damage to Glassco's reputation. One of Tish's most under-appreciated skills was its ability to stay on message. They had their talking points and consistently stuck to them until, almost without anyone noticing, those campaign themes became internalized by poets, critics and academics across the country. At first, Glassco pushed back. In one poem, he dismissed the Tish-leaning poems popping up in magazines as 'poetics about poetics about poetics'. He also took a stab at a spoof sound poem, a lark called 'A Catbird' (representative line: 'k'tuf à tuf à tuf à tuf à tuf à te kerry'). But it did no good. The more successfully Tish practised its dark arts, the funnier Glassco's ascots and dinner jackets looked. Until he himself was moved to write in a journal from the early seventies: 'I have been rejected as a serious writer, and acclaimed as a clown'.

Of course, these trends didn't leave Montreal untouched. As its taste-making clout faded, the city's poetry scene, in the eyes of the country, sank as well. Montreal became a victim of its past vitality. True, Irving Layton and Leonard Cohen continued to be attention-getting figures, but by then both men were full-time globetrotters and part-time residents (Cohen, who spent much of his time in Greece, only visited Montreal to, as he put it, 'renew my neurotic affiliations'). The mood was ripe for what happened next. In 1967, after taking up a writer-in-residence post at Sir George Williams University, George Bowering set off a Tish boomlet in the city. Younger poets, energized by Bowering's presence (he later returned to Vancouver in 1971), sought to establish a grittier local alternative – dubbed the Véhicule poets – against what they deemed as the city's genteel tradition. The old guard, Glassco among them, soon found themselves treading in the waters of a strange interregnum. The public context their talents once enjoyed had soured. Unfashionability foist upon them, they were now the 'other Montreal'. The last of a line, defiantly backward-facing, obstinate espousers of discredited ideas.

As is often the case in these generational skirmishes, a real weakness in Canadian poetry was being exposed. Tish wanted nothing to do with the 'culture-objects' flooding the domestic market, produced by Eastern Canadian poets for whom form was, in Davey's words, a 'showplace for the human mind'. And who could blame them? Many of the formalist tics that drove Tish crazy can certainly be spotted in Glassco: too-pretty gratuitousness, too-ponderous wordplay, a grapple with language that doesn't know when to let go. Even the elegiac accent Glassco made so signally his own, that ravishing mix of decorum and dread, laid a trap for him. Descriptions of 'the ragged matter' sometimes led to moments where Glassco didn't evoke, but embellished; where applying the idea of decay to surfaces caused him to lay it on thick. 'I see these silent ruins wear/the speaking look, the sleeping air/of features newly cast in death'. Glassco's trouble is that he absorbed, but never came to distrust, the classic cadences of English poetry. 'Later poets learn their craft from earlier', writes critic William Logan, 'but they must provide the originality themselves, in resistance to what they learn'. So when Glassco's poems fail, they fail not from a negligent handling of his devices, but from a too-confident embrace of them. They fail for being all too aware of how it's supposed to be done.

Such an assessment, no doubt, squares up with what readers may already surmise about the period. And that's because – as is also often the case in these generational skirmishes – history is written by the victors. It can be a surprise, then, to find poems by Glassco that burn with self-assurance, emotional resonance, many-rooted wordplays and memorable speech. These traits also exemplify everything that, for a period, allowed that phalanx of mid-century Montreal poets to dominate the skyline. This was a group that made their mark as precisionists, believing in the power of a word fitly spoken (which is why they were frequently good at the level of individual lines. Smith's 'The beauty of strength/broken by strength/and still strong', for example, or Glassco's 'nothing endure that does not gain through ruin/ The right, the wavering line'). They transformed Canadian poetry by their belief in verse as a test of prowess, a performance that could be objectively evaluated (which explains the shrewd critical prose many of them wrote: those evaluations, after all, needed to be defended). Together they strived to create an audience for world-class poetry that had a premium on intellectual idiosyncrasy, was technically mettlesome and brandished an exacting sense of diction (but also allowed for moments when that diction might take leave of its senses). All of these ideas were ploughed into the production of exemplary and enduring poems, some of which rank among the glories of Canadian poetry: Scott's 'Lakeshore', Klein's 'Portrait of the Poet as Landscape', Gustafson's 'The Newspaper' and Glassco's 'Gentleman's Farm'.

We think of these names, if we think of them as all, as yesterday's thing, their use-value used up. When they aren't being ignored, they are among the most faintly praised of our top poets. And yet their influence persists in ways, and on fronts, we no longer think to look for. Call it the shock of the old. This 'other Montreal' showed an uncomprehending country that heightened vernacular could be a powerful medium for the scrutiny of complex experience. What is more, they codified the sound and rhythm of the casually elegant, schooled-yet-spontaneous Canadian poem. Poets as varied as Richard Outram, Robyn Sarah, David O'Meara, Amanda Jernigan and Bruce Taylor owe a debt to them.

For Tish, they were CanPo's 'burden of lumber'. Today, however, there are signs that it's Tish, and not the 'other Montreal', that faces obsolescence. George Fetherling once argued that Tish ended up being far more influential than *Preview* or *First Statement*, the two magazines that brought modernism to Canada in the 1940s. Up to a point, this seems true. While the newsletter folded in 1969, and its editors scattered, the forces it helped release dominated for decades. Indeed, Tish's contempt for 'bad trips' still lingers. But then, that's exactly the problem. What has Tish bequeathed to us except the permission to resent elevated language? Spreading an opinion toward a certain kind of verse is not a legacy. Opinions get replaced. Legacies – legacies with legs – require poems that reward scrutiny. But because Tish never cared much about relating means to ends (the better to flog their stuff as 'process') their poetry doesn't demand anyone's full attention. Tish's first-thought, best-thought hard sell may have won the argument, but the poems paid a heavy price: an insanely high throwaway rate. That's what it means to be junk.

At the time, however, they were the anti-heros, intolerant of what bored them. And for this manifestoing brat pack, the poems of this 'other Montreal' were as outlandish as anything in Palgrave's nineteenth-century anthology *The Golden Treasury*. Glassco, beaten down, began paying attention. Maybe he felt they had point, maybe he wanted to show he wasn't stuck in his ways or maybe the avant-garde winds just threw him. Whatever it was, two years after he published his *Selected Poems*, Glassco went on to self-publish his last, and oddest, book of poetry, *Montreal* (1973). An 'epic-macaronic' whistle-stop tour of his memories of Montreal, the poem turned its streets to metaphoric rubble, a ugly no-man's land. The city was now a place full of old stuff. The voice is held together by interspersings of French and Indian sentences embedded in sprawling, theatrical, ample stanzas that swing between free-verse and rhyme. It's a portrait of the fogy as loser, blackballed by fate. The whole thing has the feel of a panic attack.

Now as a daring driver, beating the traffic lights,
Outwitting taxis, speeding and switching lanes,
Barely missing fenders of the double-parked,
My eye alert for cops, my ear disdaining
All furious frustrated honkings, I fly like a wild goose
Over all your hallowed ground, O Montreal,
Annihilating Jeanne and Maisonneuve
Dorchester and Saint-Denis
McTavish and McGill,
Crushing my memories of your streets, passing
Into another world, moving
Into another country of the anarchic mind

With its sophisticated notes mingled with maladroit moments, *Montreal* seemed to embody for Glassco a genuine confusion about how to continue writing poems (one critic called it 'half-cocked' another critic said it had 'the shock value of the worst Tish poetry'). Canadian poetry would, of course, go on to do different things, things Glassco could scarcely have imagined. And one can't help but feel in this poem that the shape of that future – our reality – had started to download some of its own confusion into his life.

For all the pleasure-principles he represented – technical giftedness, unimpeachable wordplay – Glassco is the saddest of all Canadian poets. He forged a fatalism that, poised between vigour and elegance, was new to us. You came for the style, but stayed for the woe. When he passed away in 1981, so too did the most cavalier heyday of Canadian poetry, a circle now under deep anti-formalist suspicion, effectively given the heave-ho. To borrow John Bayley's example of Wordsworth, they are 'like one's parents' clothes – always out of fashion'. But surely one of the great tasks of twenty-first-century critics will be to help us think again about these figures, among whom Glassco stands tall.

MICHAEL HARRIS

ONE OCTOBER EVENING in 1969, Leonard Cohen drops by a Bishop Street flat to sit for an interview. He sports an old blue raincoat, a guitar and, of course, a pretty 'friend'. Already big news in Canada, the 35-year-old Montreal poet is on the cusp of global fame following the release of his first folk album two years earlier. The interviewer, on assignment for a local magazine, is a 25-year-old university student named Michael Harris.

Sharing 'a mutual dislike of interviews' – as Harris describes it in his introduction – the two men decide 'simply to talk'. They discuss celebrity, film, perfection, friendship, clothing, bad reviews, God and songwriting. Harris is polite, careful in his prompts. Cohen is, well, Cohen: agile, civilized, saturnine, deadpan. (Harris: 'Do you consider yourself a craftsman?' Cohen: 'I consider myself a craftsman in the way that a man who draws caricatures with his toes considers himself a craftsman'.) The singer-songwriter comes across as both the most honest person on earth and a walking one-man show. There was nothing remotely like him on the Canadian scene at the time, and his example proved irresistible for young poets in search of models – young poets, as it happens, like Harris. With only a slim chapbook to his name, and troubled about the health of his poetic creativity – feeding it, mining it, protecting it – Harris is anxious for advice. 'What kind of secrets, or forces, do you allow yourself to let other people know?' he asks Cohen, 'How much of you comes out? How much of you is still secret?'

Harris's question is far from ordinary. Concern over the mystery of one's poetry, and the secret energies that go into writing it, is the telltale sign of a poet who aims to bushwack his own path. But in Montreal, such individualism is also a geopsychical imperative. The city has long cast itself as the malcontent of Canadian poetry. It staged the modernist battles of the late 1920s and 1930s, largely forewent (even ridiculed) the nationalist tup-thumping that swept the country during the 1960s and has given the country nearly all of its major poet-critics. Seen in this light, Montreal poetry is more than a singing school: it's a splinter group. It's a CanLit denomination that broke away, staking out a deracinated space in the national consciousness. Montreal poets such as Cohen perfected a way of hovering, a way of placing the poetic self 'in between' – close to Canada, but not touching it, alert to its ideological trappings, but free to escape.

Throughout their bull session, we get the sense Harris is learning from Cohen – from his solitariness, his independent-mindedness, his unique outlook. One lone wolf, as it were, is teaching another how to fend for himself. 'I wanted very much to be a poet in Montreal because I wanted very much to have this conversation', Cohen says. 'To have to put out my work somehow and have it stand for a certain kind of life in the city of Montreal'.

This is the ambassadorial role Harris now holds. He is his own man, of course. But he can best be understood by the company his poetry keeps, a loose coterie of poets whose literary ideas were forged in a line of development that has continued uninterrupted for nearly eight decades. A number of approximate analogies exist – the New York School of the 1950s, the postwar group of Rome's *terza generazione* – but Montreal's longevity as a verse nexus is exceptional. From the perspective of a postmodern and peripatetic era, it might appear anachronistic to tie poets to place. Perverse, too, since it seems as if an historical accident (poets residing in the same vicinity) is being forced to say more than it has any right to say. Yet, I can think of poems by Montreal poets that do things other poems by Canadian poets don't, and often feel the experience of living in a bustlingly mixed and bilingual city – a hot zone of linguistic impurity – gives one access to ambitions difficult to feel elsewhere. To satisfy those ambitions, Montreal wordsmiths have had to evolve new effects, language re-accented and realigned into what A.M. Klein called a 'double-melodied vocabulaire'.

Across three generations, this circle of poets – including John Glassco, Peter Van Toorn, Robyn Sarah and David Solway – form a distinguished society. Their sharp stylistic differences would appear to argue otherwise. But their of-a-pieceness is clearly evident when we acknowledge the way their virtuosity encodes itself in open, accessible, undeceptive ingenuities. Ranging from temperamentally private to hot-blooded, from down-to-earth to magisterial, their poems accommodate innovation without visible strain. All practise a reader-friendly risk-taking – nudging words in new directions, opening possibilities up – founded on the awareness that someone is going to read the results. Their most original poems (Glassco's 'The Burden of Junk', Van Toorn's 'In Guildenstern County' or Solway's 'Stones in Water') prove that stylistic breakthroughs need not be gaped at uncomprehendingly. Experiments can be consensual acts; surprise can exist as a shared shock. The ethic – which, needless to say, Harris shares – is one of courtesy: to set the poem ticking, is to set the reader's imagination ticking too.

Born in Scotland in 1943, Harris immigrated to Canada at the age of six. For most of his adult life, and until his retirement in 1997, he taught English literature at Dawson College. In 1970 he published his first book, the misconceived *Text for Nausikaa*, followed, in 1976, by the much-improved *Sparks*. Not quite a trail-blazing beginning, but by the mid-eighties he was firmly established as an estimable local figure, a familiar name to readers of *The Atlantic Monthly* where he began appearing regularly, and a favourite on the poetry-reading circuit with two national CBC prizes to his name (awarded in 1985 for a long poem called 'Turning out the Light' and then again in 1989 for a sonnet cycle called 'Spring Descending'). If he is recognizable at all today it is likely for his twenty-five year tour of duty as founder and editor of Signal Editions, the much-acclaimed poetry imprint of Véhicule Press (a post I now occupy).

Yet Harris has also written surpassingly beautiful poems that rank with the best of his generation, a group that includes Robert Bringhurst, Michael Ondaatje and Don McKay. Interested readers can find this work in his last three books: *Grace* (1977), *In Transit* (1985) and *New and Selected Poems* (1992). What it is about these collections that has warded off their deserved kudos is anybody's guess (though as early as 1986 we find David Manicom warning the situation was fast becoming 'farcical'). Unaccountable neglect is, of course, a frequent theme in the lives of Montreal poets (a frustration beautifully captured in Klein's 'Portrait of the Poet as Landscape'). But Harris also seems the sort of significant figure who would go unnoticed no matter where he lived. Terrible at self-promotion, eschewing all fashions, his poems make dreary grist for the academic mill. He illustrates none of the trends (anti-colonial poetics, the evil egocentricity of the lyric voice, Heidegger-as-verse) running rampant in contemporary Canadian poetry. He has nothing to say on the subject of ecology, ontology, theology, quantum physics, cultural politics. Nor does his work call out for the kind of code-breaking that reviewers have lavished on glamorously difficult poets like A.F. Moritz, Tim Lilburn, Anne Carson and Erin Moure. That said, Harris's poems do have a following, and there's no mystery about what causes his admirers to sit up and listen.

It begins – and ends – with his music. Everyone is praised for the musicality of their verse at some point or other. But few poets deserve the compliment. Music in poetry is an event, an outcome a poem builds deep into itself. We distinguish poetry from prose by its line-breaks, yet the magic that music can bestow on an utterance – memorability, authority, verve – depends less on line-breaks than on tapping a deeper wildness and unpredictability in the words being used. I don't mean line-breaks are unimportant in finding these qualities; merely that they are the least important. No poet can succeed for long without a good ear for breaking a line, but a line-break alone won't lead to a phrase that anybody will forever want to murmur to themselves.

Instead, music is about good line-making; about diction and syntax irreducibly fused, and the sound-signature enjambed into place. Music thus bodies forth from a poem's form, and form (or a decent definition of it, at least) is the structure that emerges when every line

– run-on or end-stopped, short or long, dropped on a pile or stacked inside a stanza – reciprocally amplifies what surrounds it. Music, in short, is high-watt word-order. It doesn't so much deploy language as redeploy it in directions that push vocabulary past its commonsensical limits. The words we use, words depleted by daily conversation, stand apart in a poem because they're put in configurations that suss out new mouth-filling nuances. Poets able to do this – heighten common speech into lyricism – are rare. The reason is that you need an ear able to ignore the consensual gist of a word and experience it as a dense bundle of acoustic meaning. But if music is so uncommon, what is it that we're often praising? What we're praising – at least in Canada – are poets who codify sound as a trick of tone and personality (Al Purdy), or poets whose voices are the idiomatic equivalent of lip-synching (Margaret Atwood), or, as in this passage from Ann Michaels, poets who scent their lines with diction chosen solely for its implied sublimity:

> Time is like the painter's lie, no line
> around apple or along thigh, though apple
> aches to its sweet edge, strains
> to its skin, the seam
> of density. Invisible line
> closest to touch. Lines of wet grass
> on my arm, your tongue's
> wet line across my back.
>
> All the history in the bone-embedded hills
> of your body. Everything your mouth
> remembers. Your hands manipulate
> in the darkness, silver bromide
> of desire darkening skin with light.

This sort of perfumed imprecision is, as Donald Davie once argued, nothing more than a smokescreen to cover the getaway of a poet unwilling to stay behind to properly render what he or she has tried, unsuccessfully, to conjure. None of these lines find their pitch as lines – as scrupulously crafted sound-units of meaning – because none have been written with the ear. In fact, the words have been rushed through their aural implications so that they exist vacantly, in a kind of sonic disconnect from themselves. The collocation of syllables in 'silver bromide / of desire darkening skin with light' doesn't draw its music from the living, blood-warm principle of natural speech; it is, instead, 'poetic' phrasing trying to disguise as music what is really an artificial act of verbal creativity.

This is something of a trend in contemporary Canadian poetry, this tendency to regard words as cosmetic, useful for the simulation of sagacity, rather than as substances with their own weight and temperature. Jan Zwicky's poetry is often brittle for exactly this reason: it's made with language sucked dry of its spoken density, language vampirized into empty intensifiers ('beautiful', 'shining') and feeble abstractions ('dream', 'love', 'darkness'). Harris constructs his descriptive cadenzas the opposite way: by replenishing language, by giving language back its kinetic nutrients. Or, to use a line from Seamus Heaney, Harris writes poems that achieve the accuracy of words 'founded clean on their own shapes'. That accuracy helps activate many of his metaphors: Emily Dickinson perceiving her blood as the 'running red / foam of wheatfields at sundown'; how surf is 'the sea's / seemingly natural turns drawing curtain after curtain / on its own endless wash of applause'; or couples 'whose fingers thread jealousy together'. In each instance, the phonetic pith of the words (i.e., 'running red', 'endless wash of applause') has been absorbed into the attempted image, creating a point-for-point matching of form to action. It's this copycat equivalency – where assertions are enacted rather than evoked – that's responsible for Harris's most satisfying effects. Here's the start of 'The Woods':

> I know the mole's slow heart
> troubles still with the mole's dull blood
>
> and her glass eyes have filled
> with dark. She lies made of mud

at the end of her burrowing,
still as sediment, a sludge.

No word here takes up the menial task of merely 'meaning'. The message of these lines – a mole preparing to hibernate for the winter – is conveyed by the escalating heaviness of the details ('slow', 'dull', 'dark', 'mud', 'sediment', 'sludge') and by the slowing heartbeat of each couplet. Notice how the speech rhythms, in their drowse of monosyllables and open vowels, begin decelerating from the first line, and then, by the end, how the entire thing culminates in the sluggishness-suggesting stresses of the last line, an effect heightened by that impeccably placed comma: 'still as sediment, a sludge'.

When attention is paid to things at this pitch of perception and vocabulary, especially when done with such casual legerdemain, the results are often construed as 'well-crafted', a faintly condescending term that implies conservativism and lack of intensity. Language, we're told, should be practised as an easy, even reckless, obligation; too much scrupulousness stifles. Yet the painstaking fitting-together of vocabulary to capture the 'realness' of an object isn't a mark of compliance; it's a mark of dissatisfaction. Precision expresses a dilemma, not a solution. It's a writer's rebellion against the unthinkingly assumed terms of a previous depiction. Take this image: 'Not a soul about/but the spinsterish/birches'. These lines exemplify the chief virtues of Harris's style: a plainspokenness that catches the full sense of every word and focuses it, creating a vivid and believable snatch of voice. One notices the run of internal rhymes ('Not' with 'about' with 'but') and the liquidity of the phrasing ('spinsterish' sibilantly meshing with 'birches'). Most masterful, however, is 'spinsterish'. Notice how it reinforces the feeling of isolation by metaphorically buttressing the description. But doesn't the word also have a kinesthetic allure, a visceral thrum that brushes against your senses? Such quiet pyrotechnical surprises are the foundation of Harris's poetry. Again and again he gently pushes a word against the direction of its common usage, freeing loose its latent charge.

If Harris is more original from poem to poem than many of his peers, it's due to his habit of overhauling words like 'spinster'. Which is to say that Harris represents the subtler experimental departures of Canadian poetry. You don't hear much about this group because we expend our publicity on envelop-pushing that only appears to be far more brutally eccentric. But to be frustrated by the limitations of diction is not always to move toward breaches of decorum; for some, like Harris, it means discreetly striving for a wider medley of aural possibilities. The genius of lines like 'the glaze of the moon is a lighter liquid set loosely/on the mercury of water' or 'the golden rain/of urine boiling its froth in the toiletbowl' or 'a kiss/is just a cushioned push/of face' is that they appeal directly to the ear. This means their persuasiveness is a listened-for property, the result of an alluring loading-up of monosyllables or the lovely tension between words combined for their alliterative and assonantal colour.

Many poets will fail to see anything daring about finding plausible and reliable ways of gamesomely logging the physical world. They may respect crisp formulations like 'lighter liquid set loosely' or 'boiling its froth' or 'cushioned push', but they hunt elsewhere for their radical jolts. There are no such jolts in Harris's poetry – just the steady hum of words completing a circuit. His innovations involve nouns and verbs wired in small but decisive ways. The causal sophistication of Harris's technique is extraordinary, more so because his soundscapes don't need to be decrypted; he isn't a hard guy to crack. He writes aggressively but transparently, using a style that differs from ordinary speech only in appearing more energetically economical and less vague. It is, in Clive James's words, 'the miracle of simple words producing great sonorities'. The marvel of this sort of miracle is not much remarked on these days. Made deaf with our large-gestured prosy pretensions, we belong to an era that has forgotten how difficult it is to write well:

> Metal-still   on the shed-roof tin
>   until it cocks its head
> to eye the world
>   which has begun to crack
> its own black shell

until its claws pull
its body in
with soft trigger-pressures it's up
and up higher
all up in an arc wheeling down swooping
and screaming smoothly down dead
on the twisting trail
of a dragonfly which turns
quickly in the silver
signals of its wings
until the swallow takes that silver
for treasure in its beak
and the beak's blunt scissor
shuts down hard
and harder then the bird pitches down
the sheer cliffs of air
slipstreaming God
to the shed-roof where it sits
and eats

and is
out again spinning
a thin blade turning
on a dotty moth dazed from every side by light
and stoneblinded surely by
this cararact of black

and is an air-ace barnstorming
stealing the stomachs of the watchers
with its dolphin's bounce from an air to an air
and twists tricks turnings for the joy of it

and flies butterfly-fluttery
at all the edges of the sky

and there turns as quickly
as a liar in a lie

Anyone who writes this way is not a person who thinks lightly of his task. Called 'Barn Swallow', the poem does more than merely describe one; it revises language into something abrupt and fast-moving, adapting it for avian life ('it's up/and up higher/all up in an arc wheeling down swooping'). Harris's success at creating such effects – and giving them the buzzing intimacy of direct speech – depends on a fluency that achieves full flight from perfectly-weighed words. Like Hopkins' 'Windhover', which seems a clear influence, the artifice is all aural, with the accelerated vernacular served up to better air the mood of speed.

It may seem an overstatement to suggest that such scrupulousness doomed his reputation, yet one can't help but wonder if Harris's low standing is due, in part, to a career that disappeared into its enthusiasm for precision, a precision whose greatest practical consequence – a slow, insight-marshalling method of composition – made him easier to ignore. Perfectionists are viewed dourly in Canada. We like our production Balzacian; recognition depends upon it (compare the three books Harris released between 1977 and 1985 to George Bowering's thirteen or Patrick Lane's six, all published in that same period). In an essay called 'Tradition and the individual talent of Charles Bruce', Richard C. Davis argues that our need to 'celebrate a never-ending procession of new versifiers' has led to a publicity treadmill where 'some other poet is in the ascendant and last year's darling recedes into anonymity'. Harris's judiciousness about what he allowed into his poems, and subsequently into print, brought about a veridical self-excision: he simply wasn't seen. After all, it isn't so much that Harris writes good poems, but that he writes the kind of good poetry – compacted, uncluttered – only very patient poets can pull off. Such unhurried artisanal industry works against the widespread notion that a poem is simply something you've had the luck to see or hear or taste, and that, awarded to you virtually complete, your only job is to punch up its straight-to-the-page transcription. We don't want our words carefully sought and selected, we want our words thrown off with a flick of the wrist.

As long as enough of us think that way, then slow producers and quiet operators such as Harris will fare poorly. Of course, if he found himself behind the curve it didn't help that he looked at the world a little differently than his contemporaries. Everything I've quoted here comes from a spectacular collection – his third, published in 1977 – called *Grace*, which was inspired by the few miles of green rusticity and wildness that hemmed a tiny farm he owned in North Hatley. Like the acrobatic barn swallow, the book did an end run around the Canadian poem as it then existed. It's difficult to imagine Patrick Lane or Susan Musgrave writing lines like 'its dolphin's bounce from an air to an air/and twists tricks turnings for the joy of it', or even of having such thoughts. Not to say the subject wouldn't have attracted their attention, but nothing in their poetry suggests they possessed a similarly astonishing ability to think themselves into the skin of a creature at once so tiny and fiercely alive. It bears remembering that, thanks to Tish, much of the country during this time was working within the shape and framework of the radically de-formalized poem. Homey gesturalism and low-key irresoluteness were *de rigueur*.

But for Harris, poetry meant something else. It meant walking the land, training his eyes, getting the measure of things. For Harris, a poem was a device that caught, with mingled excitement and terror, observed details in their environment. *Grace* made an excellent case for this sort of poetry, poetry whose descriptions existed in the music of their own happening, A few reviews sensed something ('a technically dazzling blend of sound and dense imagery', 'Immediate authority, impeccable rhythms', 'real poetry, the kind that raises the hair on your neck') but critics never warmed to the book. As a result many readers are probably in the predicament of never having heard about the keen-eyed, acoustically lively, adrenaline-rich poems Harris wrote about some pigs, moles, frogs and sheep – poems that leap these thirty years and smash squarely in the mind. Here are the last seven stanzas of 'The Gamekeeper':

> … the gamekeeper's gone
>
> whose crow's a tattoo
> at the top of a tree, losing his grip
> at the too-thin tip

of the cold that is pricking him bare.
                    He thinks war
and it's war though the summer's surrendered
          and raised its white flag
a million times over
and it's snowing.

Now the waddling porcupine's swaying his quills
          all at sea in the swaddle
                    of his winter fat;
he is slow in the sudden
          and no match at all
                    for the silk and soft skins
of winter. He chews bark,
for the gamekeeper's gone

whose snakes took green with them
          and wove it in a bundle
                    and buried it under a rock,
for the earth had stopped in tatters
          and lay down dead-white,
                    dead-skinned, belly-up
and not right. Then the wind coiled hugely,
          struck and coiled and shed its white
a million times over
and it's snowing.

Plump rats and grey weasels channel blindly
          their fright, clawing squealing
at their tunnels: to core them, seal them, escape
          from the light, from the ache
of a world wide with snow; but their black brains
are caught, are furnaced with the spark:
the gamekeeper's gone

whose starving, still hopeful, pure panic of deer
        tiptoe the brittle-twigged landscape to silence
to a deadhalt
at the appletree; and the appletree's victory stays
                stiff-necked, full of thrash
in its iron-bare head of black antler,
in the slow-moving barrens of its branches
                where the sky falls to pieces
sinking deeper and deeper
a million times over;

and it's snowing on the otter
whose eye is a film of ice.
It whispers blessing to the shivering field-mouse
whose heaven is black with snow.
It is snowing on the hare
whose fur is a layer of winter.
It falls against the houses,
against the drinkers in the bars,
a million times over. The gamekeeper's gone.

The fields harden fast
around their stone.

Sound – as a series of sonic heightenings and deepenings, intensifications and exaggerations – gives this poem its shape. Note the cascading sequences of internal rhyme, the smoothly slipping enjambment, the constant anaphoric bloom of imagery. Note, too, the stark final couplet, upon which all that flourish crashes, and how the lines get their power from the momentum still riding in from the rest of the poem.

But sound also gives 'The Gatekeeper' its psychology: the poem thinks with it. This cognition-via-sound is responsible for a great deal of the innovation in *Grace*; namely, Harris's attempt to connect the Canadian cadence to a more concretely sensuous music is an attempt to create new perceptions. Nothing necessarily unprecedented, mind you, just perceptions impossible to chime into existence using any other cluster of sounds. What made Harris so anti-zeitgeist in his penchants, in other words, was that instead of citing the physicality of a wintery landscape – lots of that in Canadian poetry – he improvised ways in which the landscape could give him the words it needed to utter itself. He didn't just describe an apple tree, but devised the linguistic logic that let him see it as something 'stiff-necked, full of thrash/in its iron-bare head of black antler'. Those lines are striking not only for their mimetic rightness – a rightness largely monosyllabic, streaming with vowels, and made memorable by the jolt-awake energy of 'thrash' – but also for the way they covet spoken rhythms. You can hear it in lines like 'whose crow's a tattoo/at the top of a tree, losing his grip/at the too-thin tip/of the cold that is pricking him bare' or 'the earth had stopped in tatters/and lay down dead-white,/dead-skinned, belly-up/and not right'. Both examples have that intense, off-the-cuff precision of words that have been chanced-upon rather than schemed. Harris gets his meaning across clearly and swiftly, but by compressing such shifts of pace and perspective into such a short space he also creates vivid moments of phrasing that stop readers short and force them to rethink language. A case in point would be the wonderful syntactic oddity of 'he is slow in the sudden' or the fascinating verb-adverb joining of 'channel blindly/their fright'.

Harris stands alone. I can think of no other Canadian poet who so successfully turned ordinary English into a semaphore for sense impressions. There are many able to strengthen passages of description with a well-chosen word – itself no mean feat – but few who possess such unique onomatopoeic gifts. Speculating on why this is so brings us to a truth that, for many writers, has been too inconvenient to credit: the relative drabness of Canadian vernacular. Ken Babstock makes a interesting reference to this in an interview with Don McKay, how he finds himself drawn to 'breeds of English' that are 'more colourful and jagged and active'. Is it any surprise, then, that surrounded by a diction without intrinsic music, music becomes barely a concern at the level of our style? Instead of extending our sentences to encompass the width, breadth and depth of the English language, we've two-dimensionalized our ear, shrinking its sensitivities down to idea and intent. What is interesting about Harris is his readiness to embark on a searching departure from this monotone norm, to repair the effects of its dullness by conjuring out of Canadian speech – using tiny touches, minimal modifications – a more interesting 'English'.

But this also reflects the culturally synoptic condition of most Montreal poets, who are constantly forced, on a daily level, to shift between different registers and syntaxes and thus are more open to cross-influences than they might have been had they lived in Toronto or Vancouver or Calgary. Cohen, who has not only recorded songs in both languages but modeled his writing after Québecois writers like Marie-Claire Blais and Réjean Ducharme, was a great benefiary of this circumstance. The city itself, in other words, lures our poems out of the verbal ghetto of what Solway has called 'Standard Canadian Average'.

Harris further refined his gift during the eight-year hiatus between *Grace* and his fourth book, *In Transit*. The Anglo-Saxon speech-rhythms were recast into simpler felicities of expression. Seizing upon this tenderer voice, and placing the emphasis on travel, coupledom and family, Harris made (to use Lowell's famous line) a 'breakthrough back into life'. He now drew his words almost exclusively from the warp and weft of daily speech, and at his best – a long elegy called 'Turning Out the Light' which episodically ledgers his brother's death from cancer – he spoke in a spare, unsentimental, easy-to-absorb vernacular. Indeed, one of the amazing things about Harris's new voice was the way it swiftly caught readers up in its effects:

> The morning drip
> eases red cells
> into the bloated arm
>
> which hangs from his body
> like some enormous slug
> feeding quietly at his shoulder.

The nurse's fingers
leave grooves in the underside,
and a dent in the top

where her thumb rests.
Then fluid fills the arm
and it is round again,

leaking a little pink
which pools on the sheet
at his elbow. She uses that arm

until the vein is not available;
then she uses the other arm.
Twice a day,

on the column
by his head, his life
hangs, upended.

These lines, taken from 'Turning Out the Light', are intended, in their direct plainness, to act quickly on the emotions. They aren't meant to unseat perfection, or upset expectations: they're written out of an awareness of the response they'll likely get. But this directness, too, is no less a formal experiment, no less an exploration of prosodic physics. True, in its conspicuous flatness and simple diction it may feel an inch away from prose. But what is poetry, after all, but a game of inches? And for a gifted poet an inch is margin enough for ambitious acts of departure. Here Harris uses basic nouns, adjectives and verbs to help defamiliarize the scene. Everything is made new through perspective, giving us the expected – 'the bloated arm' – in an unexpected way: 'which hangs from his body/like some enormous slug/feeding quietly at his shoulder'.

The image is precise and alive, but the sound of its simplicity is also ripe with unsentimental intelligence. The problem with style, you see, is that despite its accuracies, it always revises things upwards: style is always happy. Harris's minimalism here is the mark of a style learning to subdue its grace notes to a sad situation. You might say, then, that Harris discovered an idiolect for the experience: a tight, estranged-from voice, free of rhetorical add-ons. It's a kind of anti-style that illustrates what can be done with a plain-speaking argot. And for that reason it's important to acknowledge the resourcefulness coordinating each audio effect. Harris never leaves the ideal of poem-as-song very far behind. Beyond the lovely rhythmic balance between the tercets, his signature music-making can be seen in the way he doubles-down a six-syllable constant across two lines in 'Then fluid fills the arm/ and it is round again'; or how the soft alliterative bursts of 'leaking a little pink/which pools on the sheet' are rounded off with the firmer cadence of 'at his elbow'; or the piercing quick-trot precision of 'Twice a day,//on the column/by his head, his life/hangs, upended'. As is often the case with Harris, the rhythms of ordinary speech undergo the most irreducible and refined modulations, in which shifting a single word can spill away half the poem's energy.

It doesn't always work. Harris sometimes seems to want to feel his own earnestness and pushes things, so that 'every pore is a mouth/ dumb with spent agony' or daisies 'scarcely veil/the sullen face/of the earth'. For the most part, though, his bewitchments are cannier. Language is pressed into disclosing perceptions so delicately stricken – 'His fear is the house/where soundlessly the cancer/roots in the humid dark' – you enter their nakedness and fluency immediately. The secret is an unguardedness that seems found rather than made, giving us a poem that says extraordinary things while conveying the sense that these are things an ordinary person might actually say: 'Evenings we watch/the darkness descend/in its needle//and the morphine/rise in the drowse/of his smile' or 'Your eyes were wide open/when the world fell away,/my lovely brother'.

Such limpidity brings Hardy to mind. A few frivolity-free notes also recall Lawrence and Frost. At other times, we even spot a Williams-like brevity. What Harris shares with these poets is a yen for poetry that gets its life force by using distilled directness as a stay against the 'literary': relax the concision-promoting strictures and the effect that snares the reader – the sense that language is drawing on firsthand rather than predigested experience – is lost. In other words, while the candour of Harris's voice is built with durable sounds and rhythms, it isn't the candour, as such, we trust. We believe what Harris says because he creates a plausible music on the page for his statements. What seems an efficient way of telling a tale is actually artlessly mesmeric: an art that disguises its artfulness by dressing it in savoury and inventive speech. We can see this at work in a description like 'the syringe's slim/savage jab'. The phrase hooks us precisely because it is slightly more agile and textured than one might find in real conversation, but it does not stretch credibility. Or here, where Harris's brother, a child in 'schoolboy grey' required to answer *Here, Sir* during roll call, begins to stutter:

And the S began in a blush of trust,
with a tearing sound
as of long-ripping paper,
a valve not properly fitted,
as the lungs deflated slowly on and on
transfixing the master suddenly
charmed by this hissing serpentine sway,
the long consistent unstoppable sibilants,
esses upon esses and my brother almost
out of breath, eyes closed,
every muscle tense stepping out into
the sheerfall of accelerating seconds
tongue pressed aching relentlessly
against the incontinent buzz of his teeth –
until the throat stuck shut on its glottis
and his twisted face crimsoned
at the guttering ends of exhaustion –

This passage, set inside a longer narrative, consists of ninety-eight perfectly ordinary English words spoken more or less every day in endless unremarkable combinations. Yet Harris yokes them into a particular arrangement and suddenly all cylinders are firing. It brings home, of course, the mystery of poetry, the power generated from certain words existing beside one another. But it also suggests the way in which Harris has kept a weather eye (and a diamond-stylus ear) on the English language, learning to fit its assonantal and alliterative effects to new functions. Let's not overlook, for example, how the 'sheerfall' of his brother's stammering seems to take place in real time with the 'unstoppable sibilants' that transfix the reader as it does the schoolteacher. 'S began in a blush of trust' serves as an especially lovely mantra for Harris's evocation-as-enactment aesthetic – not to mention it's one of those formulations just begging to be remembered on its own. Sound not only serves sense, it helps Harris's lines linger in the mind.

But while the experience of having a crisp phrase forever force itself upon you is one of poetry's deepest satisfactions, there are subtler spells poetry can cast, and chief among them is what Clive James has called 'sayability'. Harris poems, in other words, demand to be read aloud. There's no better illustration of this than the seventeen-line, single-sentence stanza above which, if recited, seduces your mouth into reliving a little boy's anguish. Savouring each bouquet of 'esses upon esses' becomes oddly cathartic as Harris transforms a remembered trauma into a triumph of form: a syntactically dynamic aural simulacrum that traps our 'tongue' and gives it back to us with his brother's breakthrough – 'a deep, pure sob saying, Sir, Sir! and a last,/ escaping, joyous, I'm Here, Sir!'

Speech running free on the joy of its hard-earned fluency is a rare triumph in 'Turning Out the Light'. Speech thwarted is the poem's major theme, speech defeated ('when they ask me what I want/I find that I can't speak') by the eloquence-smothering texture of grief. Like so:

> Lunch is a spoonful
> of raspberry Jello.
>
> Afternoons mean sleep
> or the introduction of long needles

into the breast-bone or hip,
or deep through the flesh of his back,
for a plug of liver or an extract of marrow.

The finger-pricks come twice a day,
Even the sound of the softly opening door
has him cry out and gag
on the dregs of his vomit.

Each day they
change the soaking twist of sheet.
They will continue this
until they get it right,
until the right one fits:
it will be spotless,
and dry, and neat.

Throughout 'Turning Out the Light', as his brother's dying is described and redescribed, Harris deftly incorporates his own anguish and awe at what he is seeing. Much of what makes the poem so moving is owed to these thumbnail portraits of decay. The unnerving 'sound' of these portraits, the direct access they seem to give us to deep emotion, comes from wedding a certain sense of line with a certain turn of mind. We can see this in operation in the above excerpt, where Harris narrates his brother's suffering using the shorthand of hospital routines. An eye for detail is working alongside an ear that is able to heighten, through concision, the intensities inherent in unexceptional speech. The result is a catalogue of expanding compressions. Confined to his brother's deathbed perspective, the narrative's tendency to stall, then reticently brood, on each specific incident ('Lunch is a spoonful/of raspberry Jello') amplifies what isn't being said while staying clear of any prose-like coarsening into autobiography. Harris thus reminds us of the unresolved implications that can freight the choices we make in our vocabulary.

We see this clearly in his manner of secreting a disquieting word in almost every line, from the gently unsettling ('introduction', 'deep', 'plug') to the near-provocations ('cry', 'gag', 'dregs', 'soaking'). What Harris is after is a tonal truth: an everyday idiom flensed of its banality, leaving a subtext thick with complication. There is no 'charm' here (for useful comparison one need only recall the poems in *Grace* where the image-making was ecstatic and copious). Harris's intonation is so nuanced he has the Dickensonian ability to endow ho-hum words with severe particularity, making them crackle: 'it will be spotless,/ and dry, and neat'. Those two lines – faultlessly punctuated, plangently emphatic – are pushed, unbearably, to the brink of their insinuation. Unsentimentality is given stinting economy of scale. Harris's invention of an exacter, plainer poetry to capture this effect is one of his finest achievements.

There's more. In fact, the delight of reading Harris, for those new to his poetry, will come from the salutary surprise of encountering work I've neglected to mention. The skylarking wordplay of 'Miss Emily and Death'; the knockabout wit of 'A Visit to the Galleries'; the intricate harmonics of 'Dolphin'; the tender, tensile stride of 'A View From the Kitchen'; the ceremony and brio of 'Epithalamion'; the imagistic flexing of 'Uncle Edward'; the brisk élan of 'Spring Descending'. To read these poems is to be struck by Harris's amplitude of thought and feeling – there is no prosy drift to his voice, only an urgency that make the poems greater than the sum of their lapidary parts.

A show of appreciation is vital because in a time like ours, when immense-mystical modes are prized over even-tempered finesse, a human voice like Harris's is at a disadvantage. It doesn't fit our notion of originality as repudiation, the cutting of ties. This isn't to say talent like his attracts no admiration, but it's welcomed within limits. The poems are accepted as well-written; but because they aren't a forecast of the future, they're seen as old news, a dead end. Yet Harris's ambition is perhaps the most ancient and most rarely attained: a natural speech. He gives poetry the feel of real talk, creating ingenious forms so colloquial in their syntax and sense-making that we rarely experience them as the exciting experiments they (quietly) are. Harris isn't the obvious maker of an entirely new kind of poem, but he embodies what the late Stanley Kunitz described as the poet's true vocation: he is a generalist, 'a person speaking to persons'. Very few Canadian poets understand language's singing side as well as Harris, yet he transcends the specialism of his art and touches the bedrock of our own living accents even as he reinvents them. He can do this – assert his panache without appearing the least bit the poetry pro – because his poems make their first appeal on a level which demands from the reader no more than an ability to understand the language. And as if to gently remind us of that fact, there appeared, in the April 2002 issue of *Books in Canada*, a delightful sonnet called, appropriately, 'Speech':

> When I had teeth, no accent at all
> was safe from me. I'd Irish
> groined and turd and tank-you
> Lard. I'd Scotch the ballads where
> those drowning lords were richt laith
> to weet their cork-heeled shoon.
> I'd do Canadian if I knew how,
> but settle now for American, its
> boo-jhwah Appalachiana
> that drawl y'all git from The Tee Vee.
> Still I'd like to report my love-life hasn't suffered.
> In flagrante, I moan like a heifer at stud,
> a moose with no teeth, a cleft-palate dog.
> Thank God I can croon the word Love.

This comes as close to seeming spoken as any poem I know. The quick and frequent changes of vocal angle, the near-delirium of its spiel, feels exquisitely homemade and points up the close-at-hand sounds Harris likes to use: the stylized patois of 'I'd Irish/groined and turd and tank-you/Lard' or the mad amalgam of ad-libed mannerisms in 'American, its boo-jhwah Appalachiana/that drawl y'all git from The Tee Vee'. Of course, these lines are also serious probings into idiom, and bespeaks a poet who conceives of his experiments not theoretically, but musically, executing them with all the mischievous-ness ('I'd do Canadian if I knew how') that characterizes his Anglo-Quebéc mindset.

I'm aware, of course, that many will regard my remarks about Montreal's poetic outsiderism as an irritant rather than a definition. But such irritants are useful reminders that there are always other interpretations, other hearings, other truths being held in check by the canon-compilers. We already see these subtle crowd-control tactics at work against distinctive poets like Richard Outram and George Johnston, who are exalted for their excellence and simultaneously excluded from serious literary debate. All the better, no doubt, to preserve the career convergences, the large-scale professional dress-ups: everyone writing the same thing, reading the samc thing, until both poem and reader are conceived in the poet's own image. But for Montreal poets, readers are not an ideological idea. You might even say that Montreal poetry is defined, if not driven, by the knowledge that a real mind waits at the receiving end, a mind with expectations of being interestingly addressed. This facing-the-reader voice – let's call it the 'boo-jhwah Appalachiana' – belongs to a different sort of Canadian poetry: a poetry of one-offs and unpeggable sensibilities, a poetry of memorable phrase-making, solid sounds and language-refreshing surprises. As it happens, it's exactly the sort of poetry that's always the last to catch up in our march to the next prize-giving season.

'There are many ways to tell your secret', was Cohen's answer to Harris forty-two years ago. 'I think that a decent man who has discovered valuable secrets is under some obligation to share them. But I think that the technique of sharing them is a great study.' The good news is that Harris's poems are in no hurry; its secrets will wait for whomever can stop for them.

ADAM KIRSCH

THE POET-CRITIC gets no sympathy, and considering the charge-sheet against him – adversarial, addicted to dicta, motivated by an axe-grindingly acute sense of right and wrong – why would he? He is, in most eyes, a hyphenated hothead. Until recently, however, that hyphen was still a badge of special authority, so that practitioners writing critically about their craft were regarded as poetry's ideal readers. Not everyone agreed (Northrop Frye thought poets made bad critics because they were too obsessed by their own processes), but Alfred Kazin summed up the standard view in 1967 when, with considerable professional envy, he described the poet-critic as always 'right in the middle of the parade (and if he is good enough, he will be leading it)'.

That was then. Today, as Irish poet-critic David Wheatley reminds us, 'there is a temptation to read the hyphen as a subtraction sign'. Chalk it up to life after theory. As soon as powerful new methods began to dominate English departments, the poet-critic gig lost its prestige. Literary criticism for the general reader – the sort championed by poet-critics – took on a belletristic odour; no matter how formidable the close reading, it would now exist on the margins of a more sophisticated cogitating. Worse, by seeing off Arnoldian objectivity ('the object as in itself it really is'), theory discredited the probative force that powered the poet-critic's prose. Standing on postmodern ground for their higher surmises, academia outgrew aesthetic evaluations; artistic merit, as a concept, became an ideological fairy tale. What eventually filtered down to street level – if the industry-wide outbreaks of shock at negative reviews are any guide – was a hypersensitivity to strong opinions and the taste-correcting urge lurking inside. Show us somebody dedicated to sifting out the best from the merely good, and we'll show you somebody with a hidden motive. As a result, the poet-critic lost the gig altogether. Criticism by poets, once the conscience of the art, is now exposed as a theatre of special interests, an acting out of *parti pris*. Thus his plight: taking sides, the poet-critic can't be trusted. He speaks for no one, except himself.

Adam Kirsch isn't the sort to be scared off by a little historical irrelevancy. From the start of his freelance career – around 1997, just shy of twenty – he has devoted himself to criticism that turns back the clock and resheathes poetry in high seriousness. He has sharply developed preferences, a well-stocked mind and very specific ideas about poetry's characteristics as an art form. His assignments, after a very busy decade, have ranged widely and include Anne Carson, W.S. Merwin, James Tate, Paul Muldoon, August Kleinzahler, Glyn Maxwell and Yusef Komunyakaa. He has also sized up, and sometimes dressed down, the work of Charles Bukowski, Hart Crane, Robert Lowell, Ezra Pound, Samuel Johnson, Wordsworth and Shelley. That he is a poet himself was eventually confirmed in 2002 with the publication of *The Thousand Wells*. But to anyone paying attention, it was already obvious by his habit of filing arrestingly ambitious four- to five-thousand word pieces that carried out their flaw-detection duties without heed for margins of error. Only someone personally implicated in the ways poems can fail would credit his doubts to that extent. And only a critic would strive as hard to make those doubts plausible to those who didn't share them. That, in a nutshell, is what it means for poet and critic to share one body.

Yet Kirsch's odd-man-out status also testifies to how rarely the two come together with such unshakeable purpose. Poets might flirt with the odd Olympian pronouncement, but know better. The rules of engagement are too risky, the results too easy to ridicule. Having wasted no time finding his stride, Kirsch remains focused. He continues to place his poet-critic multi-tasking at the service of a profoundly unfashionable 'premodernist' vision that emphasizes form, discipline and tradition. He continues to assert the right to press large claims upon readers, deriving his authority – and arbitership – from Eliot's belief that, as Kirsch put it in an early review, 'only criticism that aims to change poetry is worthy of the name'. Needless to say, this requires a conviction that, for many, is unthinkable because untenable; an irony-free zone that breeds reactionary, pontifical states of mind. Kirsch is too careful a student of history not to understand the dangers (and, luckily, there's always the back-chatter his reviews inspire to remind him. David Lehman: 'a constricting and reactionary aesthetics'; John Palattella: 'a narrow and pedestrian sense of style and propriety'). But self-justification, you suspect, is precisely what eggs him on. It's also the most compelling thing about him: his determination to re-exalt the poet-critic stance. The clout might be gone, but the duty remains. Except that where the poet-critic once held the one true line, he is now forced to draw it in sand.

The Modern Element (2008) is a collection of twenty-seven reviews that set up shop in the same big idea. All poet-critics possess a home truth that underwrites everything: where things went wrong, what tendencies are being neglected, which direction to take next. For Kirsch, it is poetry's 'neurotic obsession with the modern'. *The Modern Element* has thus been assembled in reaction – and at times over-reaction – to what Kirsch thinks was a very bad deal. The modern as 'mastery of complexity' (what Matthew Arnold campaigned for) should never have been allowed to give way to the modern as 'surrender to complexity' (the definition that Eliot established and that still prevails). In other words, it was the classic mistake of sacrificing long-term potential for short-term gain. Modernness as an aesthetic category has been mortgaged for the instant gratification of modernness as a temporal category. The poetry that results – one that makes a point of its modernness and whose idea of risk is tied to making that point – is too surface-seduced to create a shareable experience between reader and poet. This, Kirsch argues, leads to 'fraudulent self-exposure, which makes no inner demand on poet or reader, and otiose experimentalism, which mistakes novelty for discovery'. His critical study *The Wounded Surgeon* (2005) was an earlier attempt to explain how this notion of modernness, if left unchecked, can bait us into crude misreadings. The explicit disclosures of Berryman, Lowell, Plath, Bishop, Jarrell and Schwartz? A technical trick, Kirsch reminds us – one that established artlessness as a radically new kind of artfulness. But so successful was the innovation that we devalued what their poems did while fetishizing what they said. *The Wounded Surgeon* was thus an attempt to return these careers to their first principles. Confessionalism, Kirsch reminds us, was a ruthless stylistic victory over the refractory idiom of extreme feeling. 'The suffering that afflicted this group of poets', he writes, 'becomes significant only because they examined it with the surgeon's rigor, detachment, and skill'.

Providing reminders is, as it happens, a large part of Kirsch's strategy. Many of his best reviews do nothing more than dust off a once-fighting tenet – 'objective correlative', for instance – and get it back into the fray. Poetry, he reminds us, is about playing the long game, about developing forms that not only make meaning, but make it stay put. Suffering the wound of a modernness that has bequeathed us a set of expectations without the means of satisfying them, Kirsch offers his cure: poets need to reclaim 'the mastery of traditional form, which alone allows meaningful departures from tradition' and thus enter into a richer relationship – 'the nimble transcendence of the old opposites' – with inherited standards.

For this reason, Kirsch's takedowns of John Ashbery and Sharon Olds are no surprise (both *ouevres*, he claims, are shipwrecked by their radicalisms, philosophical and sexual, respectively). Nor will anyone be scratching their head over the generous tributes he pays to Derek Walcott, Czesław Milosz and Dennis O'Driscoll (the terms of his praise for O'Driscoll can just as easily be applied to Walcott and Milosz: 'worth, mastery, possibility, control'). What may catch readers off-guard, however, is his admiration for the 'astringently bizarre' Frederick Seidel. Indeed, Seidel seems to be a poet who not only resists the terms of Kirsch's expectations, but slightly reconditions them ('one of the very rare contemporary poets who can be transgressive, not in the fashionable way of the seminar, but in the disturbing and baffling way of the nightmare'). This needs to be pointed out because the knock against Kirsch – and poet-critics more generally – is that he is too predictable, an amateur, as it were, who has professionalized his prejudices to the point where, often, there's no need to read him. But who would have forecast the even-handedness of his essay on Ginsberg ('in *Howl*, Ginsberg achieves a telescoping of ideas and images of which Donne would be proud')? Or Koch ('buoyant, clowning, exclamatory – a rhapsode of friendship and love')?

Where Kirsch really flips the script is in his bracing evaluations – admiring, analytic and ambivalent in equal measure – of formalist poets James Merrill, Geoffrey Hill and Anthony Hecht. Each is a career audit in which Kirsch wolfishly investigates whether risks, to use Frost's words, 'were weakly lost or richly spent'. Given the scrupulous formalism of his own poetry, you would assume his sympathies would prevent him from pushing his skepticism so far. The real occupational hazard of being a poet-critic, however, is that you are harshest on matters about which you are most qualified to speak. Luckily, Kirsch's concept of modernness also means his sympathies are with readers rather than poets. Nothing up his sleeve, he always brings along his own criteria for what he alleges and always makes sure he expresses himself with the utmost clarity. This kind of straight talk depends on the ability to communicate the feel of a poem, and to communicate, when the situation requires it (as it often seems to), what feels missing. One unfortunate side effect – betrayed most embarrassingly in the wind-and-wrath essay that ends the book – is a condescending regard for American poetry as nothing more than an error gratefully waiting for Kirsch's correction. Indeed, if *The Modern Element* has an autobiographical subtext, then you might say these reviews are the wish-fulfillment of a young man who enjoys the vanity of his own good sense, but is restless under a dispensation he is helpless to change. This would partly explain his penchant for dramatizing careers as an exciting battle against the odds (Walcott's struggle, for instance, 'to convince himself and the world that originality is still possible, even at this late hour').

But front-line situations – with the fate of contemporary poetry hanging in the balance – bring out the best in Kirsch. An incomparable context builder, with a near-perfect nose for comparisons (the echo of Eliot's *Four Quartets* in Ashbery's 'Grand Galop' was neat, but Ashbery's distance from Wordsworth's *The Prelude* was immensely clarifying), Kirsch is excellent at placing poets in their historical moment, aided by an ability to evoke the way the climate of a period manner can suddenly be made to pivot into the private weather of a poem. Painstaking and patient, he builds his evaluations from the foundations upwards, putting intimidating figures (Yvor Winters) or unfamiliar careers (Les Murray) into revelatory perspective, or providing provocative redescriptions of poets (Billy Collins) with whom we might already be *au courant.* Kirsch can do this because he isn't obsessed by the little choices that hold together poems, but by the large choices – the consensual glue, you might say – that hold together our definitions of poetry. He is always tracing specific effects back to general causes. His great gift, in fact, is the speculative statement with immersive reach; the statement that extends far beyond the needs of the review to enter deeply, and alter, conventional wisdom. The easy sophistication of these speculations can be breathtaking. On Merrill:

> A poet gives the impression of strength only if his linguistic powers seem to meet and overcome the challenge of significant statement. Simple things said simply are graceful; difficult things said with difficulty are impressive; but simple things said with difficulty are merely showy.

Or take this exemplary paragraph:

> Solemnity however has always been Hill's besetting vice. Solemnity is to seriousness as sentimentality is to emotion: the attempt to induce a feeling that refuses to occur spontaneously. What's more, solemnity provokes a kind of resistance – mockery, or sheer disbelief – which genuine seriousness never does. And it takes courage for a poet to realize that such resistance on the reader's part may be justified, that it demands a genuine reform of his poetic methods. That is why there is something truly impressive in the stylistic evolution of a Yeats or a Lowell. Hill, however, has never embraced the kind of humility necessary for such a change. Instead, he has been the Coriolanus of contemporary poetry, proud of his refusal to compromise or condescend.

Force of belief is only one reason Kirsch has made such an impression. The serenity of his polemic is the other. Kirsch always keeps his temper, if never his tongue. For all his willingness to take extreme positions, he is rarely rude or intemperate. Polite hard-headedness is, in fact, his secret weapon: he simply refuses to believe that what a poet has put into a poem automatically belongs there. His now notorious Jorie Graham review is the most dramatic example of this hard-headedness, and also its most valuable expression because it is the sum of Kirsch's manifestos (absorbed into it, for instance, are Glück's 'narcissism', the 'discourteous[ness]' of C.D. Wright and Ashbery's 'elephantiasis of indirection'). Reading Graham's book, Kirsch meets a mind that is most unlike his, and thus finds himself at the extreme end of his dilemma with the modern element. In her failure to create what he calls 'objective correlatives for inner experience', Graham produces not poems but 'a shorthand, a private idiom, which the reader is left to translate'. To prove it, he sets out to translate it. Whether readers are brought any closer to that proof is arguable (I think that Kirsch makes a haymaker of a case) but they'll witness something even better: exhilaratingly bloody-minded detective work that gathers up the evidence of the poetry's shape and sound and strives to solve the quality of its meaning. Keeping close step as both accomplice and jury, Kirsch tests each line for the information it brings; and his patient marshalling of clues in strategic, cant-free, blow-striking ways produces a fascinating set of instructions in how to read. You don't have to buy into the Kirsch Method to find the exercise useful.

That method does, however, suggest why reading Kirsch can be an uneasy pleasure. His moralizing bias toward poetry within 'formal mastery' draws out formulations that force him to sacrifice his creativity as a prose writer. Ideas are flow-charted into larger ideas to create complex, diagrammatic discussions. But Kirsch pays a price for such brain-work: he has a weakness for a dry-as-dust parlance that raises doubts about whether he can muster the stylistic nimbleness needed to get a fix on, and fix in place, constantly shifting definitions of genres, conventions and forms. 'Like many modernist poets', he writes about Graham, 'she wants poetry to serve as an evocative transcript of mental processes, rather than a finished and self-subsistent object'. This is true, but the sentence has too much textbook in it – put more of them in a review, for paragraphs at a time, and unsympathetic readers will think that the ground has been brilliantly well-laid for a thoroughgoing misunderstanding of the book. Kirsch's prose can't see beyond its own precocity. Or take this: 'It is in the negotiation of these two demands, meaning and form, sense and rhythm, that poetic beauty is created'. This is a sentence constructed entirely out of Parnassian publicity-kit words. And a favourite touchstone like 'mastery', no matter how hard-pushed, has a tendency to linger in the mind as sentiment, not argument. In his Larkin essay, he defines a poet's sacrifice for his art in the most drained lingo: 'It means hollowing out one's self, in order to allow all the bitterness and joy of life to take up residence there and find expression'. There is something too easy about that sentence, or rather, Kirsch makes things too easy on himself. His prose, when it praises, sometimes forgets to register any struggle, which leaves us uncertain about his certainties.

This brings us to a part of the poet-critic's playbook that Kirsch seems to have skipped. Like poetry, prose can be understood as memorable speech. Prose on poetry, however, is a different kind of speech altogether: aphoristic, intuitive, compressed, unpredictable, peppy. Poems do many things at once, and if you want to capture that restlessness you need sentences that can run together different kinds of experience. (The poems we love, we love for the way they are written. The same goes for the criticism.) Many poetry-reviewers don't take the challenge seriously enough, or the solution: a critic needs to coin his own terms. Neologistically poor, Kirsch sticks to a fairly standardized vocabulary, arguing through definitions. The result are essays that can't help but radiate an egghead *gravitas*.

To be fair, *The Modern Element* does give us some quotable aperçus (the New York School's 'atomic-age *jeunesse dorée*' or Les Murray's sexless novel-in-verse *Freddy Neptune* as 'an *Odyssey* of erocide') and lots of memorable stand-alone indictments. Hill: 'one does not read *The Mystery of the Charity* with a sense that poetry's responsibility has been enacted; it has only been addressed as a topic'. Glück: 'the lasting and distinctive impression [her poems] make on the reader, is not of a mind curious about mystery, but of a mind that enjoys regarding itself in proximity to mystery'. Collins: '[his] devotion to the ordinary is not a disciplined response to disenchantment. It is, rather, a peculiarly

American form of mental laziness'. Winters: 'his canon seem[s] like a toy kingdom, a Monaco of poetry existing in placid unrelation to the empire all around it'.

Kirsch's chops as a critic are well-known; as a poet, less so, which proves that it's easier to build a profile as critic than as poet (which, in turn, activates the poet-critic's biggest fear: being better at the wrong thing). That said, *Invasions* (2008) is an advance on the 'silent, parcelled and controlled' poems of the award-winning *The Thousand Wells*. Sticking to a single form – a sonnet-like sixteen-liner – Kirsch's second book explores the deeply divided time-sense of an imagination obsessed with mirrorings and facades, bogeymen and spooks (exactly 'the music of doubt and self doubt' that he notices, and praises, in David Yezzi's first book). Reminiscent of the paragraph-stanzas of 'One Weekend' from *The Thousand Wells*, the form allows a fascinating toughening of Kirsch's earlier tone: we now get slow-moving syntax, balky lines, disconsolately rumpled phrasing. While Berryman and Walcott would be a good place to look for something similar, the debt to Lowell – specifically the heavy thinking poet-diarist of *History* – is overwhelming. It's clear, though, that the influence has been salutary, pushing Kirsch to be less brightly epiphanic, more anxiously suggestive. 'Larkin', one of the book's best poems, sums up the British poet thusly:

> If genius is to carry the pristine
> Shock of perception to the bitter last,
> There was no purer genius: philistine,
> Uncompromising, foul mouth stuffed with rust.

That ending, especially the very fine parting image, approximates Lowell's knack of catching the corroded aspects of a life while also serving notice of Kirsch's own gift for using rhyme (pristine/philistine, last/rust) to further encode the grimness. In 'Withdrawal', Kirsch expresses the floating media-saturated fatalism of a post 9/11 world:

> The good it did was negative. The mail
> Put off its weaponized white coat of spores;

The jets no longer seemed to fall
Or pivot madly toward the upper floors;
Such things returned to their old habitat
In nightmares and the crawl on CNN.
But where did the rainbow come from, pledging that
The flood subsiding wouldn't rise again?
It was just something swallowed with the dose
That fed the brain its missing chemicals,
Coaxing it from its darker purposes
Back to the daylight we assume is normal.
Now as the milligrams decrease, the ache
And sizzle of the synapse slowing down
Warns that these months of peace were a mistake;
Things were not wrong inside, but all around.

'Things were not wrong inside, but all around' is as memorable as language gets. The well-managed flow of this, however, gives a hint of how it can, and does, go wrong: observations are wrenched into an effortful word-placing that always keeps an obligatory eye on the rhyme scheme. Kirsch's experiments at writing a more improvisingly intuited poetry hits, for lines at a time, pay dirt: anecdotal after-images, confessional hints, self-dissolving details. But as with his first book, continued attempts at a more colloquial phrasing can't escape an ever-so-slight drift toward antiquarianism:

There are things created of a size
We can't and weren't meant to understand,
As fish know nothing of the sun that writes
Its bright glyphs on the black waves overhead.

The result is a begloomed, piecemeal rhetoric that feels like padding, and a cookie-cutter form that requires it. What constitutes poetry has always been an open question, but never quite as open as today when the alternatives available have made a poet's prosodic choices nearly impossible to anticipate. To argue, as Kirsch does in *The Modern Element*, that rhyme, done expertly, can be 'considerably more surprising than the most estranging experimentation' is to be a poet who has settled his own questions about form. For that reason, despite Kirsch's conviction that traditional forms are a path to the present and not the past, I can't help but feel that the best explanation for his choices in *Invasions* is provided by Paul Valéry, who said that the chief pleasure of rhyme is the rage it inspires in its opponents. When Kirsch describes, in a poem about a burial, the tossing of earth onto a casket and 'the streaky clumps/That scatter with a soft unanswered knock', he might as well be writing about the public reception of his own poet-critic sounds.

JAMES LANGER

IT USED TO BE a good day when a book as fine as *Gun Dogs* (2009) was assigned to you for review. It still is, but jadedness now threatens to creep in. The poems in James Langer's debut are musically alert, with marvellous rhythmic and tonal variety. Such formal sophistication was once unicorn-rare in this country. Today there is barely enough time to keep up with new expressions of it. Canadian poets seem to have caught the habit of writing well.

It didn't happen by accident. A fully eloquent poetry has been available in this country since E.J. Pratt. But for decades Canadian critics and reviewers avoided this body of work out of the belief that literary style was for foreigners or phonies. No longer: poetic form has become a hot-button issue thanks to a group of tyros who have made it impossible to talk about anything else. The upside is that it's an exciting time for serious readers of Canadian poetry, here and abroad. The downside is that an admirable book like *Gun Dogs* – which might have emerged as a triumph when fewer such books existed – trails a herd.

Or worse than a herd: a sub-genre. *Gun Dogs* is a prize example of what Newfoundland poet Patrick Warner has labelled 'the School of Stacked Vowels and Clustered Consonants'. As a member of this school, Langer has a knack for finding words that, placed together, crackle and buzz. Read his collection with a pencil in hand, and you'll leave behind pages scored with marks beside every attractive sense-heightening description ('sandstone grit that girders the barrens'), compressed evocation ('snow eddied, amassed, erased the trails') and compound phrase ('fog-clot', 'murk-light', 'mud-thrum').

Judged on technical merit alone, there doesn't seem much Langer can't ace (a fascinating sonnet called 'Half-full' is constructed out of alternating end-rhymes of 'half' and 'full'). Indeed, the reason his translation of the first 64 lines of the Anglo-Saxon staple 'The Seafarer' is so successful is that Langer himself writes with an Old English doggedness. He loves nothing better than to create a sense of linguistic abundance. But even fans of this sort of thing will be forced to confront lines over-egged into noise and show-offness. Or ear-catching moments ('Loon's a loose cannon, booze-hound') that merely grease the workings of the poem: they help set up the next bit of wordplay. Too often, it's all effect, but no after-effect; enhanced flavourings, but no lingering finish. For Langer, language that sounds good means well. The danger is we also see a poet, to use Clive James's words, 'looking for spectacular ways to say not very much'.

For all its extra zing, *Gun Dogs* will leave you with the sense of a gob-smackingly gifted poet biting off a lot more than he can chew. That said, the late American poet-critic Thomas Disch had a useful test for gauging a collection's worth. Pretend you were editing the year's best: how many would tempt you? I'd say five: 'Home Suite', 'Gun Dogs', 'Gangrene', 'North of Boston' and 'Chalk Outlines'. Enough to hold our attention? Absolutely. Enough to hold its own during a poetry boom time? Not quite – yet.

IRVING LAYTON

MY WIFE AND I were leaving for Rome when I got the news. The cab was waiting, and, just as I was about to shut the laptop, my inbox lit up with an e-mail from David Solway. 'Bad news', it began. There was no time to react. We were late. So after checking-in, after boarding, after finding our seats, after taxiing down the runway and after switching off the reading light, I stared out into the vast darkness we were sailing through, and quietly cried.

It isn't a stretch to suggest that what Layton meant to me, and to nearly two generations of Canadian poets, chimed with the 'ruins and travellers' cheques' of Rome. Italy adored Layton. The man often derided elsewhere as wilful, graceless and disruptive was regarded by Italian poets as brilliant, passionate, audacious and masterfully contrarian. He remains one of the few foreign poets you can find in translation on bookshelves in Italy. To our embarrassment, the Italians have done a better job of keeping him in print than we have.

For Layton, Rome – a city he described as his 'Italian lady' – represented a chance to escape into, and speak out of, a richer culture. After his death, I was amused to hear the CBC say Layton fought for a 'Canadian' voice in our poetry. Layton didn't have a Canadian bone in his body. The story of how Israel Lazarovitch became 'Irving Layton' is the story of a man at war with any such cultural denominator. 'A dull people' is what he called us, 'without charm/or ideas'. We were a tiny backwater of wood-hewers toiling at the edges of the world's indifference, and he wanted none of it. He was the first poet from this country to disown his assigned historical self, that checklist of boondock 'Canadian' behaviours. Everything about Layton flowed from that decision. He was, as the Italians say, *fuori dagli schemi*, outside existing plans. He seemed to have no collective feelings, and no one ever caught sight of him in a crowd. To meet Layton was, in fact, to be impressed by how idiosyncratically himself he was, in every ornery fibre.

While his peers Purdified themselves to the ordinary and local, he forged a genuinely transatlantic voice, a voice whose forthright lyricism, bawdy enumerations and biblical amplifications could travel everywhere. And did. We forget that this is what it means to be a world-class poet. It means setting your sights above being 'voice of the land' or 'the world's most Canadian poet'. In Layton's case, it meant writing with a mischief and eloquence that took ordinary language out of the ordinary and brought it within hailing distance of the best of Lowell and Hughes. It meant writing poems shot through with reverence, vulgarity and wit – poems that in their intricate play of piety and blasphemy were not only unique in twentieth-century English poetry, but near-miraculous. And CanLit's revenge? Repackage Layton as a cautionary tale: The Genius Who Lost His Touch.

It's true that the sustained interiority that made reading Layton a deep-sea dive was drained away over time so that we found ourselves, late in his career, splashing around in very shallow water. What you were given in his last books was one range of voice, one kind of opinion. But this scold, when taken too far, becomes exasperating, and my own defence has always been threefold. First, that Layton is the kind of poet whose failures of measure and common sense are necessary to his successes: the searing registering of colours and sounds and smells, the aggressive underscoring of intellectual and political ironies, the fast and sudden punches of phrasing. Second, that publishers are ultimately responsible for creating books, not poets, and McClelland & Stewart had a role to play in abetting (and milking) Layton's productivity and lust for self-display in the latter years of his writing. And third, I like to repeat Layton's lovely riposte to a Toronto poet who jeered that Layton had published 40 books of poetry with only one good poem in each. 'If true', Layton said, 'then that's 40 more good poems than you'll ever write'.

Because, finally, what else is there to say? 'A poet's real biography', Joseph Brodsky noted, 'is in his vowels and sibilants, in his meters, rhymes and metaphors'. When you're done summarizing Layton's denouncers, grading his uneven career and highlighting his romantic conquests, the hardest thing to keep in mind is that he wrote not only good poems, but great ones. To measure his achievement by the shock it produced, however, is to measure it by the smallest imaginations of the time. We saw this in the media reaction to his death, which was a reminder that journalists always found it difficult to present Layton without condescension. It was no surprise, for example, to see obits stealing labels from each other, like 'trailblazer', '*enfant terrible*' and 'controversial'. These words continue a tradition that began the moment Layton published *Here and Now* in 1945, whereby he is simultaneously exalted as rogue and excluded from serious literary consideration.

If Layton's poetry remains more audacious than even the most sympathetic reading can admit, it's because he dared see intelligence, technique and strong emotion as collaborators. His death is heartbreaking. But today, as I walk around Piazza Venezia and recall Layton's splendid lines on his own visit nearly 45 years ago – 'The fountains of the city flying/Upward in the illusive act of dying' – I can think of no better image for his final release and enduring achievement.

MEDBH McGUCKIAN

'A DREAM dreamed in the presence of reason' was Jesuit Tommaso Ceva's definition of poetry. One way or another, all poets fiddle with that formula. Medbh McGuckian has fine-tuned it. She has hit on a dream-to-reason ratio perfect for replicating what she calls 'the feminine subconscious, or semi-consciousness'. Think middle state as a mental state: sensations mingle until language is a vapour of impossible-to-visualize surmises. McGuckian's poems don't make sense, they make mist.

Her debut, *The Flower Master* (1982), set the standard. Written around the time of her first child's birth, the book attempts to tackle the passionate ambivalence of her maternal feelings. Each poem is a series of richly evocative assertions that harm their own logic ('A man will keep a horse for prestige,/but a woman ripens best underground'). Opacity rides up hard against precision, in a constant bestriding of clauses, but never quite overtakes it. What comes through, pictorially, is a mood of lightness and transparency suffused with half-sexual strangeness ('I begin to scatter/to a tiny to-and-fro at odds/With the wear on my threshold'). The effect is startling; seductive even. But, for all that, no less of a letdown. A reader kept on standby – unsure what happens next, struggling to understand what has happened already – is a reader with nothing to keep in his head.

The Currach Requires No Harbours, McGuckian's ninth book, is more of the same: dense, diffuse and dimly apprehensible. Of course, her anti-depictions have a function: to scramble male tenets of poetic form. Against control-freak articulateness, McGuckian offers an exploratory seeping forth of sounds. By letting language have its way, she hopes to be led to insights otherwise unreachable. Yet McGuckian's digression-prone method is actually a spectacularly ornate free-association game. Far from freeing buried meanings, she has refined a mellifluousness no less confected for being slippery. Orotundity piles up, longeurs go long. The problem, you soon realize, isn't McGuckian's obscurity. It's her decision to double-down on it: not simply to seal off her non sequiturs from rational inspection, but to overwrite the act. The poems, in other words, make a big show of handing themselves over to ideas too deep to be grasped. It's an attention-losing ploy because it's so self-indulged. That said, if you do sometimes find yourself paying attention (and you will) a big reason will be the lush music of her expression:

> Days that belonged to war and peace
> at the same time, they were always so:
> darkened cinemas, the strength of lamps
> reduced as low as possible.
>
> Peace being restored at different speeds,
> the sea disarmed, England calm,
> and the shelf upon which it sat
> more certain of the greens and golds,
>
> or what she might look like
> while looking – her hummingbird nature,
> her maple-tree nature. Hers is the first
> of many languid arms to reach out
>
> like a lifted horizon in a landscape's
> perfect swaying, her opaque red plumage,
> lips and heels like patched sails
> in the same damp winter's afterglows.

Here, from her poem 'Regaining Control of the Night', we have some atomized perceptions prettily captured in four stanzas. It's a beguiling blend of pinpoint grammar and just-short-of-evanescent imagery. McGuckian isn't always so semi-articulate and, by playing it straight, can achieve vivid enrichments of ordinary perception: 'the way the moon attaches/her self-closing, liquid glance/to the perfect leaf'. But she can't resist: she will always strike inward to a deeper voluptuousness. Which means that *The Currach Requires No Harbours* will be enjoyed best by those who find it easiest to detach their expectations from a poem's actual result. Take the following:

> The trans-lake mountain,
> cruel where the black
> passes over, is tender in its silver-toned
> puckerings of preparation.

Every word after 'mountain' operates outside the bounds of normal usage, but because McGuckian – a name that too closely rhymes with McGuffin – doesn't coordinate the consequences of those new identities, the sentence is a bit of a put-on. The words aren't badly chosen, they're arousingly chosen; or, as she once said, 'a word has only/an aroma of meaning'. But what is 'an aroma of meaning' if not arbitrariness with delusions of grandeur? We can say this much for McGuckian's poems: they're utterly hers. She has a reputation for a mind on its own wavelength, and it's well-deserved.

DON McKAY

WHEN Roo Borson won the Griffin Poetry Prize in 2005 every table in Toronto's vast Stone Distillery erupted with applause, yet the mood was solemn: Don McKay had lost. The distress that rippled through the room on that June evening (it was his second unsuccessful nomination) was a reminder of the extraordinary affection that exists for the sixty-five-year-old word wonk and birder. And truly, is there a name in Canadian poetry that looms larger? Whose reputation stands higher? Not since Al Purdy has a single poet meant so much to so many. McKay is pre-eminent, inescapable, ubiquitous.

To get a more specific sense of his stature, one need only read other Canadian poets. As it was with Purdy, scores of younger devotees have become dab hands at replicating the sound and sense of McKay's poetry. You can spot him, for starters, in Ken Babstock, Adam Dickinson, David Seymour and Jeanette Lynes. In fact, it's now nearly impossible to read a first book of poems, especially if minted by Brick, that doesn't glitter with McKayesque coinages. Older, mid-career figures have proven no less susceptible (a recent example is Brian Bartlett's series of bird panegyrics from his last collection *The Afterlife of Trees*).

If all this affirms McKay's popularity, it also betrays how utterly franchisable his methods have become. He bears no blame for this, of course. We're sometimes quick to dismiss poets who are easy to mimic, but the ease with which a style goes from uncommon to cribbed often belies its hard-won birth. Purdy's pioneering plain-talk, which inspired decades of helpless plagiarism, didn't really exist until his sixth book, *All the Caribou Horses* (1965). And similarly, for many years, McKay had to make due with vigorous but tire-spinning attempts to find a vernacular keyed to local landscapes, creatures and seasons – what, in his first book, *Air Occupies Space* (1973), he called 'this/demotic am am am among the trees'. Only with his fourth, *Birding, or desire* (1983), did those experiments grip ground and accelerate into the much-celebrated (and much-copied) McKay voice – a run-on-at-the-mouth zaniness that converts everything seen and heard during leisurely country walks into high-speed fugues. This is 'A Toast to The Baltimore Oriole':

> Here's to your good looks and the neat way you shit
> with a brisk bob like a curtsey, easy as song.
> Here's to your song, which
> though 'neither rhythmical nor musical' (*The Birds of Canada*),
> relieves me of all speech and never deals with what is past,
> or passing, or to come.
> And, as a monument to the sturdy fragile woven
> scrotum of your nest,
> I hereby dedicate baseball.

Piety-tweaking colloquialisms ('the neat way you shit'), perversely exact metaphors ('scrotum of your nest'), and offhand venerations ('I hereby dedicate baseball') not only comprise the heart of McKay's verse toolkit, but have come to represent a better way of paying attention to the world. And by better, I also mean faster. His next books, *Sanding Down This Rocking Chair on a Windy Night* (1987), *Night Field* (1991) and *Apparatus* (1997), are the work of a poet who taught himself to stay in sync with the jolts of Canadian speech, and gain a higher pixel-resolution to boot. As with most breakthroughs that become mass-produced, McKay's discovery was privately motivated: the need for a cognitive music that could keep up with the idiosyncrasies of his thinking. Incidentally, this is where comparisons with Purdy end. Syntax, for Purdy, tends toward stability. It exists in a steady state. McKay's goes frantic. Jauntiness floods his lines like an amphetamine ('ok ok ok ok/here they come' is how he uncorks a poem about chickadees). McKay's insight into style as a stimulant has inspired entirely new post-Purdy trends. Conventional line-breaks have given way to jump-cut enjambment. Single-voice speakers have been replaced by multi-tasking narration that splices together various registers. These are welcome developments. But as diminishing returns begin to set in with a growing list of look-alikes, it does make one worry: is McKay overrated?

Last year, McKay published his eighth book, *Strike/Slip* (2006). The title is a geological term, describing a fault-line where two plates slide (or 'slip') in opposite directions. While the term is rich with metaphoric potential (i.e., modes of seeing slide past each other), it's also a fairly accurate description of the instability – or better, the interrupted stability of McKay's wordsmithing. There is the recognizable 'look': a looping-over and layering-under of thoughts that creates, on the page, a spine of erratic line-lengths. There is the trademark tang of his disjunctive phrasing, with its near-indefinable mix of humour, tomfoolery and awe. Setting, too, returns. McKay's world is almost wholly rural. Woods – walked through, stood in, listened to – are at the heart of his oeuvre, and his prototypical narrator emerges once again from these new poems, a pastoral *flâneur* who makes his daily rounds of pond, cliff, river and pine seeking first-hand revelations.

This time, however, our hero's 'oh' and 'ah' moments are drawn mostly from mineral epiphanies – 'Who is so heavy with the past as you,/Monsieur Basalt?'. And, all over, are his birds. McKay may have come to realize that 'everything derives from rock' but he's still made room for chipping sparrows, rock doves, thrushes, dipper, pine siskins, not to mention 'squat/swart psychopompic gulls'. Along with Eric Ormsby and Eric Miller, McKay is probably one of our great decoders of avian eccentricity. There's even a case to be made that McKay's poems aspire, almost as ends-in-themselves, to the condition of birdsong – that what they're after are full-dress impersonations of warbling. *Strike/Slip* certainly does nothing to dispel that idea. 'Song for Songs of the Common Raven' is constructed from a jumble of rising and falling notes that accelerate into each line-break. The intended effect is one of hovering, of lines lifted out and suspended, caught on-the-fly:

You could say it carries, you could say
dwells. *Corvus corax*: even in Latin
you can hear that smoke-and-whisky brogue –
croak, curruck, and (swallowing the syllable)
tok. You could say a fierce
unsayable secret had possessed the voice,
which has to speak and must not tell and so
is hallowed out and rendered terminally
hoarse. Of its brutal
seismic histories, its *duende*,
it says nothing. Nothing of the flowing and bending of rock,
of the burning going down and coming
up again as lava. Of rogue gods
loitering among the hemlocks nurturing the urge
to break out into body it conspicuously
does not sing. While sending messages that might
say 'Watch your asses, creatures
of the Neogene' or might say 'Baby,
bring it on'.

A hoot, yes, but what's happening here is hardly new. *Strike/Slip* is a re-gifting. We unwrap it to learn we've been given a poet we already know very well. I imagine there must be readers who feel that, when it comes to McKay, business as usual is time well-spent. My feelings however divide on precisely that point. On one side, a satisfaction from contemplating the attributes McKay is fêted for. On the other, a powerful sense of deja-lu. To be sure, the book differs from the others in one important way: an environmental anger that has grown stronger over the last decade (and about which more later). But it's hard not to suspect that a repertoire of trusted techniques is simply being recycled. Indeed if younger poets have taken from McKay what is most easily imitable, McKay has, in a sense, followed them. A great deal of his work since *Another Gravity* (2000) is lavish with superfluity. 'I have 2.6 ideas', he once joked, 'and I say them five times each', but his reluctance to revise and refine past a certain professional comfort-zone is anything but funny. It's the rare poem in *Strike/Slip* that would not be improved with a blue pencil. Everything feels slightly inflated, slightly unnecessary: from phrasal tics ('Whatever I say now', 'We might as well say', 'we say' 'What I want to say', 'as they say') to we-get-the-point overwriting ('Still, something settles,/something stays. Something sedimentary/accumulates').

Take another look at the poem quoted above. As lively as it may appear, McKay has padded it with sententious overstatement ('You could say a fierce/unsayable secret had possessed the voice,/which has to speak and must not tell'), intellectual filler ('Of its brutal/seismic histories, its *duende*/it says nothing') and fussy intensifiers ('conspicuously'). A straight read through *Strike/Slip* should be enough to convince anybody that these poems love the pied-beauty sound of their own voice: Songs for the Song of McKay.

The result is a book that's easy to praise – streaked with eccentricities, rich in grace-notes – but hard to love: bad line-breaks, disposable banter, misdemeanours of metaphor and poems too thinly-textured to rise above whimsy. It sometimes seems that the best way to read McKay's new book is, essentially, to skip. A line here, a phrase there. (His definition of earning a living as 'Work plus knack/plus luck' is great, but to discover it many readers will have punished themselves by reading almost the whole of 'Utter'). McKay is clearly awake to the language as it exists right now, finding new words to put into poems ('J-stroke', 'nooks', 'rah-rah', 'yucks', 'scritching', 'po-mo', 'Velcro'). But few reviewers and critics have been honest about the way he has grown increasingly prone to a sham writerly authority, where gimmicks are left to do the work of feeling and perception.

Two recent studies that claim to look hard at his poetry, *Don McKay: Essays on His Works* (2006) and *Field Marks: The Poetry of Don McKay* (2006), say virtually nothing about this. Edited by Brian Bartlett, *Don McKay: Essays on His Works* is the first major conspectus of McKay's career. It features essays by friends, colleagues and mentees like Ross Leckie, Stan Dragland, Robert Bringhurst, Sue Sinclair and Susan Elmslie. *Field Marks* is edited by Meira Cook who provides an introduction to a taster of 36 poems by McKay (who himself contributes an afterword). Both books pay McKay the tribute of placing his poetics front and centre. Both books make smart, plausible arguments for

McKay's importance. Both books are filled with the sort of articulate commentary McKay's poetry has consistently received, commentary that tells you our man is blue-chip, world-class, a winner. It is criticism of veneration, one that beatifies every twitch as a bold train of thought. Such criticism is one of the perks of having a cultic reputation. Another perk is the assumption that you are read best by those who like to read you most. Perhaps, but perhaps these two books also confirm the risk of reading McKay so affectionately: one appears overly charmed by the tricks he uses to create his acoustic *mise en scènes* – the double takes, the stop-on-a-dime rhythms, the volte-face verbs. McKay is considered such a good poet that readers fall over themselves to find that goodness everywhere, especially his hither-thither diction, his whatnot moments. Doubts, if expressed, are expressed only to be chased. His gifts are real and undeniable, but it seems as though we've struck a deal with our skepticism. In return for poems fizzing with stylistic vitality, we pretend not to notice what's vapid, repetitive and muddle-headed. Estimations of McKay's poetry that avoid his howlers can't really be of much use because they create the suspicion that the critical consensus he enjoys is a better deal than he deserves. A balanced assessment thus seems desperately needed, even at the cost of harshness.

McKay does not write in traditional forms ('I am out of sympathy with the institutionalization of form as an 'ism''), and instead sides with a more intuitive, from-scratch prosody. A student of nature's organic unpredictability, he tries to give anything prefab the slip. In doing so, he has conceived a feverish life form of his own: rangy, lapidary, nimble and arrestingly arrhythmic. From a technical view, McKay's poems are fascinating experiments in structural tolerance. Errant and impulsive, they're held together by a tonal glue best defined as a balancing-by-keeping-moving equilibrium. 'Jamming' is how McKay once described it, and it's a method he's marvellously good at, as we can recognize in early humdingers like 'I Scream You Scream', 'March Snow' and 'Three Eclogues'. His has a rare instinct for the sort of syntax that can generate evasive links and elided assertions, that can encourage sentences to 'open doors at both ends' in order to create phrasing loose-meshed enough to allow different feelings to enter and disperse. Here, in its entirety, is "Stress, Shear, and Strain Theories of Failure":

> They have never heard of lift
> and are – for no one, over and over – cleft. Riven,
> recrystallized. Ruined again. The earth-engine
> driving itself through death after death. Strike/Slip,
> thrust, and the fault called normal, which occurs
> when two plates separate.
> Do they hearken unto Orpheus, whose song
> is said to make them move? Sure.
> This sonnet hereby sings that San Fran-
> cisco and L.A. shall, thanks to its chthonic shear,
> lie cheek by jowl in thirty million
> years. Count on it, mortals. Meanwhile,
> may stress shear strain attend us. Let us fail
> in all the styles established by our lithosphere.

One of the pleasures of McKay's poetry, when he's writing well, is how he keeps us on the qui vive. We read with near-vertiginous anticipation, always looking ahead, always peering into the concavity of the poem's emerging articulations to get a fix on what's coming next. The above poem – a defrocked sonnet – is one of the best in the book. Written using a kind of trippy, geological shoptalk, it addresses the provisional order of things in large part by turning itself into a pun on the 'ground rules' of human life on earth. The poem also mirrors the notion of 'shear' by using sudden variations in diction to create exciting musical disturbances. ('Do they hearken unto Orpheus, whose song/is said to make them move? Sure'.) Everything is in play – associations change hands as fast as McKay changes his mind – but nothing feels arbitrary. The verbal overlaps and mental links add up to a cogent voice and point of view. Unfortunately this method doesn't always bring out the best in McKay. It can, in other poems, distract him into delivery that has plenty of stylistic rumble and wow but not much in the way of substance. 'To whom we turn to be/momentous, to be/monumental, to be/meant'. That's the scat-singing of a poet with an ear tuned to the gesticulatory improvisations of speech. It's also uncomfortably close to sounding like a quick trot with a few pet mannerisms. And the better McKay gets at this ad-lib talk, the less his poems seem to say. An exemplary intellect has long been part of McKay's M.O., but more often than not the pleonastic poems in *Strike/Slip* resemble intersections where a Hard-to-Grasp Insight is always passing through, forcing McKay to mobilize lots of fast-action diction to catch it:

> Protero, palaeo, meso, ceno:
> I had, I thought,
> a thing to say as I approached
> the columns of angular basalt. But all those
> rough chateaux were shut, their epochs
> slammed, their hours immured.
> The spells of textbooks
> echoed, so much gabbling Greek.
> I thought of earth,
> how it remembers us and calls our
> nutrient-rich bodies and nostalgia-heavy heads
> home to its humus.

McKay is often thought of as a poet of landscape, but to compare these lines from 'Apostrophe' with the exact noticings of more detail-hungry nature poets, like Eric Ormsby or Harry Thurston, is to see how thoroughly McKay's eye depends on having a big idea to see through. His poems may be scenery-stimulated but it's rare to find a description that is honestly happening before our eyes and not intermediated by filters. In this case, 'columns of angular basalt' are being intellectualized on behalf of a typical McKay theme: nature and our inability to ever fully know, own or control it (hence the speaker finds the rocks 'shut', 'slammed' and 'immured'). Also typical is the way McKay rigs this meeting of man and mineral into a kind of morality play on the lyric 'I' (in the second half of the poem the speaker goes on to sermonize against poetry's tendency to regard the 'deaf, blind' moon as private property). Human beings are allowed a place in McKay's poems but never pre-eminence. In fact, discrediting the single, arrogating point of view is what, in part, helps enable McKay's discontinuities and detours. The problem is that it's a philosophy, and a prosody, that also encourages him to fall back on a facile exhortative mode whenever inspiration peters out on him. This is clear enough in the above example, where the first six lines are lucid, and the next six – everything from 'spells of textbooks' to 'home to its humus' – ludicrous. But McKay wants to get into business as a deep thinker, and this technique is what he uses to think deep. His self-skeptical attitude drives him to dissolve fixities, and the dazzling outcome – keyed-up, syncopated, tangent-generating – provides cover for his duller literary-grandiose register. The form allows him to say, and get away with saying, anything at all, while the homiletic mood bestows preposterous dicta ('I thought of earth,/how it remembers us') with poetic sanction even if they don't prove credible as art.

To put it another way, McKay has patented a betwixt-and-between style that can sell readers on the idea he is pursuing a complex course of feeling, one that readers can themselves observe in transit as it develops and intensifies on the page. When these shifts are married to real focus, the payoff is memorable: 'Presto-critter', he calls out to a dipper, 'you are the creek's own/bright idea and your quicknesses – dart, tilt, zip-across-the-rapids,/perch – inflect its flow'. When not, we get something structurally runny and imprecisely reverential. Words are used with casual elasticity; they are used 'poetically'. Take McKay's decision, later in the same dipper poem, to write of a 'creek's continuous/music of wash and loss'. *Music of wash and loss*? Once again, one wishes this unconventional poet were better at noticing, and nixing, triteness. But the real question is: why doesn't anyone else flinch? In order for a metaphor like 'music of wash and loss' to sound good, you have to have a weakness for a certain kind of sentimental pictorializing. And if McKay's stardom is any indication, it clearly sounds good to a lot of people. The quickness of his ear might be irresistible, but shouldn't a poet who lets himself write about 'the song of mother rock' or how 'pain finds/words and tastes them acrid and metallic/on its raw tongue', or how red pine 'swayed in the air like gospel choirs' or how 'bones fall in love with the wind,/which teaches them to whistle' – shouldn't such a poet lead to *some* head-scratching about why his crackling style needs to lug such bunk?

Doubts, real ones, do exist. Richard Greene, Zach Wells, Shane Neilson are three poets who have written minority reports on McKay's frequent moments of mediocrity. (They are also, tellingly, three poets whose poems show no evidence of having joined the choir.) But, insofar as we can keep score, criticism becomes irrelevant when a poet can play to the gallery. *Strike/Slip* is in fact so perfectly what we now expect good Canadian poetry to be (an expectation McKay is partly responsible for creating) that the book radiates the almost constant pleased-with-itself attitude of a poet who knows where his reader's quasi-reverential buttons are and what it takes to push them. Indeed, if McKay's talent is to always appear busy with some philosophical mega-concept, his genius is to find language that lets readers bask in the deception that they've been made to ponder it too.

How he does this is an interesting question. His verbal charms provide, I think, only part of the answer. Our historical moment has a lot to do with it too. McKay is very lucky to be writing at a time when his concerns can appear not just pastoral but progressive. Nature poets have always been ecological in the sense that they are acutely aware of being intruders on the scene. The difference for McKay is that his intruder-consciousness brings profound prosodic responsibilities. He has based those responsibilities on a visceral experience of what he calls the 'thinness of language'. The phrase comes from *Vis à Vis* (2004), a collection of essays that, as he writes in his introduction, attempt to 'come to grips with the practise of nature poetry in a time of environmental crisis'. The phrase concerns language's inability to fully capture the essence of what a poet perceives. According to McKay, underestimating this 'thinness' leads to a costly nomenclatural arrogance, or what he calls 'the centralizing and reductive influence of the name'. Meditations on the shortfalls between what we see and the words we use to describe it have roots deep in our poetic tradition. But having caught the Gaia tide at exactly the right moment, McKay connects this 'centralizing and reductive influence' to our ecological carelessness. The poetic mindset that forces its felicities on the world, he argues, draws on the very same appetite that makes us resource-guzzlers.

McKay dramaticizes that idea in *Vis à Vis*'s opening essay by describing a grim sight he discovered along the Saint John River: a raven strung up with baler twine from a roadside tree, tail gone and a shotgun hole through the back. McKay regards the raven as an example, writ small, of what can happen when the world is reduced to the grasp of our will. Since there was no obvious purpose to its death, the creature functions as an expression of human power, a casualty of our possessive relationship to what exists around us. But this lethality is, for McKay, epistemological at root. Romanticism's belief in the nameability of the natural world is itself a kind of willed domination. What McKay proposes as a corrective is a 'poetic attention' that can act as 'a species of longing which is without the desire to possess'. Only by contemplating – rather than ideologically appropriating – one's surroundings can we preserve the autonomy of 'wilderness', defined by McKay as 'the capacity of all things to elude the mind's appropriations'. Along with Tim Lilburn and Robert Bringhurst, his poetry not only develops this idea into a thesis ('knowing, not owning' as Bringhurst succinctly puts it) but has helped give the emerging Canadian school of eco-poetics its sound: hyperfocused and high on its promised insights, often drifting into an intimidating, even combative vagueness determined to quarantine the sacredness of nature and isolate it from the contagion of 'naming'.

At a time of ecological crisis, the idea of a poetry that promises to lift away the false categorizations of nature to allow readers to wordlessly confront its underlying reality – or 'wilderness' – is deeply attractive. But while there is much to be said for that kind of writing and thinking, the incongruity between its aspirations and the trivial effects of its literal practise are too obvious to overlook. It is baffling to be told, unvaryingly and insistently, that McKay intends his poems to resensitize our stance toward the 'otherness' of nature, when his tendency is to quite obviously write *over* nature, to soap it so respectfully in 'poetic attention' that its earthy quiddity is washed away. His poems don't really arise from a lived-in sense of place but from an intellectual reaction to it. Words connect with other words, but never fasten to their subject. To describe flying birds as travelling in 'rough/asymmetrical gestalts' or to describe their wings as 'shifting like fine/polyphony', could, I suppose, be understood as geopoetically poignant. It is also poignantly useless. What aspect of reality do those two images sharpen or magnify or intensify? *Strike/Slip* marks the escalation of McKay's environmental concerns with poems about industrialization and misguided forestry practices ('The broken prose of the bush roads/'The piles of half-burnt slash'). At least that's the script the poems stick to. But too often, the considerable resources of his ear – the weighing up of syllables, the testing of conjunctions, the clocking of verbs – are brought to bear on rhetoric. Too often, to read him is to merely track the vain drift of his man-bad/nature-good logic; passages that, despite the green ideals that set them in motion, are just pieces of writing lightly scented with the smelling salts of serious thinking.

> Everything is listening at me:
> the stumps oozing resin, the birdsong
> bouncing off my head like sonar,
> the bludgeoned air with its fading
> after-echoes. I think of people
> herded to a square, staring
> at the man on the platform.
> Whatever I say now
> will be strictly interpreted
> and parsed.
> Is this the way it works,
> locking you, stunned, in the imperative,
> making a weapon of each tool?

These are the first lines of 'Après Chainsaw', presumably written 'without desire to possess'. What that eco-motto seems to mean in practice is that the chaff and loose-ends of suggestive vocabulary ('oozing', 'bludgeoned') and historical allusion (that Holocaust-evoking 'people/herded to a square') are made to stand for a poem that really isn't there. Perhaps the reader's own expectations need to be wilderness-friendly, not so driven by the aggression of needing to understand. After all, why else would the poem seem to anticipate, and reprimand, my presence: 'Whatever I say now/will be strictly interpreted/and parsed'. But then, how are we ever expected to separate honest speech from hot air? McKay's career makes one realise just how badly we lack a way of talking about poetry that isn't framed purely in terms of its anti-quantifiable impulses. McKay wants to expiate our environmental guilt by purifying poetic language of its self-centeredness. This purification has led him to evolve an idiom that doesn't seek to control what it describes. The blowback, however, has been a large-scale reification of vagueness, where the almost-image – what we get in the above poem – assumes a mystical quality, a fundamental essence immune from questions of relevance. In the past, when a Canadian poet used a word he meant something specific by it. Today our words live a dozen different lives, each of them indifferently. *Strike/Slip* is heavily invested in the aesthetics of imprecision – the barely-describable, the unfathomable, the fuzzy. We get 'tongueless tongue', we get 'praising the unsayable to the angel', we get 'the camber of its nothing as it/lifts, as it glances, as it vanishes'. This – inert and nonevocative – isn't poetry, but philosophically encoded filler; not poetry, but born-again Georgianism that tries to wring maximum wisdom from everything it lazily leaves unsaid.

To the relief of his fans, *Strike/Slip* was given the 2007 Griffin prize. But the worry isn't over. There is yet another, even more exclusive trophy for which McKay is still in the running: posterity's attention and praise. He certainly delivers real pleasure of a special kind in poems like 'Pond' 'Abandoned Cable', 'Dipper at Parkinson Creek', 'Pine Siskins', 'Ascent with Thrushes' and 'Abandoned Cable'. But because of his acclaim, expectations of another order are raised, without ever being satisfied. In that gap lies the difference between an interesting poet and a great one. McKay is now the main attraction, and for many of our younger poets, the way forward. His popularity operates on the principle that anyone who doesn't exalt his work hasn't really understood it. Perhaps. And perhaps his popularity reveals us to be a country of astonishingly easy graders.

A.F. MORITZ

'EVERY SACRED THING that wishes to remain so', Stéphane Mallarmé said, 'must envelop itself in mystery'. Anyone who has spent time with the French symbolists will be familiar with the theological swoon of their theorizing. Mallarmé and his stablemates Paul Verlaine and Paul Valery may have rejected Christian principles, but it's hard not to feel they were really religious poets who merely transferred their devotion to matters of style.

Poetry, of course, has always had an affinity with religious belief, but what makes symbolism so interesting is that it marks, arguably, the first major example of literature aping religion's own turn from a curiosity about cosmic questions (life, death, suffering) to an exclusive interest in the creativity that 'solved' those questions (rituals, signs, icons). Mallarmé, who assumed the office of symbolism's high priest, argued for a poetry that was supernatural in its logic, that resembled a 'religious mystery'. To put it another way, poetry was a province of secrets – secrets that needed to be protected in exactly the same way religion seemed to safeguard its own: by privileged concealment.

Mallarmé believed that religious answers were satisfying because they always withheld something, they always mystified. Mystification became for him, therefore, the truest, most authentic poetic experience. 'To name an object', he wrote, 'is to suppress three-quarters of the enjoyment of the poem, which derives from the pleasure of step-by-step discovery'. There are good reasons to be skeptical of the 'enjoyment' Mallarmé had in mind (the painter Edgar Degas reportedly fled one of his readings, screaming 'I do not understand!') but there's no point ignoring that the Mallarméan aesthetic – the paring down of language to its essence and the simultaneous building up of its opacity – was modelled on religion's own radical cryptography. Jesus, after all, also taught by setting puzzles. He relied on parables and metaphors, and his sermons were often densely subtle. Compression ('The Kingdom of heaven is like to a grain of mustard seed') is at the root of all his lessons. Thus if symbolism can be understood as a spiritual task, an ambitious search for 'orphic' riddles to replace the reality it intended to explain, then scripture is poised on the edge of a similar paradox: it deciphers the world only by enciphering it anew.

But there's a difference between addressing mysteries and manufacturing them. 'Therefore I speak to them in parables', Jesus says in Matthew 13, 'because they seeing see not; and hearing they hear not, and neither do they understand'. They do not understand, in other words, because of conventional assumptions which keep their eyes and ears closed. Aware any attempt to speak plainly would likely increase the difficulty of his divine insights, Jesus realized what he needed, and what parables provided, was a method of short-circuiting the everyday mind. The genius, therefore, of Jesus's riddling (a riddling that was never esoteric in its diction, but simply the relocation of ordinary ideas into unusual, defamiliarizing contexts) lies in the way it fruitfully frustrates readers – frustrates them into *thought*, that is, rather than lulling them into dwelling on their own bewilderment. Scripture doesn't end with the mind's confusion; it merely begins with it.

The richly insinuating power of Jesus's sermons was exactly the sort of thing symbolism longed to recreate, and here we can point to the sense-scumbling texture of Mallarmé's own poems (the aureate diction, the scrim-like syntax, the private allusions, the confounding imagery) as best exposing the sacred basis of symbolism's literary intentions. But to believe, as Mallarmé did, that 'everything that is sacred and that wishes to remain so must envelop itself in mystery' is to believe that the sacred is nothing more than a reverence-inducing mood, an ambience created by 'enveloping' a subject. Without an appreciation for the motives that fashioned scripture's suspenseful form, symbolism was free to perceive the sacred as a problem of style, an achievable literary effect. Symbolism, in other words, threw away the religion but kept the religiosity, converting it into an exoticism practised for its own sake. Confusing scripture's evocative difficulty with its evasive appearance (one that helped shift the gears of twentieth-century poetry) ensured that mystery is now no longer regarded as a means – a tool able to preserve the rich ambiguity of an insight – but an end. Thanks to Mallarmé, poets today can claim the privilege of posing mysteries without the burden of showing fealty to truths.

I've taken the long way to A.F. Moritz's new book, *Night Street Repairs* (2004), because it's clear to me that if there's a contemporary Canadian poet making fresh use of the symbolist ambition (as well as serving as a fresh example of its failings) it's Moritz. Since his arrival here in 1974 from Niles, Ohio, he has published fourteen books of dense, delicate, indefinable poetry. Among the most notable being *The Tradition* (1986), *Song of Fear* (1992), *Mahoning* (1994) and *Rest on the Flight into Egypt* (1999), which was nominated for a Governor General's award. His career has generated an extraordinary amount of interest, and is haloed with a seriousness that continues to prove particularly irresistible to our younger poets (his influence can be observed in the recent work of Ken Babstock, Karen Solie, George Murray and Eric Miller).

The apostolically solemn figure he cuts among contemporary Canadian poets has a great deal to do, I think, with the reverent melodramas of his writing; writing, you might say, that thinks secularly but is religious in its enthusiasms. By 'religious' I mean, of course, it resists the workaday. It frees its subjects from a straightforward relationship to the ugly, plodding prose of their own literalness and lifts them, instead, toward a higher, purer referent: 'our world' – as Moritz defines it in the very last lines of *Night Street Repairs* – 'which is *the* world, although it is not here'. But by religious I also mean it draws a veil across its message. Mallarmé-style mystery mongering, in other words, which locates its greatest authority, creativity and ambition in a poem's most obstinately runic moments. Many of Moritz's admirers routinely define these moments as 'surrealist' in their underpinning, and it's easy to see why. But the fact is when Jeffery Donaldson in *The Literary Review of Canada* describes the opacity of Moritz's 'curious voicings' as a 'sleight-of-hand extracting of prophecy and vision from a world of everyday details'; or when Chris Jennings, in *Arc*, makes the case that Moritz's obscurities allow 'the labyrinthine logic of a vision to establish it own validity'; or when Richard Green argues, in *Books in Canada*, that Moritz is able to make 'theological statements that are nearly impossible for poets who are more "accessible"'; or best of all when Moritz himself explains that his poetry

> creates a strange, 'illogical' story out of visible things, wrenching them from their normal positions and their obedience to laws of nature and habit, by making them subject to an invisible meaning which, it asserts, is their deeper reality.

– they are, all of them, placing the poems squarely in the Mallarmian tradition, the poeticizing of the sacred. This, however, raises the crucial question of how to properly read Moritz's new book. What I may feel has been given an unwarrantable vagueness ('Somewhere near here is where I fell behind, / or looked away, a moment only, lost you, / and you went on oblivious') you may feel has been permitted its allowable mystery. What I may feel has been undecodably distanced ('a global drift of broken bricks your loss / shovels down to hunger from apex and appetite') you may feel has been cryptically enriched. Accusations of obscurity have, I admit, become reviewing's most overused dig. And it does seem rather philistine to level that sort of grouse against poetry as sophisticated as Moritz's. After all, 'making sense' may not be much of a priority with him, but his poems can be deeply attractive in their difficulties.

Night Street Repairs is an excellent case in point. One of his most charismatic collections to date, it serves up a richly palimpsestic verbal music pieced together from small moments of cut-and-run logic. The poems are elastically discursive, generous in their eccentricities and full of looking-glass skirmishes with language. It's telling, however, that whenever Moritz's poetry is working at the height of its powers, as it surely is here, its principal flaw is also at its most conspicuous. This is because any 'good' Moritz poem – like any 'good' symbolist poem – draws all its heat to its surface, leaving itself busily vacant. It is intense and interesting, but has no quiddity. It is fat with allusive density, but offers thin purchase on the imagination. I'm well aware that Moritz has run up a reputation as an ambitious poet who grapples with serious ideas, but I can't think of a poet who uses a vocabulary less viscerally suited to his subjects. His rummagings through a topic turn up very little except lots of 'deep thoughts' – thoughts, in other words, which are pregnant with significance, but impossible to fix in the mind. The result is a kind of spirit-speech defined not by its lofty unreadability but by its intellectual frictionlessness. If Moritz's poems are difficult, in other words, it's because the thinking has no traction. It's a directionless traveling-away-from that leaves the reader with nowhere to look:

> Some thundering *Aeneid* goes on inside you
> like light and like a river: barbarism,
> repression of barbarism over an entire
> earth, praise of peace, and pity for the lost,
> lament for the necessary, the healing, pity.
> You remain calm. No one looking at you knows.
> Your father sang the indifference of god
> before he died, and the measure of divine
> indifference we can reach – a laborious song:
> difficult to make the unstrung beautiful.
> In his aftermath, what's left? Experience
> that song does not change and light does not make clear?
> Knowledge that tyranny alone will hold
> the killing back a little? But you don't know
> if, for that, its worthwhile to move the air.

Reproduced here in its entirety, 'A Filiation' is steeped in the visionary mood and vatic gravity of Rilke, Leopardi and Holderlin. But in fact such a poem would have been impossible to write without Mallarmé's innovation of turning poetry into a ritual. The large-voiced diction busily tilting the tone toward the magisterial ('barbarism', 'peace', 'divine', 'beautiful', 'tyranny') is being used to sell the idea that Moritz is onto something deep. The poem thus becomes a showpiece for profundity. Moritz no doubt *wants* to shoulder high seriousness, is *trying* to invest his talk with a sense of moral risk. But while the poem appears to be toughing it out, there's no felt strenuousness to its statements. Insight has yielded to the appearance of insight. A line like 'difficult to make the unstrung beautiful' may be striking to readers who find such lines striking, but the thought is a closed-circuit, transmitting only to itself. It doesn't move us, or surprise us, or shock us; and this is because very little is riding on its success or failure. The poem's intellectual turbulence is therefore a false front since there's no danger to the thoughts. The poem may seem to churn with the implications of its ideas, but the language itself is never agitated by them.

And so rather than inaccessible, it might be more accurate to call Moritz's poetry non-negotiable. We are asked to accept specific images and statements as significant without being told why. You never know, in other words, if Moritz has gotten hold of a real problem. All of which creates the troubling sense that, for all his 'invisible meaning' and 'deeper reality', Moritz is faking it. As another example, we can point to the way his poems always return to the same evocative emblems: city, city in ruins, machine, body, river, sun, moon. Moritz, to be sure, has written appealing, atmospheric poems using these emblems. But emblems are not emotions, and throwing yourself into the suggestiveness of that sort of visual vocabulary isn't necessarily the same as wrestling with genuine questions of doubt, perdition or spiritual estrangement. These emblems – and the private logic that locks them in place – instead allow Moritz's poems an arm's-length brinkmanship, a brazenness exempt from any kind of true exertion:

> Your grieving breasts that flowed inexorably
> with youthful light: the dark air veiled them, holding
> Venus, Mars, and Saturn far away,
> and scream of tires and click of blades,
> the dew gathering around you on black trees,
> tenders roofs and smokestacks that knifed up
> in gutted woods. And my hand that over you
> hovered, still farther than the fearful evening.
> Then you hardened the space between us. The latch
> clicked into its place, light sound
> bursting to fill with burning a night now still
> more quiet in its fury, more decayed.
> And the hand yet hovers, the same, years after

on that lurid step, not touching the door that closes
your ever joyful dying smile and the dawn stars
that always were fading in your look, even at noon
among canoes, bright water flags and beach stones:
other stones of the hand's poor hoard.

This passage, taken from 'Dedication', is typical of the way Moritz uses vague, loose-fitting phrasing to prove his case. The lines teem with coercive images that toll loudly ('Your grieving breasts', 'scream of tires', 'smokestacks that knifed up', 'gutted woods', 'fearful evening', 'lurid step') but whose distress is left unexplained. It's one thing for mysteries to be difficult. It's quite another to trivialize that difficulty by outsourcing it to glamourously hazy adjectives like 'grieving', 'fearful' and 'lurid'. Margaret Avison, for example, is often difficult but rarely allows her poetry's obliquities to deform its truths. When she writes 'Moving into sky/or stilled under it/we are in the becoming/moved: let wisdom learn/unnoticing in this', she uses a past-participle ('moved') and a gerund ('unnoticing') to turn a seemingly impenetrable idea into an alluring, communicable insight. Avison's syntax is so dazzlingly scrupulous it poses the riddle and simultaneously solves it. The lesson here is not that poems have to be accessible – Avison's are anything but – but that even mysteries have to marry words to their full meanings.

Mallarmé was the first to wreck this pact with language, the first to cherish words chiefly for their 'orphic' appeal. Moritz's decisions about his style, with all the over-generous freedoms he extends to it, flow from Mallarme's radicalism. But some breakthroughs can also be a defeat, and Moritz's embrace of Mallarmé's watershed act points specifically to what's missing in his own poems. It's not that they're badly written; it's that they refuse to exist in a more clear-headed relationship with their words. As Avision shows, difficulty isn't necessarily an obstacle; it can entice in all sorts of healthy ways. Truths that appear remote, St. Augustine wrote in *Against Lying*, 'are more ardently desired, and for being desired they are more joyfully discovered'. Concealment is intended, ultimately, to provoke disclosure, not prevent it. The belief that the not-said should be kept safe from the 'crudeness' of precise thinking – as if transcendence were a membrane a poet might tear if he pressed too hard – is symbolism's legacy. And such a legacy has proven useful for promoting careless writing above its station, and luring readers into mistaking self-admiring evasiveness for intellectual toil.

If the 'meaning' Moritz hands us too often seems like a menu with all the items crossed out – we're invited to a feast, but are barred from the food – I suspect it says less about his talent and more about the limits of the symbolism sponsoring it. The influence was certainly much more obvious in his early work. Indeed, the further back you go (and here the well-edited *Early Poems*, published by Insomniac in 2003, is particularly useful) the more foreclosed the symbolist thinking. The early poems are too perfect in their furtiveness, too confirming of their coded intents. This also affected their music, which tended to be monotonal ('Deep in the house / a heavy door is closed, / all is so still the dust ascends') and featured a small and velveted voice, its range elliptically smothered ('I am the dark man / so dark / that in the shadow or memory you would say / my flesh grows green').

But from the wan artifice of these early poems, Moritz has significantly extended and aerated his verse line. He is now much more talkative, and ever since *Mahoning* has been obsessed by long poems – long, orchestral, chord-crashing poems. If one feels Moritz has built his poetry to a larger-than-normal plan, it's likely because the poetry is now all climax, full of rhetorical nadirs, crests and zeniths. It is a voice comprised entirely of epic accents. Being a big spender of syllables, however, doesn't necessarily mean you stop being a miser of sense. Mallarmé regarded opacity as a kind of fevered, counter-intuitive eloquence, and the allure of this idea is something from which Moritz's poems have never recovered. Except now he spends twice the time saying half as much three times as obliquely. The anti-inevitability of this sort of writing can certainly be compelling, and there are lots of successes in *Night Street Repairs*, ranging from evocative out-at-elbows lines, to marvellous pell-mell passages, to poems fascinating in their mix of coherence-jamming impulsiveness and cool ratiocination. Moritz, no denying it, can be very good. Yet in poems like 'The Labryinth' I can't help but see a poet trying to steel his imagination's tin resolve, where the run-on manner of the writing, the difficult-to-interrupt haste of the thinking, conveys the panic of a mind pining for something *real* to happen to it:

> Reciting confused obsessions
> under the midnight cope –
> as far as we had come then
> (you remember it all but listen
> with hope to my retelling) down
> that spectral lurid alley. Snow
> was falling on the iron
> latch of great rotted wooden doors
> where it ended. And there we saw
> how we, like all the rest, might reach
> completion not with infinite
> reluctance but relief: because
> we too were tired. The streets
> empty then – it was Christmastime –
> the dome of St. Paul's rose up
> before us now and glowed in sullen
> dominion, floating without motion over
> that ancient gate, over rooftops
> engraved on the glowing night
> dead but for the faint nervous
> roaming of the snow. That moment
> our souls flew out through astonished
> eyes and hovered among the stone
> apostles standing far up
> on the walls, too high for human
> sight to make out the faces ...

This is only the first third of the poem, but it's enough to illustrate Moritz's strategy: keep the poem talking (and talking and talking) in the hope that readers won't notice the language is ducking its responsibilities. And what are those responsibilities? Expressive syntax, focused diction, tonal appropriateness, rhythmic momentum, exacting line-breaks. In a word, form. What's missing in the above lines is the self-generated adhesiveness of good poetry, the coherence that emerges when exactly the right choices work together. Despite its carefully mortised look on the page, the poem actually exists in a stylized avoidance of form: the language is free but not vigilant. Moritz might counter – and a line like 'Reciting confused obsessions' could be invoking such a claim – that his poems represent a different idea of form: form as intoxicated imprecision. Seen in this light, 'The Labyrinth' is an example of what can happen when the indescribable infiltrates language. And indeed, it's this notion of form that's often alluded to in *Night Street Repairs*: 'The coherence/of the world is that it has all fallen apart in some minds and remains/intact and beautiful in others'.

But while there's no doubt Moritz's poems feel the world's indecipherability very powerfully, that's *all* they feel. This is what contributes to the murmuring monotony of his ruin-ruminating imagery, the complacent sameness of his forceful language. Moritz's idea of form leads to poems where the quorum of a few high-octane words is enough to keep the all-purpose prophetic mood going. And that's exactly why sonorous, meaningful-sounding phrases like 'spectral lurid alley' or 'the faint nervous/roaming of the snow', or 'glowed in sullen/dominion' represent a characteristic symbolist defeat: their evocativeness is purely ceremonial, and is never linked to a recognizable human predicament. Moritz wants to appear as a poet straining to capture difficult-to-name feelings, but his poems are never challenged by the mystery of those feelings, only coddled by it. And so when you write poems that use hazy figurative thinking to swiftly accede to the de facto unfathomability of the universe – when at the first sign of trouble, you rush toward mystification – then you're the kind of poet who has learned to make things very easy for himself.

It should also be mentioned that the exaltedness of this sort of writing, the gigantism of its gestures, is inseparable from what makes Moritz's poems so fascinating. Moritz loves language for the exhilarating inscrutibilities it can idly arouse, but the high note of *Night Street Repair* is a clutch of poems ('To See The Day', 'Simplicity', 'Translators', 'To the Moon' and 'The World') where that love is lavished on a more demanding ambition: charged-with-conviction lucidity. Language in these poems is focussed by argument, not freed by incantation. Which isn't to say Moritz curbs his celestial-scale intensity; he simply refuses to let that intensity overwhelm his earthy concerns. He refuses, in other words, the symbolist's quid pro quo – expressive accuracy for transcendental approximation – and steers his richly deflective voice closer to the grain of his thoughts.

What one notices, therefore, isn't the immensity of Moritz's sensitivity toward the unsayable, but how the unsayable forces him to enterprisingly find the unexpected corner of a context, an angle of implication other poets may not have thought about or know how to use. The counter-realities and alternative perspectives precisely evoked in these poems only further endorse a truth much of *Night Street Repairs* ignores: that there are many interesting ways of talking about the world without always vigourously grieving the aspect of it impossible to put into words. This is important to keep in mind, because one can forget – as Moritz often seems to – that the right words exist and can be counted on. In 'Translator' with its polyglot 'patched oxblood shoes' ('The left one knew Latin and the right knew Greek') or 'The World', with its trees forever standing 'in silent massiveness and flight', Moritz's vatic tendencies find themselves in a productive tension with this trust in language. These poems anxiously read reality's otherness in a bid to find a solving normalcy. None exists, of course, but it leads to a sense-searching both intuitive and deductive, and a poetry that speaks with a sidelong, concatenating clarity. Take the conclusion of 'To the Moon' where, in lines of lapidary calm, the moon is movingly summed up as a trope for a life trapped in a state of unrequited decipherment:

> Let's say, peaceful moon, you don't express anything.
> Still on your face imagination comes to rest,
> the dream that you are more than rock
> and a reflection, now and then, of natural light:
> a sign and so like us
> even when brightest you darken and hide
> whatever's deepest in you, and endure this failure,

this being an inexpressive, slowly eroded
face of forces you strictly contain – impulses like children
in love with twilight, its plain song and free glide of birds,
but confined now to their bedroom, to their window
because night's coming, it's almost time for sleep.

There is something marvellously un-Moritzian about the directness of this, the way it borrows Moritz's devout cadences but crushes the melodrama from them. You might say, in fact, that these lines win their simplicity by resisting the 'inexpressiveness' of the object they were created to comprehend. It is a striking description of the moon, and we know it is striking because the language harms its own hermeticism long enough to fix, in the excellence of its phrasing, the idea's lovely unusualness. The lines don't bait our curiosity by their insufficiency, but stimulate it through the careful rationing of an insight.

The difference between the two tactics, as it applies to Moritz, deserves debate because the adjective 'neglected' has dogged his reputation for so long (mostly centred, as far as I can see, on the embarrassment of his never having won the Governor General's award) that any talk about his poems is less an engagement than a reflexive appreciation. Moritz is not reviewed, in other words, as much as protectively profiled. As a result there's been no interest in confronting the possibility that, despite its many metaphysical pistons, his language is barely firing. Moritz is seen as an original, someone whose 'beautiful inexplicitness' (to use his own phrase) has innovatingly complicated the innocent simplicity of the contemporary Canadian lyric. But as with the symbolists, the attributes of Moritz's strong exceptionalism transmit a weak subversiveness. His poetry appears distinctive merely because it displays a fluency that has symptomized itself. Every new poem reacquires the same must-have items – impressionistic, allusive, vatic-sounding, hymnic, oratorical – as though Moritz were doing nothing more than checking off a shopping list.

'In an age of disbelief', Wallace Stevens wrote, 'it is for the poet to supply the satisfactions of belief, in his measure and in his style'. But as long as Moritz only offers the rhetorical surface of belief, the satisfactions of his measure and style will prove too thin a soil for the reader's imagination to take root in. For twenty years, Moritz has regarded poetry as religious theatre: the equivalent of spine-tingling polyphonic chants echoing in a cathedral. But as the Talmud reminds us, 'The Torah speaks in the language of men'.

bpNICHOL

He dashed off comic books, hatched operas and banged out television scripts. He futzed with fiction, tinkered with radio plays and monkeyed with children's verse. As a member of the sound-poetry ensemble Four Horsemen, he chanted and nasal-droned for audiences across North America. He favoured collage, comic books, typefaces, puns, doodles and blank pages, and had a soft spot for the letter 'H'. Remembered best for the nine-volume *The Martyrology*, one of the longest long poems in Canadian letters, bpNichol – the beaming, shaggy-haired avant-gardist who died in 1988 at the age of forty-four – became internationally famous for his hand-drawn visual poetry. He called himself a 'language researcher'. Mad scientist was more like it.

Alas, Nichol's super-caffeinated productivity is also, in a sense, hearsay. 'Barrie', writes his close friend Paul Dutton, 'could have a few minutes time in an airport departure lounge, or standing at a bus stop, and out would come the notebook and pen'. But much of what he did with that notebook and pen remains scarce, housed in private collections and rare book rooms. A young man in a hurry, Nichol was in love with perishability. 'I was interested in the half-life of the poem', he said in an interview, 'the decay, and the fact that things faded away'. Fired up by innovations that allowed him to publish his work when and how he fancied – the mimeograph and the photocopier – he championed the 'quick thing': pamphlets, broadsides, handbills and cards.

These items appeared in limited runs, often editions of one, which Nichol distributed by subscription, sold cheaply or gave away. His ephemera even transcended paper: poems were stitched on pillow cases, printed on matchbooks and – in one pioneering format that dropped straightaway into obsolescence – saved on 5.25-inch floppy disks only bootable on an Apple IIe. Nichol seemed to regard all these try-anything-once odds and ends as a kill switch for good taste. 'Instant garbage for the nation's waste baskets' is how he summed up his publishing activities, a slogan perfectly embodied by an early microbook that instructed readers to promptly burn it. Nichol's *samizdat* war against the traditional book resulted in many tactical victories – exciting, unclassifiable confections of word and image – but ended in defeat: a corpus, in Dutton's words, 'unavailable, widely unknown, and far too little appreciated'.

Of course, the challenge of celebrating an artificer whose key artifacts are near-impossible to scare up (or afford: the 1972 silkscreen collection *The Adventures of Milt the Morph in Colour* will set you back a cool thirty-five hundred) isn't lost on admirers. Indeed, distress that Nichol will be typecast by his most conservative work sharply divides debate about his legacy, with accusations that the syllabus-friendly *The Martyrology* – the only book by Nichol still in print – has been used, in Christian Bök's words, to 'sentimentalize his subversiveness'.

In a bid to claw back the diaspora of Nichols' output, his selected poems, prose, comics and essays have been pickled in sundry reprintings and repackagings. These include *H in the Heart* (1994), *bpNichol Comics* (2002) and *Meanwhile* (2002). The best effort is *The Alphabet Game* (2007), which, by printing his greatest hits alongside 'obscure treasures', serves as a useful periodic table for Nichol's preposterous range. bpNichol.ca was launched in 2008 as an online lumber room for hard-to-find audio recordings and digitized versions of unobtainable volumes. All of this curatorial activity, however, barely scratches the surface. That's why, for the last two decades, Ottawa poet jwcurry has been doggedly itemizing every last morsel by Nichol, as well as everything written about him. When completed, the eight-volume *Beepliographic Cyclopoedia* is estimated to smash the scales at four thousand pages. Nichol would have cherished the irony: the poet who married his creative adrenaline to the demands of fruit-fly publishing, memorialized by a book of such Brobdingnagian proportions.

The Captain Poetry Poems (2010) is the latest 'lost' work by Nichol to be caught up in the ongoing salvage operation. Originally published by blewointment press in 1971, when Nichol was twenty-six, the booklet was tossed off during one of his most workaholic periods. (He had won the Governor General's award for poetry a year earlier for *four* books.) A twenty-five-page flood of text, gag panels, thought balloons and hyperbolized letters, *The Captain Poetry Poems* tells the story of the eponymous superhero and his struggle to find happiness. Bald, beaked and wattled, 'Cap' – Nichol's pet name for him – is hardly the rock-jawed conqueror. In fact, with his visor, spandex, wings and six-pack abs, our man looks like a mutant chicken. Cap is a sad sack: self-conscious, plagued by doubts, undone by indecision, torn about his purpose in life. Nichol shouts encouragements from the sidelines ('O CAPTAIN POETRY SEE IT THRU') but, plum out of ideas, Cap finds himself in a *Groundhog Day* funk ('O he sings like a madman, talks like he's sane,/and does it each day again and again'). And popping up everywhere in the book (in one case even cradling Captain Poetry's head) is Nichol's most intriguing and disquieting alter ego: Milt the Morph, the dementedly smiling, empty-eyed troublemaker.

It's obvious Nichol intended the book to be both a send-up of the poetic tradition and a kiss-off: he writes of Cap, English poetry's greatest defender, 'yur slippers made of paper/yur words made out of milk//yuve seen better days'. *The Captain Poetry Poems* is a running ledger on whatever the hell occurred to Nichol when writing it; Boy Wonder serving notice of his independence. The iconoclasm of the project inspired Michael Ondaatje to make a short documentary on Nichol, *Sons of Captain Poetry*, released at the same time. But except for one excerpt reprinted in a few anthologies – an amusing quarrel between love interest Madame X and Captain Poetry ('dear Captain Poetry,/your poetry is trite') – the chapbook is a largely overlooked slice of Nichol's fugitive canon. Younger fans may not even know it exists.

Toronto's BookThug, however, thinks Captain Poetry deserves rediscovery. With the help of Nichol's friends, the feisty press has assembled a corrected edition, out now, incorporating material missing from the original. Also included is an afterword by *blewointment*'s then-publisher bill bissett, recreating the mid-winter scene as the tiny crew cranked out copies ('zoom inside th cabin n see us printing ovr dayze n nites'). The crying need for a 'corrected' version may have something to do with enduring rumours that the blewointment book was so rife with errors Nichol basically disowned it. (It was the last title from the press to bear Nichol's name.) Forty years later, BookThug is waving under our noses the edition Nichol would have approved.

An excellent case can be made for considering the reissued *Captain Poetry Poems* more historically significant than the dozens of similarly totemic keepsakes still waiting to be rescued (even if, as the editors warn, it 'may not be the "best" work in Nichol's oeuvre'). This is largely due to the addition of a never-published prose coda by Nichol ('some words on all these words') that drops two surprises. First, he proposes that Captain Poetry is one of the missing links to *The Martyrology*. (For Nicholites, this is akin to unearthing the papyrus napkin where Sophocles jotted down the idea for *Oedipus Rex*.) Second, and more striking, is Nichol's claim that Captain Poetry was created to satirize stereotypes rampant in Canadian poetry during the 1970s: namely 'the macho male bullshit tradition', as he puts it, 'where if you were male & wrote poems you had to make damn sure you could piss longer, shout harder'.

No doubt Nichol had in mind poets like Patrick Lane, Al Purdy and Irving Layton, all of whom incorporated the 'piss longer, shout harder' swagger into their debates about poetry. Nichol, however, never bought the Hobbesian vision of a literary scene. This was the entire point of the 'gift economy' he is so often associated with. Through zines like *Ganglia* and *grOnk*, Nichol tirelessly promoted and published a vast range of work by those he admired, and did so without expectation of quid pro quo. Fame just wasn't a going concern for him. 'Behind *Ganglia* and *grOnk*', Nichol said in an interview, 'was a strong idea: to focus on certain work, to argue for that work, and to put enough of the work forward so that readers could get a feeling for the sheer quantity of people who approached the text in this way'.

Nichol was thus both a tastemaker and community-builder. His own example – most notably through the beguiling manifestos he and Steve McCaffery collaboratively wrote and circulated through the Toronto Research Group – helped turn Toronto's small-press scene into a large ensemble act, spawning cooperative projects free of us-and-them demonizing or the sizing-up and dressing-down of peers. A practising psychotherapist (for years he belonged to the talking-cure commune Therafields), Nichol lived as though he were barely able to hold back some vast exuberance, and it gave everything he did an extra positive charge. More importantly, he had a knack for schemes that made a virtue out of this very insouciant unseriousness. He helped rewrite the rules for his generation, not only by offering those around him a new set of permissions, but by handing them an unexpected challenge: to give their experiments the direct evidence of human touch.

That's why, when a publisher reissuing a book like *The Captain Poetry Poems* explains that 'all efforts were made to present the material in the spirit of the original', a caveat is required: the 'spirit of the original' is rooted entirely in its material. The new edition keeps the comic book size, but everything else is upgraded, tidied up, made reader-friendly. Lost is the on-the-fly quality of its original appearance. As was Nichol's wont, the book's design – mimeo sheets stapled along the top edge – was employed as a counter-agent to the squareness and predictability of the 'big-presses'. He practised a warts-and-all avant-gardism, and as such the original *Captain Poetry Poems* got its revolutionary mystique from the way it conspired against itself. It seemed aware of its own forgettable fate, even relished it. (Run across a copy today, and it will be yellowed and foxed, its decay a poetic device against timelessness.) Captain Poetry was part of Nichol's ongoing attempt to free poetry by killing it and resurrecting it as junk art. At the time he published *The Captain Poetry Poems*, he was on a creative spree, spending big on what no doubt appeared to be triflings. 'They'd pick it up', Nichol said of one of his early books, 'and they'd see there are three words to a page and kind of flip, flip, flip, and they'd be through it in 30 seconds and say, 'What the fuck was that?'' But those works gave many younger Canadian poets their Keatsian 'On First Looking into Chapman's Homer' moment. It was literary gunpowder and blew their minds.

Nichol's most interesting work is premised on a simple idea: poems are made up of combinations of words, which are made up of combinations of letters. This allowed him to break down lexical identity in ways meant to remind readers that every word is one letter away from every other word. Sometimes he did this by taking words apart in the course of the writing. We see this a lot in *The Captain Poetry Poems*: 'up the creek/the cup reek/EEK!!' Language was basically sonic Lego that could be recombinated into original typescapes. In one early example, printed on a postcard, 'turnips are' becomes 'rustpin', 'stunrip', 'puntsir' and 'tipruns'. Another postcard explores the interlocking possibilities of 'owl', 'low' and 'cow'. Nichol's most extreme manifestation of this idea was homophonic translation, in which he translates the sounds of a foreign language rather than its sense ('c'est l'hommage dansant' becomes, for instance, 'sailor magic danse on'). More than a poet, Nichol was a problemist. He created calligraphic conundrums meant to provide readers with 'as many entrances and exits as possible'. His word for this was 'borderblur', which he defined as that sweet spot where 'language &/or the image blur into the inbetween & become concrete objects'.

He began to think this way in the late 1960s, emboldened by the example of 'concrete poetry', a growing international movement that exalted language's typographical medium as its one true message. Words were 'concrete' material that could be spatially shaped. Concrete caught on with no real sense of what the rules were, making it hard to pin down a definition of what the new genre covered. This suited its practitioners to a tee. Indeed, concrete's 'assault on the decorum of the printed page', to use Stephen Scobie's words, was something Nichol grasped intuitively. Increasingly disappointed with the traditional lyric poetry he was writing at the time, he seized on concrete's major principle – the poem as pictorial rhetoric – with the glee of a boy given access to a secret identity and magical powers. It was the birth of a new kind of Captain Poetry.

Visual poetry gave the idea-a-minute poet a way to stuff his thoughts into nutshells without getting bored. Nichol wanted to say as much as possible with as little as possible, and concrete poetry, by identifying the minimum visual properties necessary, allowed for the sly surfacing of subtext (in one lovely example, Nichol replaced the letter 'o' in 'cloud' with the billowing of parentheses). Best of all, the form was something he could do to please himself. It was still high stakes – concrete, after all, was bred by crisis, as a challenge to lazy values – but there was no right or wrong. Nichol tracked truth by sight, stalked surprise in the white space of the page. In the best examples (like the affable and awesome 'Allegory Series'), you feel him feeding his excitement into his shapes and images. Whether typeset, typewritten or hand-drawn, it's impossible to ignore the intelligence his best visual poems radiate.

At their worst, though, Nichol's visual poems are just the wish-fulfillment of a poet who liked the look of his own irreverence. They bespeak an exaggerated confrontation with convention. Nichol was interested in short-circuiting reading habits unchanged since the Gutenberg revolution, but too often, the results merely project his interest. This is why Nichol's visual poems leave many readers cold. Staged cleanly in open space, they give him away not as a hot-blooded rebel but a Spock-like formalist. Calibrated to convey the sonic weight and density of language untamed by sentences, the poems are full of causeless, do-nothing effects.

Let's take one example from *The Captain Poetry Poems*. On page sixteen we have three A's, two upper case and one lower, overlapping in a trippy Escher-like pattern. Embedded inside – as if readers were stealing a rare look into the soul of the letter itself – is a rolling landscape with a cloud-filled sky and, peeking out of the corner, Morph the Milt. The message is obvious: each letter is a rabbit hole into its own world. Still, Nichol has simply produced the stylized *idea* of a rabbit hole. How can you possibly respond? True, it has a quirky vigour that tells us an actual hand drew it. But it's a typographical bagatelle planted foursquare on a page.

This complaint can be extended to visual poetry in general. Self-enclosed, emotionally static and cut off from public life, these optical mannerisms are the closest contemporary poetry gets to the automata vision of nineteenth-century craftsmen. In one of his most celebrated books, *ABC: The Aleph Beth Book* (1971), Nichol uses a stencil to 'overlay' each letter of the alphabet into multiple-exposure versions of itself. The twenty-six 'glyphs' are like mechanical toys or whirligigs. They amaze at first sight, but deaden in the gaze. They look better the less you expect of them.

Twenty-five years after his death, the same might be said of Nichol. He still means a lot to many poets, but he matters less. The proper historical setting for his achievements was in the late sixties; he came of age in a period in Canadian literature when there was widespread sympathy for oddity, and experimental poetry was the marquee event. As a scene, however, we have drifted several parsecs away from that. The indie lit subculture has shed its prepublication stage of adolescent rebellion. Post-Nichol, the Canadian avant-garde has become warier of grassroots movements, and is now more professionalized, its sense of self more academically located. Additionally, today's experimentalism no longer has the same power relationship with its audience. Thirty years ago, the avant-garde took advantage of what economists call 'information asymmetry': its poets knew much more about the game they were playing than their readers. Today we suffer fools less gladly. Our bullshit detectors are better, and keeping people interested in convention-flouting is hard work. Nichol's poetry has fallen short of a crucial threshold: the new that stays news.

Those who flip through *The Captain Poetry Poems* and wonder what it all means will never know. You had to be there. Indeed, *The Captain Poetry Poems* only underscores that the long aftermath of Nichol's death has become a love affair with holy relics. The work may wear badly, but the legend is imperishable. Yet, *The Captain Poetry Poems* also demonstrates everything worthwhile about Nichol: his free-agent sensibility, his bemused distance from the mainstream-verse universe and its 'umpteenth poem on me and mom', his belief that joy could infiltrate poetic conventions and eat away at their genetic structure.

In photographs, Nichol's smile has a rapscallion edge. He mastered every encounter, be it on the page or in person, with charm. The result was an all-in creativity that never curdled into what Daisy Fried once called 'evilly subversive'. What made Nichol's work so head-turning was that it was a free and unembarrassed expression of art as play. He fulfilled Baudelaire's definition of the artist as an adult who can 'recall childhood at will'. In turn, it allowed him to see with astonishing depth into the fantasy life of children (he wrote for a number of children's shows, including *Fraggle Rock*). His many winning moments – his 'Pataphysical Hardware Store' catalogue included a pencil with erasers at both ends and inflatable thought balloons that could be taped to someone's head – point out the most galling failure of our current crop of experimental phenoms: humourlessness. For all his *épater* ethic, Nichol was too much fun to dislike. Making the individual uncomfortable – Nietzsche's ambition – wasn't Nichol's thing. He was that rare bird: an avant-gardist without an axe to grind. He was seditious, anarchic, optimistic. You kind of miss the guy.

DAVID O'MEARA

ADD UP THE air travel, and Canadian poetry's carbon footprint is huge. Ralph Gustafson tramped across London and Manhattan. Irving Layton was always packing for Greece (where Cohen waited). Al Purdy got boozy in Mexico and Russia. Earle Birney skin-dived off the coast of Fiji. Gwendolen MacEwen toured Egypt. P.K. Page was a resident of Australia and Brazil. And Don Coles' 'wander-years' included Stockholm, Florence and Munich.

Canadian poets clearly get around, and, fittingly, their ports-of-call are as much stylistic as geographic. Ever since ancient Romans first caught the bug, travel has proven to be a kind of theatre. Whether the backdrop is uncharted rainforest or a cobblestone piazza, being abroad spurs psychological auditions, tryouts of self-invention under exotic test conditions. This premise – that we are freed by not feeling at home – also extends to language: a change of scene can uncork euphoric new noises. Flaubert believed travel helped 'enliven one's style'; an idea Layton echoed when he praised a junket overseas for 'replenishing my stock of metaphors'. Of course, there are pitfalls: overconfident familiarity with customs only glancingly experienced, stolen snatches of a tongue one doesn't speak, cultural name-dropping. It was exactly this sort of pretentious cosmopolitanism that pushed Kingsley Amis, in 1951, to issue his famous diktat against poems about foreign cities. But the xenophilic itch to match untried sounds to unfamiliar surroundings is why the best Canadian poetry on distant settings – such as Daryl Hines' 'Arrondissements', a dazzling sonnet-sequence on Paris' twenty districts – ranks among the best Canadian poetry. In each spot on the map we find a poet outside his comfort zone, taking a leap.

The owner of a well-thumbed Baedeker, David O'Meara is constantly drawn to what he called in his first book, *Storm Still* (1999), the 'flawlessly foreign'. Wales, Japan, Italy and Tunisia are some of the far-flung places his poems have described. O'Meara, however, isn't interested in package excursions. He prizes, and convincingly registers, alien encounters, situations where 'our normal props of distraction', as he explained in an interview with *Ottawater*, 'have been disturbed'. Sightseeing, in other words, is about being blown off course: it stirs up (or ought to) soul-searching about how we live, the rules we follow, and our true intentions: everything about us that's 'half-hid// and too uncertain to crack open/easily'. Similar self-interrogations – by turns haunting, lively and unsentimental – occur when O'Meara dwells on other subjects: small towns in Ontario, hockey photographs, thirteenth-century Italian labourers, dilapidated movie houses, stammering, glass, boyhood and the zeitgeist itself, exuberantly summed up in a long verse-letter to Auden. It also bears mentioning that when he isn't globe-trotting, he likes to take walks. His second book, *The Vicinity* (2003), was a paean to pedestrianism, filled with sharp-eyed reports on urban odds and ends. (O'Meara's flaneuring is largely headquartered in Ottawa, where he bartends.) Point being, O'Meara doesn't need to undertake a transatlantic flight to write a good poem. But sometimes his gifts – energetic verbs, spring-loaded syntax, a love of slang – don't come fully into action unless faced with the disorientation and toil of travel. Want to arouse O'Meara's senses and excite his sensitivity to language? Drop him into 'the salt-cracked sufferance of the Chott-el-Jerid'.

Take 'Arriving Early'. Included in his new collection *Noble Gas, Penny Black* (2008), the poem finds O'Meara standing on a platform at night in the South Korean city of Sunch'on. He's just missed his bus connection, and, along with it, any chance of rendezvousing with his girlfriend on her birthday. It's a variation on a favourite theme: people sidelined by setbacks, demoralized by the gulf between dream and reality, or simply loaded down by the impedimenta of daily life. Things – love, health, especially the weather – rarely go as planned, leaving O'Meara to preserve the disappointments inside formal shapes that become 'landmarks/of each near-disaster'. But O'Meara has another favourite theme: despite long odds, we keep making choices that give the competitive edge to hope. This explains why our stressed-out traveller, faced with no real alternative, hands over 'just short of three digits Canadian/for a two-hour taxi ride'. What ensues is a high-speed chase in which O'Meara's cab eventually overtakes the bus ('I raised one mental/finger as we shot across its prow') and fast-forwards him ahead of the passenger he narrowly avoided becoming ('every inch a gain on where I might have been/if I'd been back there'). Zipping along in rhyming sestets, the poem calmly captures the anxiety and burning-rubber adrenalin of the episode, but also the bemusement of a man who, his sensible side now eating his dust, has been awarded a fresh start. Arriving early, he is reborn:

> Paying the fare, it felt a bit Caesarean,
> that surprise advance arrival, stretching my legs, pearled
> out from the warmth of my fiberglass shell, into a world
>
> I didn't expect to be waiting in. At least, not yet.
> Twenty minutes ahead, I was point man, postulate,
> herald to the very tidings of myself. I leaned
> against your arm, and pictured my double lagging behind
> down off the bus, puzzled, alone, rattling your doorknob,
> pacing the lanes while we're out on the town. Poor slob.

Two-timed by your evil twin: is there a cheekier metaphor for the way travel eggs us into behaviour so unlikely we no longer recognize ourselves? Even the language picks up new tricks. Check out 'Caesarean', an adjective that not only alludes to the speaker's premature appearance, but also to how Caesar in 49 BC ignored edicts and marched his army across the Rubicon toward Rome, unopposed. And check out the verb 'pearled', with its suggestion of an irritant transformed into an object of beauty. Both words are uncannily right, packed with multiple meanings readers can absorb in a flash. For those familiar with O'Meara's work, there's also the sly self-quotation to keep us busy. 'Paying the fare' points backwards to the culture-shock cab ride in Storm Still's 'Ikime-Jinja' ('we'd paid the fare. I was standing there/somewhere among the months/and nothing recognizable'). And the trope of taxi as time machine ('into a world/I didn't expect to be waiting in') brings to mind *The Vicinity* and O'Meara's comment about the driver in 'From a Dawn Taxi' ('It's a whole/other day there and he's already in it, while/I'm in the back, with the night's final fringes'). It's hard not to see those earlier poems as perspectives O'Meara has revised, improved, outgrown. And given the evidence, it would be hard to disagree: the clean-lined fluency, the invitingly informal tone, the crisp and unforced rhyming, and the speaking voice that, by skillfully modulating short phrases against longer descriptive sentences, rides its own melting. Frankly, I don't think he has written a more perfect poem. Indeed, encoded in its taut and effortlessly colloquial stanzas is the sense that another 'poor slob' is 'lagging behind' – O'Meara's Prufrockian alter ego: practical, earnest, but without the swing in his step, the swagger.

The person who has 'arrived', in other words, is O'Meara himself – or, rather, a style readers can recognize unmistakably as his. 'Arriving Early' is a breakthrough poem: coherent, memorable, wholly successful. In this context, 'early' becomes an inside joke; there is, after all, no appointed hour for a poet to come of age. The adverb might also be a playful insinuation about being a quick learner. Or maybe O'Meara is teasing us: his ear racing into accents and formal patterns ahead of readers, leaving them unprepared for such effects.

In many ways, the O'Meara who shows up in *Noble Gas, Penny Black* is still the same guy. The distinctiveness of his poetry – its unpredictability and variety – comes from what he overhears, not how he sees. It comes from his invention of forms, line-shapes and stanzas that try to preserve the bent ways in which we talk: the cadences of our deadpan, offhand, unembellished conversations. We see Canadian influences – most traceably Don Coles – but, along with many of his peers, O'Meara probably couldn't exist without the examples of contemporary British and Irish poetry. Like Simon Armitage, Glyn Maxwell and Paul Farley, his ambition is to informalize form – free it from fustiness. The result has been a prosody both ardent and anti-ornate: language that looks plain but sounds rich. O'Meara uses 'real' names for things – Corona, Lucky Strike, Docs and Jolt Cola – and likes the challenge of finding fresh vocabulary for blah subjects (a tossed ball, a root cellar). His images make an open appeal to what we might already notice for ourselves: 'hacked-out/silhouettes of spruce', 'a room/of cream walls pouring into baseboards', 'toy-sized election vans/squawking anthems/and slogans from mounted bullhorns'. These descriptions are drawn to actual scale: the telling detail tied to the telling word without inflation or shortfall. A poet who writes lines like 'Flags lift and drop – crescent, star,/crescent, star' is a poet who selects his words for their precision rather then their surprise. The surprise, instead, is in the repetition, the gently misdirecting enjambment, the ebb and flow of stresses. The reasons O'Meara once gave for the exquisite tact and naturalness of Coles' poetry can easily be attributed to his own tone and pacing. The agonized ambivalence of a poem like 'After the Funeral' is, after all, carried out by a series of calculated tone-shifts that let O'Meara speed up, slow down, stop short:

> Some stay on the hill for hours,
> still as the chiselled stone; others shut the doors
> of cars, and drive back to their hotels, or home,
> visitors
>
> to that hill in years yet to come. And some
> of us gather, as we should, to drink and bequeath
> unto ourselves the memories not eclipsed
> by death.
>
> Through the candid gloom of the bar I watch you
> mourning there among the faces, a hall of mirrors
> lit with stories and clumsy stabs
> at humour
>
> we hope will frame and explain a life. I hold
> myself in cool remove, stubborn over beers.
> Wanting, times like this, to be like you.
> In tears.

I don't think it's a stretch to propose that the speaker's internal tug-of-war – holding his grief in 'cool remove', but wishing it otherwise – mimics the poet's conflicted attitude toward artifice. In his *Ottawater* interview O'Meara claimed that, when revising his new poems, he worked hard to 'shuffle the artfulness out of them'. The spirit, if not the evidence, of that thinking can be seen here: quatrains of jagged-nerved line lengths, rhymes that sharpen the irregular textures of the spoken rhythm, syntax that creates a tight seam from simple phrases. O'Meara has always tried to resist any confected, too-sonorous connection between technique and feeling ('you lose something', he once said, 'if it's too polished') but he also clearly wants his poetry painstakingly crafted, crash-tested, durable.

This tension, specifically his need to solve it, has been a boon for him. It's allowed the troubled feelings to which his poems give vent, and given his poetry its range (since no two solutions are the same, every poem is different). Averse to distorting 'hall of mirrors' wordplay, his lines lack the verbal éclat of other poets, but are no less kinetic. The running off of form against speech has taught him to evoke a mood using clashing language-levels ('The sandwich was crap, the tea/magnificent') or astutely reworked colloquialisms ('The further auctioning off/of towns and hills that flashed below – going, gone'). His best poems, in fact, reveal him to be an emerging master of elegantly purled plain-spokeness. Less satisfactory poems show that, while flattened phrase-making can be potent, casualness too aware of itself, and thus making a show of its coolness, leads to overkill: over-advertised ambivalence ('All-Inclusive'), over-dressed offhandedness ('The Day of Invasion') and over-demonstrative understatedness ('The Game') .

All this, of course, might have been said (even the quibbles) about his earlier books. What sets *Noble Gas, Penny Black* apart is the how the grimmer, glamourless aspects of travel have been interiorized – or inscaped – into what one might call a *paysage demoralisé* of private scenes, details and incidents verbally underpinned by the chastened syllables of a man sobering up and coming to grips with what he sees in the bathroom mirror. There are moments of weakness ('Let's ditch this city', he begs, 'these jobs, all the bother/of having things, and keep only each other') but travel is confronted for what it always was: running away. Escapism ends up exiling O'Meara's speakers, with the poems ruthlessly tracking the distance between who-one-was-then and who-one-is-now. 'After the Funeral', in other words, is also about another kind of death: the traveller who once 'felt strange on the Earth, and pictured it as an astronaut' finally lands in adulthood.

Newly world-weary, O'Meara still appreciates the curious and bizarre ('Wasn't Japan weird?') but is emotionally closer to the holidaymaker who, jaded, quickly tires of his trip. So often in these tableaus, travel seems a gesture of defeat, where 'the reversing surf slaps us flat, our only reward/some crotch sand and a mouthful of salt water'. The tone is jet-lagged, slightly depressed, drained. It's a world where everything unknown and undiscovered has been beaten flat by tour groups, where sightseeing consists of 'a mental box to add, then/tick off of our itinerary'. Life is now a travelling from – shock-inducing marvels, as well as treks that promise new kinds of never-seen, recede into the past. Happy memories linger, loom large ('Do you remember the clattering gates/of the bakery where we worked that summer' he asks) but O'Meara can't connect. More often, he sounds like a man running on empty: 'I'm prepared/for another entrance into the day, but stall'. As with 'After the Funeral', we get a sense of two halves at war with each other. The 'I' and eye previously used to depict himself in tough-mindedly sympathetic ways ('Lucky/your life, lucky my own') stare out from the no-place, or between-place, of a mind beset by regrets, and haunted by ghosts of less disaffected former selves. O'Meara is bummed out. And like any brooder worth his salt, he lets his thoughts turn to old girlfriends. Lost love has always perfectly embodied the search for lost time, and we can see why in the tender conjurations of 'I Used to Live Around Here' ('There's a part of us left in these places:/a held hand, a look, a dumb joke') and especially the five-part 'self-unsettling tale' of the book's capstone poem, 'The Old Story'. It ends:

> They sat there, the two of them, flanked
> by the Crystal Palace of whisky bottles, glassware,

and mirrors, the time-rubbed caramel
of wood. On bar-

stools, with brass, slouched in repose.
And talked, the band tuning up, but let
down by the turnout. And shot shit
on how they met,

what they'd meant when they said,
how they'd not understood, holding back
what they had to. Case study
of a love life. A wreck

is how it looked – theirs and theirs
but never really theirs. Then nothing to offer,
just sex, the letting-go factor, the inklings of trust
and commitment. Dear

Abby, the band's raw twang was
soundtrack to what's always on their minds.
Dear Willie Nelson, Dear Will Oldham. They agree
to be friends.

The first four parts dissect, with forensic doggedness, the days leading to the breakup. The quick-stepping, asymmetrically shaped stanzas enact the process of saying good-bye through a 'double exposure' of superbly arranged, miniaturized recollections. It's basically a postmortem: we're given all the early (often ill-boding) impressions, questions and speculations that add up to a garden-variety twenty-first-century courtship shipwrecked by incompatible 'plans and pet peeves'. Balanced between blunt and epigrammatic, 'The Old Story' is packed with special effects: suggestive semantic turns ('theirs and theirs/but never really theirs'), scene-stealing imagery ('glacial clouds tossing hail/at the window as the late became very'), and extended acrobatic riffs:

... Smitten, they traded quibs
on old hairdos in photos, Wim Wenders, dumb secrets,
all the creeps

and dead ends
they once dated. And rushed over at the end of their shifts,
called when they couldn't, and might for example, in a restaurant
notice a faint drift

of freckles
on the collarbone one itched to slide a fingertip over,
but mostly just wanted and wanted and wanted to be
with each other.

O'Meara binds together everything – the accretion of asides, the unceasing patter, the snappy yet sensual small-talk – on the sharpest, most impulsive bends of syntax. He not only mixes high and low, but holds our attention simply by working the switch between the two (this toggling echoes key contrasts in the book: going/staying, returning/can't return, looking forward/back). Wise, articulate, with a woundedness socketed into its wit, the poem comes across not as the result of hard thought and hard choices (which it is), but as an unprompted chemical reaction, a run of lucky breaks out of which a kind of grace emerges.

The real message of 'The Old Story', however, is that O'Meara's reputation as a seasoned nomad also encompasses the wear and tear of time travel. 'We're tourists/to our past', he writes at one point, comparing his backward-looking to vacationing that rarely yields deep or lasting effects. But for O'Meara, the autumnal mood is often a hardship to be endured. Far from passive, his nostalgia bottles up an Orphean sense of injustice, an anger over the impossibility of ever retrieving what you've lost. This can be easy to miss. 'The Old Story' charms us with its disarming combination of insouciance and sadness, but the poem is actually driven by an obsessive, spurned hunt for meaning regarding an event the speaker can elegize but never explain. With the possible exception of 'Arriving Early' (the poem could, in the end, be a wish-fulfillment) the impulse not acted on is the main event in these poems. At times O'Meara is frightened that the moment, buzzing with possibilities, will break off and leave behind a sulky bit of uncompleted life. (In one poem, a bungled attempt to break into their locked apartment traps his girlfriend on the roof. He rushes off to get his roommate's key 'scared that in the interlude / you'd vanish, or were never there'.) This puts his poems in an odd predicament. For all my talk about how they vault into a new voice, they are mostly blow-by-blow accounts of non-events ('You turned forty all afternoon', is how the book starts). Nothing of much significance happens, and keeps happening: parting glances, sick days, vegging in sleepy Turkish cafés. This nothing-much heightens the poetry's elegiac properties, the dramatic scarcity standing in for what was already missing. It also reinforces O'Meara's darker vision of daily life as a cycle of aborted beginnings, and of aging as an experience that replicates the deadening effect of constant travel (stories are 'old' because they happen again and again).

The book ends on two poems, each dense with fine-tuned emotion. First, a hotel room on a 'northern coastline / so far from home'. A backpacker (perhaps another doppelgänger?) lies back, flipping channels, waiting for his beer to chill in the ice-filled sink. The mood is end-of-season, end-of-century and end of the earth. When he goes into the bathroom to check the progress, we're given one of the eeriest self-portraits to appear in O'Meara's poetry:

> There's a handprint on the mirror, barely
> a smudge. Another soul who passed here ...
> the same as you, once so sure of time and space
> you thought you knew what travel was.

The handprint in the mirror is a nullification: staring back is an identity 'fingerprinted' by previous consciousnesses. Faced – literally – with evidence that others have stood in that very spot before him, the speaker recognizes himself as a latecomer (the poem is even called 'The Late Show'). Here is an image of wanderlust emptied of mojo. In earlier books, O'Meara's travel poems were jump-started by the unprecedented quality of what he was seeing. Now he makes travel poetry – and makes it his own – from his sense of second-handness. It's a picture of a poet in the middle of life's journey, the dark wood replaced by a Lonely Planet guide. The speaker is thinking of 'time and space' because he's been following a science program on TV about an atom-smasher built to 'prove a theory of the universe'. Although 'barely/a smudge', the handprint is proof enough of a universe of diminished premises. Time and space – as it happens, also the two basic principles of travel – are compressed into that tiny room. The world is one-size-fits-all, its distances traversable by the wandering self, and like the stages of life, the journey is one-way. 'Ever', the book's moving coda, expresses this idea in a lullaby of hypotheticals:

> You, me,
> from the streets of Samarkand to Peggy's Cove;
> we'll see
>
> Delphi,
> Angkor Wat, the markets of Asia, the Louvre,
> maybe
>
> shade-trees
> on the Euphrates if time is kind enough,
> we'll see.
>
> Will we
> ever live in Montreal again. Maybe not, love.
> Maybe.
> We'll see.

O'Meara has a great knack for dropping a hint, and this serves him especially well here. Uncluttered and bone-simple, the poem is a master class in formal and verbal precision. Check out how the refrain (will we/maybe/we'll see) allows pressure to build up inside a minimal structure, and how, with each repetition, the tonal temperature changes. The modesty of the anaphoric form helps O'Meara say no more than he wants to mean. It allows him to wring from his lines a music rich in complicated emotion: regret, resignation, wistfulness, and, very faintly, reprimand. Mortality, the poem implies, drives travel: we hurry to make tracks before our life runs its course. It's no accident the poem's pendent-like stanzaic shapes – tercets split by a long outrider – visually evoke the needle's eye, and the unlikelihood of passing through it. The poem's question-and-answer structure is a Scheherazadian attempt at resisting the great subtractive force shadowing every docked-at destination: constantly amended by evasiveness, life remains pure potential, and the speaker thereby keeps his lover (and death) at bay.

There is something else O'Meara leapfrogs with this book: his predecessors. The voice tugging at a lover's dream in 'Ever', trying to pull it down to earth, is also speaking to Canada's distinguished tradition of travelling poets. When Layton *et al.* absconded to Greece, travel was more adventurous, with much of the adventure bound up in the exhilaration of simply being outside the country. O'Meara's era – my era – is different. Travel is common, clichéd and too easily fetishizable. Travel poems continue to be written (viz. Stephanie Bolster's explorations of Parisian zoos, for instance) except what they struggle to pin down isn't the strangeness of where they are set, but the belatedness – or elusiveness – of a promised transformation. O'Meara is therefore the first Canadian poet to extend the experience of contemporary travel into the writing itself, where the real adventure now lies – not reportage or reflection, but the trip ongoing. In doing so he has an excellent chance of getting off where every good poet, well-dusted by all the logged miles, hopes to arrive: among the few who, every generation, uphold the distinction between day-tripper and expeditionist, between the Grand Tour of the period manner and the rare, unrepeatable crossing.

ERIC ORMSBY

'C*remains* is not a pretty word', advises Eric Ormsby in his new collection, *Daybreak at the Straits* (2004). And who better to know than the man who has built a career out of an obsession with pretty words. If we could rifle through his five books using a search engine able to discern similarities of melodic texture, we would turn up reams of show-off diction: 'prismed', 'insinuations', 'luxuriate', 'simulacrum', 'nascent', 'lambency'. Ormsby's vocabulary is, of course, significantly more colloquial in its full range: not all his lines drive you to the OED. But what is admirable about Ormsby is precisely his fondness for the kind of large, Latinate words so distrusted by his contemporaries. These enhancers sometimes give his imagery its amazing, boosted presence on the page ('the skimming owl's/concavity of surveillance' or 'lethal light insinuates and tinges'). But more than that, their use can be read as a bold effort to paganize ordinary speech, to introduce some black-magical Fabergé blasphemy into its domestic plainness.

Let me explain. Received opinion tells us that rhetoric like Ormsby's is too well-bred to threaten convention. Innovations in poetry have always depended on a *volte-face* return to unprettiness, like Ted Hughes' violent-verb style in *Crow*: 'Shock-severed eyes watched blood/Squandering as from a drain-pipe'. Ormsby's words, instead, inhabit the aristocratic reaches of our language – the very music Hughes' 'tattered guts' and 'shattered brains' is meant to mock. Such opulent singing has been so embarrassed by its alleged enemy – vernacular – it's been rendered alien. Obdurate, extravagant, anti-quotidian, these words have never been absorbed into daily practice. But this is their great opportunity. They have been pushed so far outside the zeitgeist that, in their re-entry, they ring out with exhilarating oddness. Words like 'acclamatory', 'cantillation' and 'marmorealize' have the rare potential to put readers in contact with an English language newly decanted: their odour as sharp and unfamiliar as the day they were first bottled.

Yet any critic who wants to discuss these 'avant-gaude' experiments, to use Stephen Burt's term, faces a problem: our prosodic field of view isn't wide enough to capture such large effects. Our praise is scaled to fit encroachments into low diction, not loud logophilic rediscoveries. The ricochet of cockney in *The Waste Land* ('It's them pills I took, to bring it off, she said') is celebrated as an aural novelty, and rightly so. Eliot jolts our ear into recognizing how the dreariest conversations can be carriers of small stylistic graces. But it seems impossible to imagine Ormsby's dress-up words being responsible for similar surprises because such surprises, as we currently understand them, demonstrate the strength of *not* being poetic. And nothing about Ormsby's maximalist coinages in *Daybreak at the Straits* ('The clouds that lie in cinnabar striations') tells us that he's prepared to climb down the ladder of his rhetoric and lie in the rag-and-bone shop of ordinary speech. His verse-line, in fact, is right where he left it in 2001 with *Araby*: ecstatic. Ormsby is so keyed-up the merest hint of loveliness can keep him going for pages. 'Little Auguries' opens: 'The vast summer's distillate of cloud/rambled, thunder-proud'. Barely begun, the music already feels rash. And as the couplets throw off their images it becomes clear Ormsby is beyond the rescue of prudence: 'Saluting thistles sentinelled the road', 'patient worms, Penelopes/of satin, tend decennial looms', 'the magnesium of mackerel schools/kindled the scuffed canal/with incandescences of protocol'.

Poems scarcely get richer than this, rarer still a wealth so free of embarrassment or apology. Even if you know enough to expect it, Ormsby's verbal greed can take you aback. According to his memoir-essay 'The Place of Shakespeare in a House of Pain', such greed was Ormsby's first fundamental experience of the world. He describes growing up in Florida in a 'time-warped' household where his grandmother and her sisters spoke in extravagant sentences memorized from Shakespeare's plays ('*Our ears are cudgelled*, and that's no joke!').

This high-tea scat singing, while often cryptic, proved irresistible and awoke in him half-resented faculties:

> If we were driving home from Miami Beach and there was a particularly splendid full moon in sight, Grandmother would weigh in with:
>
> Sit, Jessica. Look how the floor of heaven
> is think inlaid with patens of bright gold …
>
> It irked me to hear this because it pricked my interest and distracted me from whatever solipsistic reverie I was in the middle of. Who on earth was Jessica? A dumb name, like 'Juliet', my grandmother's given name; the sort of name that foreigners, and especially the English, gave their kids. Still that unusual word 'patens' caught my ear. I liked it though I had no idea what it meant. I thought of it as denoting ingots or bars of gold; the light of the moon did fall through the clouds in long bars and lambent slabs. The description was right, I couldn't deny, but it had the effect of sliding words between me and the world outside. Undisciplined as any child that age, I did not want to see my mercurial sentiments marshaled into language. But beyond that, I disliked and mistrusted the way my grandmother reduced everything she saw to some sort of poetic form; disliked and mistrusted it, even while I myself possessed and nourished the same instincts as she.

It is fascinating and a little touching to think of Ormsby's flamboyant poetry as the apotheosis of his grandmother's eccentricities. Yet the reaction portrayed here ('I disliked and mistrusted the way my grandmother reduced everything she saw to some sort of poetic form') has become a fair sketch of Ormsby's skeptical reader, the reader who runs into a deal-breaker like 'paten' and refuses to linger any further. A balanced assessment of Ormsby's achievement has therefore been hard to come by because what first attracts attention about his poetry – the scale, particularity and vibrancy of his vocabulary – becomes, for many, the most difficult thing to forgive. This is why, when he's criticized for his sumptuousness, the censure takes its cue from the school of authenticity. Style is truer, adherents tell us, when it humbly submits itself to the expressions people actually *use.* Ormsby, on the other hand, is too off-puttingly 'expert': brimming with swank sounds and suffering no worries about what to do with them. This serene lustre has made him absurdly easy to typecast. He is one of the drawing-room 'palefaces' that Philip Rahv in 1949 famously compared to open-air 'redskins'. In a sense, Ormsby can't win for losing. His success as a paleface draws on gifts largely perceived as anachronistic, and depend on rhetorical risks that, in our redskin age, have become unthinkable. Acutely aware of practising what is, by tradition and instinct, an ornate art, many poets police their poems for any telltale pallor. Those with a taste for prettiness pay a heavy price, since cadence is only allowed if trapped in an unbearable wrestle with plainness. This tussle – displayed most dramatically, perhaps, in Tony Harrison's ease-crippling early sonnets – has become one of contemporary poetry's signature effects, even as it stems from an old prejudice. A split vision has long existed between poets such as Keats who believe language is more marvellous than the materials it works on, and those such as Clare who scale it back to its earthy pith. And to Canada's own scale-back crowd Ormsby represents an old-school fustiness: technically adroit, but with an ill-advised soft-spot for sesquipedalian polysyllables. Such a depiction begins as a friend of patience-tested readers, but ends up betraying them. This is because it leaves them unprepared for the chief pleasures of Ormsby's poetry. Take 'Vacuum Pantoum':

> The vacuum's cannistered voracity
> never gets enough: its gulf-presidium
> snootsavors carpet, its mumbo-continuum
> snuffles triple-ply with toothed tenacity.
>
> I overhear the siren in the vacuum
> bag that serenades as it asseverates
> lint-detritus or evacuates
> the peregrine residuum

that effloresces on my velveteen.
The mites in their minute imperium
are obliviated by this wolf-harmonium
whose howl's Aeolian and gabardine.

O hoover me! I hear sprawled sofas hum,
Suck on my pleats! the buxom curtains plead.
The kilim pimps the nozzle for a knead.
The louvers quiver for the slot-scoop's thumb.

Were I to give a single example from *Daybreak at the Straits* of Ormsby's humour and utterly left-field musical sense, this might be it. The phrases are gauge-busting ('The vacuum's cannistered voracity'), a little absurd ('mumbo-continuum'), and force us to stumble slightly over the crowded, cross-grain rhythms ('I overhear the siren in the vacuum/bag that serenades as it asseverates/lint-detritus or evacuates/the peregrine residuum'). To a generous new-to-Ormsby reader, all this will sound magnificently weird. A less-generous reader will complain about being excluded. This is unjustifiable, not because the complaint is necessarily untrue but because it hints at sub-literate pieties which, if taken seriously, would make you wonder why people read poetry and not traffic signs.

The logic behind such criticism – plain words can be trusted, complex words can't – comes with a cost. Namely, we surrender to the cliché that our ear substitutes for the noise on the page. To prize an idiom for being inherently pretense-free sentimentalizes language. It turns the act of reading into an assertion of integrity rather than an exercise of faculties. Worse, it injures the art's experimental resources as it reinforces existing ceilings of accessibility. There is, I agree, nothing immediately accommodating about 'asseverate', and it may even be silly to imagine a day when the word might trip off the tongue the way 'ass' does or 'severe' or 'ate'. But good poetry isn't really about accommodation; we are coddled enough by a vapid, linguistically slack media (who have done their part to make us more intimidated, less resourceful readers than we used to be). A good poet will have the ambition – indeed it will be an obligation of his or her excellence

– to slip over on readers the kind of outermost music which their self-infantilizing hunger for accessibility will have conditioned them to reject. A good poet, in short, will help a reader grow up. Of course, if you're free of this fear of bewilderment then maybe you've already embraced the idea that marvellous things are happening in Ormsby's poems. Events that point to new uses for words – and hence new harmonies. Here is 'The Song of the Whisk':

My flail demolishes
the gold of yolks;
my mesh abolishes
what it would coax.

The waterspout can frisk
while it soufflés the sea;
what's the twister but a whisk
for instant entropy?

I will erect a pinnacle
of undulant béarnaise;
with clicketing quite clinical,
paradisal mayonnaise.

Three slim quatrains, yet the sky in this short poem would appear to be the limit. Compressed into its forty-six words is a rush of witty musical ideas (the waterspout turns the sea into a 'soufflé' – a light, puffy dish – but the word is also the past participle of French *souffler* or 'puff up') and startlingly audible ('clicketing quite clinical'). Ormsby is preternaturally alert to the colorations words have in proximity to each other, and uses this skill to introduce unexpected, almost extra-verbal densities into his lines (the last stanza especially seems to thicken into a liquid literalness). A matchless phrasemaker, Ormsby sees an object for what it is and simultaneously sees it in words; this two-fold gaze confers an immediate advantage as it allows him to perceive the world with finely estranging eyes.

Take the metaphor in the second stanza: whisk as waterspout. A more conventional poet, even a very good one, would have drawn on try-too-hard rhetoric and shock tactics to coin the same comparison. Yet Ormsby does more than force an unconventional likeness: he creates a sonic surrogate. Expansions and contractions of perspective (minor household item as major meteorological event and vice versa) occur not only intellectually, but on the level of diction. Poets who write this way – who move words into clusters of meaning so intense they seem to stand up from the page – regard language not as a function but as an agency, not as a licensed tool but as a vast and complex sensorium. Put another way, language isn't reasonable for Ormsby; it's infinite. And when he's facing it, all words are potentially as useful as all other words. Complex or plain, such designations are irrelevant: what matters is the consequences of the choices he makes and the credibility of the outcome. When writing 'Song of the Whisk' Ormsby budgeted each line's clarity against its fecundity. Baroque is the ready-made pejorative for this register, yet how ironic that this exuberant push-pull makes the more sensible work of Ormsby's peers look flabby and verbose. The exceptional precision of his verb-moods ('my mesh abolishes/what it would coax') and syntactical inflections ('with clicketing quite clinical,/paradisal mayonnaise') is justification enough for the tactic; and is enough, I should think, to bring even a reluctant reader to admiration.

One reason it might not be enough is that the reader is liable to see pomp and pride where there is only sincerity. And here I use the word as Pound did – 'Technique', he wrote 'is the test of sincerity'. Ormsby chooses his words the way any poet does: because there is, as the economists say, 'a felt need' for them. The difference is that his choices also represent the moment at which a poet feels the existing inventory isn't quite doing what he wants it to do. This frustration is the incentive for sensational poems like 'River Plants', 'Florida Bay', 'The Public Gardens' and 'Mullein'. But these moments, because of the aesthetic adventures they promise, are also significant for the art itself, and as such they deserve our attention. Robert Graves' advice was to go after the real words and stay away from anything stand-in. Ormsby's poetry is likewise a fight for the essential among the ersatz. Mis-appellation is his only real opponent, and this explains the miss-no-detail pointillism in which the tiniest swirls of a seashell's surface receive lavish discrimination. He is, you might say, a neologistic perfectionist. That this leads him to employ all-jaw, big-mouthed curios like 'polyphonal' and 'diatoming' simply means that they have an intrinsic lilt he considers essential, and he won't be warned away from using them by some need to respect decorum. If the danger is that we swallow our language whole and never taste it, then Ormsby is determined to serve up undiscovered piquancies.

Yet so firmly unprogressive do these words seem that we forget how subversive they've already proven themselves to be. It was, after all, Wallace Stevens who first prodded unusual words like 'concupiscence' into delicious confrontations with vernacular. Ormsby is, I think, Steven's truest inheritor; a double agent infiltrating and simultaneously altering two separate idiomatic DNAs, literary and colloquial. The remixed musicality isn't always successful, but when such arch argot is fed into a syntactically 'spoken' matrix the effect can be riveting. Below is a section from 'Dicie Fletcher' where Dicie's tooth is being yanked out by Dr. Diore. Reading the description, it's hard not to feel Ormsby has bred his words to entirely new genetic addresses:

> When a dark oak is cracked by cyclonic wind
> and its lashed branches flail in the shrill black air
> and the whole heaven eddies with laceration
> while under the skreegh of wind the herdsman hears
> acorns pittering the rain-pocked soil
> with palpitant volleys, gatling-gravel-pings,
> so Dicie heard, from deep inside her skull,
> how the tormented third molar grunted, squeaked,
> then twitter-stumbled like a stub of chalk
> scraped across a blackboard to a shriek,
> and she blubbered as the thick-embedded roots
> tore at her gums till all at once,
> with a popping suck it clopped into the dish
> and rattled there, long-rooted, flung to defeat

This is dazzling, and much of its power rests on how the language channel-hops between the five senses. In Ormsby, the world is always being presented to us in joined-up portions rather than in an array of separate perceptions. The lines 'while under the skreegh of wind the herdsman hears / acorns pittering the rain-pocked soil / with palpitant volleys, gatling-gravel-pings' convey their details by compacting sight, sound and touch into a single signature. The fact that Ormsby experiences texture stereoscopically accounts for the sprightly oddities of his style; he bends and stretches verbs and nouns to emphasize unlikely sensory combinations. Take the line 'The whole heaven eddies with laceration'. It perfectly conveys the energy of the storm, but by placing 'eddies' alongside 'laceration' Ormsby forces the two words to underwrite strange, original nuances in each other. What is further astonishing about that line isn't how it's so alert, alive and apprehending, but how completely *typical* it is. We are not looking at a poem hitting its most potent note but at an entirely characteristic flourish. What for anyone else would be a flash of surpassing brilliance, is for Ormsby business as usual.

This easy, fast-moving abundance is why one senses in Ormsby the potential for an altogether revolutionary music, one with attendant demands on the listener to adopt a different set of aural allowances and expectations. When Ormsby describes the ant lion as a 'larval hunter with a gladiator / lunge of needle-mandibles' who rules with 'silicate / strategies, glint-facades of fright', or when he sets his watch and is struck by how 'a tiny, startled, hurrying succession / of twig-snapped seconds comes tiptapping out' you can't help think he is trying to jolt our language into an as-yet-to-be-invented idiom streaming with mixed dictions and kinetic compounds. Here is the first third of 'Microcosm':

> The proboscis of the drab gray flea
> Is mirrored in the majesty
> Of the elephant's articulated trunk. There's a sea
> In the bed-mite's dim, orbicular eye.
> Pinnacles crinkle when the mountain-winged, shy
> Moth wakes up and stretches for the night.

Katydids enact the richly patterned light
Of galaxies in their chirped and frangible notes.
The smallest beings harbour a universe
Of telescoped similitudes. Even those Rocky Mountain goats
Mimic Alpha Centauri in rectangular irises
Of cinnabar-splotched gold. Inert viruses
Replicate thc static of red-shifted, still chthonic
Cosmoi.

Like the whisk-into-waterspout metaphor, and the aroused senses-mingling sensuality of the Dicie Fletcher narrative, this poem is an example of Ormsby's habitual bestriding of boundaries. Spatchcocked with strangely assorted jargon (it sounds like the rapt voice of a fanciful but scrupulous scientist) these lines create a speech of linkages, of constantly-asserted connections. Of course they do this by leaping the colloquial register ('Inert viruses/Replicate the static of red-shifted, still chthonic/Cosmoi'). Such turns of vocabulary are everywhere in Ormsby's poetry. Just like the nonce improvisations we saw earlier ('gatling-gravel-pings') here we have precision-intoxicated descriptions ('In the bed-mite's dim, orbicular eye') that shadow their subject so closely the language seems to absorb the subject's properties. If the physical texture of the world is evoked with innovative resourcefulness it's because Ormsby understands that language has its own textures. Poets like Ormsby – and I'd add David Solway, James Merrill, Amy Clampitt, Richard Wilbur, Geoffrey Hill and Richard Outram to this vanguard of idiomatic experimenters – believe important truths reside in rapture. Of course, the catch is that such truths are only uncoverable by those who use language in this belief.

Unfortunately, with poetry's drastic capitulation to prose over the last forty years, we've forgotten that words can be precise, primal, pungent, exhilarating and identity-giving. We're living in a time of bland eloquence in which a usage like 'thing' is relied on as an all-purpose synonym. We've knocked all Shakespearean splendour, all sense of amplitude out of our language, so that now it's possible to issue thousands and thousands of decent, humble, simple, sometimes pleasing words without ever coming close to reproducing the dripping gorgeousness and creaturely life of Ormsby's lured-out-of-the-dictionary idiolect.

That said, a law of diminishing returns does seem to have set in. After five books one begins to take the virtuosity for granted and grow more aware of the shortcomings. Ormsby is a poet to whom every word in the language has, by now, its own musical value. And yet one sometimes feels that the words, when they come, fail to come at a high enough price. This free-spending with no sense of saving parsimony can be seen especially in 'Six Sonnets on Sex and Death', a sonnet-sequence whose unwittingly self-caricaturing overripeness ('Neuterness annulled his jolly knot./The vain inane inoculated all/his tousles of temptation with a shot') brings to mind Valery's complaint that Hugo 'took big words but manipulated them without effort, with such ease that they give the impression of being empty'. Elsewhere, the very strengths of the poems begin to work against them: their gilded clarity of expression makes one wish they had something to say that couldn't be so terminally articulated. Lines like 'Their webs are glitzy and their spinnerets/sequin the silks they unspool as they spin' or 'spring water laves/the skin with its brisk plush touch' reveal Ormsby to be, as expected, a very fine precisionist, but the style here freezes detail into a cult of itself. Each word is so marked by its painstaking choosenness that Ormsby creates what Norman MacCaig used to call 'so what' moments; descriptive moments, that is, rendered vividly but to no particular purpose. Sometimes, the renderings, rich with new-mintedness, are an adjective ahead of the subjects they spring from. Ormsby can take four words and fix a phrase to stop you cold, but this talent, when pursued too obsessively, also prevents him from seeing that the poem needs to be about something more than just his phrase. It also prevents him from *seeing*. An example in miniature of this anti-accuracy would be 'winter-dociled bee' which is too self-consciously perfect; the image feels gilt-covered rather than dipped in gold. And poems ('Against Memorials', 'Time as Escargot', 'Domestic Questions') constructed from this kind of word-worrying seem held together too much by will.

But these are tiny concerns, not ruinous. From the very successful ('Mrs. Lazurus', 'Lines Written after Reading Thomas a Kempis',

'Episode With a Potato') to the superb ('Rowing into the Glades', 'Watchdog and Rooster') to the outright masterpieces ('An Epistle from Rice Point', 'Soliloquy at Nightfall In the Mayflower Hotel') there is plenty in this book to confirm Ormsby as a poet prodigiously equipped for writing major poetry at a time allergic to such literary striving. The question of how much is available to the 'ordinary' reader, however, is a question worth trying to answer, because the answer will help decide whether we will ever value Ormsby as something more than just a poet's poet.

The funny thing, you see, is that 'cremains' *is* a pretty word. Or becomes so thanks to Ormsby's ear. The word experiences a kind of takeover: it's been separated from its assigned prosaic self and melodically reconstituted. This, of course, is a time-honoured trick. Whether its Paul Valéry calling poetry a language within a language, or Rainer Maria Rilke declaring that 'no word in a poem (I mean every 'and' and 'the') is identical with the same-sounding word in common usage and conversation', or Hart Crane dreaming of a form 'so thorough and intense as to dye the words themselves with a peculiarity of meaning, slightly different maybe from the ordinary definition of them separate from the poem' – they all hint at the same thing: poems create an acoustic threshold past which the normal rules don't apply. In Ormsby's case, his hearing is drawn to marginal, near-neglected sounds. It's a case of old noises given fresh promotion. The words he chooses ('encairn', 'predacious') don't always release all their savour in one lick, but he intends their music to be eventually savoured. At a time when accessibility represents a poet's own vacationing eagerness to be swiftly understood, Ormsby has never hesitated to scout out the more isolated areas of our vocabulary. Wallace Stevens believed poets needed to love words with all their capacity to love anything at all. Should we ask any less of our readers?

JAY PARINI & TOM PAULIN

How to make poetry matter? According to Clive James, ban it – with stiff penalties for possession. Criminalizing verse, argues the Australian critic, would have the immediate and incontestable benefit of rendering poems dangerous. He's got a point, and not merely because it recalls Mandelstam's joke on the Stalin era: 'only in Russia poetry is respected – it gets people killed'.

James's real target is the outreach efforts designed to cure non-poets of their indifference. A poem posted in a bus might catch the bored eye of the odd commuter, but it's hardly enough to persuade them to stop ignoring the stuff. One-time stunts won't change deep-seated opinions. To win converts you need to do more: you need to spark curiosity about your cause. And a smart way for poets to do that, apart from writing exciting poems, is by writing exciting criticism. In other words, widening poetry's core readership starts with raising – to rich, phrase-turning heights – the level of conversation about the art. Poetry's minority status is regrettable, but doesn't justify critical prose emptied of gusto, mischief and melody. You don't defeat indifference by boring people. If poetry matters, the language we use to describe poetry matters too.

Jay Parini is a well-published American poet, novelist, reviewer and biographer. He believes that poetry is important because it exercises our better faculties – 'without it', Parini says, 'we can live only partially, not fully conscious of the possibilities (emotional and intellectual) that life affords'.

This sentence occurs in the preface of his new book, *Why Poetry*

Matters (2008), and it sets the tone for a defence of poetry that celebrates the health-giving power of poetic form. We get pronouncements ('poetry is useful because it draws us closer to the earth, helping us see what lies about us'), dictums ('Only in the moment of a poem, within its steady unfolding of a vision, does life clarify') and warnings ('poets who willfully ignore the world around them risk marginality').

What we don't get is good writing. Parini congratulates himself on his lack of 'specialist jargon', opting for a plain-speaking that radiates seriousness. But seriousness is not a style. A style is something that sets out to seduce, and our man writes with a dry, definitional care that can't help but bore you stiff.

There's no reason not to trust Parini's admission that he is 'especially fond' of poets like Wordsworth, Hopkins and Frost, but you never get the sense that he's been knocked sideways by their poems. A critic who wants to excite readers about poetry needs to lead by example. Parini spends an entire chapter vouching for the redemptive bona fides of T.S. Eliot's *Four Quartets* (the poem 'offers directions for living', it displays 'the deep wisdom of a lifetime spent in contemplation'). But nothing in his praise compels us to put aside his essay and chase down the poem. A critic's main hold over readers is through words, not ideas. How you say it counts for everything.

Why Poetry Matters fails because Parini's sense of poetry's importance is directly proportional to his claims for it. The bigger the claim – poetry calibrates our moral and mental bearings! Poetry soothes and consoles! – the blander the prose. The real question, and an answer that could actually glue non-poets to their seats, is how do poems that 'matter' work? How does a poet like Eliot write a poem that does the job of satisfying emotion and intellect while getting its words to belong together? Parini is caught up in talking points, when one would rather he talk shop.

One also expects him to know what time it is. Insisting on the social function of something society happily functions without is a losing game. Whatever world that argument belonged to is gone. Don't misunderstand: that poetry is a vital cultural good is, for me, beyond argument. But poetry's fate doesn't depend on convincing readers of that. It depends on motivating readers into discovering such truths for themselves. It depends on a talent for talking openly, rigourously and arrestingly about the poems we love. And it depends especially on ensuring what matters most about poetry – that if it's there, the ear will prove it – is front and centre in any debate about the art.

For Tom Paulin, the ear is king. For the last thirty years the Irish poet, provocateur and critic has been obsessed with the 'genius' of spoken English. 'Poetry begins in speech', he writes in *The Secret Life of Poems* (2008), 'in the skipping rhymes and chants children make up in the playground and the street'.

Like Parini, Paulin has ideas about the civic subtext of those oral energies. (Heaney's 'Broagh' is a poem that 'expresses deep anxiety about the present and the future of the Northern Irish'.) Paulin has no interest, however, in promoting poetry's feel-good qualities. Poets, he believes, don't write because of what their poems can 'do' for others. They write to satisfy an aphrodisiacal itch to mate specific words, what he calls 'a meshing pattern of related and relating sounds'.

Paulin's new book rounds up 40 poems, with an essay on each. Some choices are familiar (Coleridge's 'Kubla Khan'), most are not (Frost's little-known 'The Investment'). But whatever the poem, what counts is its 'secret life' – the clockwork hidden in plain sight. Poetry, for Paulin, is a real-time event: it comes alive the instant we make contact. On the page, Keats' 'To Autumn' is just a clump of words. Jolted by our attention, those words self-assemble into an extraordinary music.

The secret to this, according to Paulin, is right there on the surface. He sees emotion as syntax; sees vowels and consonants as fundamental partners of sense. What moves him, for example, in Edward Thomas' 1917 poem 'The Owl' (about a soldier's return to 'food, fire, and rest' after battle) isn't its sentiment, but the 'painful oo sound' that Edwards subliminally stitches into his lines, and how that audio effect (based on an owl's 'melancholy cry') creates the poem's grief-logic.

Paulin's great gift is an ear that doesn't know between old and new. A sixteenth-century sonnet strikes him as freshly as a twenty-first century lyric. He also has a knack for letting us experience that freshness exactly the way he does (who else would consider 'ruck' an 'untidy, scrummy word' or describe Swift's 'disgusted attraction to monosyllables'). Paulin works tirelessly to activate what he thinks our ear might be overlooking, and sometimes pushes his readings to absurd precisions. 'Rosenberg's lovely last line', he writes, 'is as simple as ordinary talk: it is braced by four ts, softened by th, has a tiny pause after "little" and a slightly longer pause after "white".' Sure, if you say so.

But these are errors of enthusiasm. Poetry, for Paulin, is just too damn fascinating to leave alone. And his enthusiasm can't help but rub off on us. His commentary on Ted Hughes' 'Thistle' will send many readers scrambling for the rest of Hughes' poetry. Ditto for his magisterial discussion of Robert Lowell's 'Sailing Home from Rapallo'. As Paulin proves, the trick to writing good criticism – criticism that unites poem and public – is to write criticism people want to read.

ROBYN SARAH

ROBYN SARAH can't stop staring, and her poetry – largely set in Montreal's Mile End neighbourhood – abounds with things she's seen: black-garbed Hasids hurrying past, an Italian knife-sharpener ringing his bell, boys larking on a metal balcony. She is always logging some ordinary, and ordinarily unnoticed, moment ('little Eurekas', she calls them) and many poems don't seem to do much more than set a standard of alert response to her surroundings ('Bars on snow:/fence-shadow, light/from a doorway'). This spectatorship occurs inside a semi-artless style inextricable from the poet's wished-for invisibility: 'Incognito in the little shops/is how I want to go'. Like the ephemera that turn up in her pocket dramas – raindrops, twigs, bread crumbs, fluff, dust – Sarah's poems have a sublime plainness. They are at once down-to-earth and noble, homely and elevated. You might call them Canada's answer to 'sprawl', Les Murray's term for Aussie exuberance. Sarah hates filler (her *bête noire* is the annual glut of poetry collections fattened with 'warm-ups, misfires, and exercises'). She doesn't, as she's sometimes accused, settle for less; she simply believes a little goes a long way. 'Make much of something small', she urges, and lives by it. Her precise descriptive siftings – an avocado 'halved lengthwise, hollowed,/salted, dressed with lemon' or a rose in a vase 'hung on the limp stalk/of its spent neck' – promote a vision of abundance as composed of luminous bits and pieces that never take up more room than they need.

To 'make much', of course, also means to insist on something beyond a reasonable sense of its importance. This is Sarah's joke; a way of keeping herself, and her unpretentiousness, grounded. At what point, after all, does self-effacement begin to look like it's peddling its own humility? But then, that's also Sarah's advice to us: have the courage of your banalities. Anyone can write a poem about eggplants, but to state the vegetable's case as simply and deeply as she does in 'A Praga Market', fixing its traits in unshowy metaphors ('skin/like leather, just wrinkling'), requires a smallness that takes itself seriously, a smallness that dreams big. This of course brings to mind Elizabeth Bishop, a poet also notable for her humble affections ('Homemade, homemade, but aren't we all?') But Sarah's tradition is larger: George Herbert, John Clare, Edward Thomas and William Carlos Williams are all present in her style. She belongs to a school of poets who take things at face value, whose poems represent an obstinate loyalty to the near-at-hand. Only by staying on the surface, they argue, can one find the deepest sounding.

Sarah writes about her kids, her cooking, waiting for mail, snow, bird calls, running into friends on the street, daydreaming at the window and middle-of-the-day surprises: an alley filling with the music of a neighbour practising the English horn. She wants to reprioritize our penchants, to show ordinariness alone is certain good. All this, however, introduces a double bind: by its very existence, a poem represents a large claim being made for a small thing and thus betrays the modesty Sarah seeks to celebrate. This is the signature tension of Sarah's nine books. Because of it, certain ironies – creatively productive ironies – are available to her that elude more ambitious poets (poets, say, who dress up the slightness of their subjects). Sarah isn't out to prove insignificance is in eye of the observer. The world, after all, is full of people who believe certain things are beneath their notice – and part of Sarah suspects they have a point. Her poetry, instead, flirts obsessively with ideas of irrelevance: 'We are collectors all, and our/collections are collectors too,/collecting dust'. She does this through subject (e.g., the 'pink star' of a drop of wine on a page), but also through style. Take 'Carried' from *Becoming Light* (1987):

> The impulse running its course:
> carried, like a leaf on air,
> through air, to rest – not just
> the motion, but the path it makes

no leaf will make again – to this
I give what self I can,
what sight, what will.
Or winter warmed: a smell,
fresh, tremulous, and sweet,
we say spring, that breathes
from heaps of shrinking snow
gone lacy in the sun – or steams
from rivulets that run
in all directions, out from under these.

A whisker past minimal, the poem is, in part, a description of melting snow, and, more broadly, a meditation on endings – nature as a place where everything is 'running its course'. Form thus expresses what is being said through content. The irregular lines, the soft monosyllables, the run-on cadence: all this Sarah uses to mimic her theme of dissolution and disappearance. Sarah is always looking for subjects that provide useful analogies for her method. In this sense, 'Carried' is a kind of primer, an *ars poetica* demonstration of what happens when poetry finds its own level: it seeks the irreducible, returns to first principles. The poem also suggests that smallness, uncompromisingly pursued, forces adjustments to a poet's ambitions, delivering a blunt reminder of how little they mean. 'Carried' is a document of vanity cut down to size, of an ego reduced to a stage-whispered awareness of self. It's a parable about mortality, our time on earth. Sarah's poetry, it implies, doesn't strip life to essentials; it's the result of life stripping *her* to essentials.

Smallness is no small job. Unlike minimalism, it doesn't abbreviate data; it compresses information streams. That's why 'Carried' feels bigger than it looks: every vowel, consonant and syllable has received unhurried consideration. Amazing how so few words add up to a speaker 'making much', her mind at large in minutia. But this offers a related lesson. Because smallness occupies a bigger intellectual area than is visible to the reader, it can only be written by those who have the whole of English poetry in their heads. Smallness believes the universe has been optimized for its love of precision, its high care for nouns and verbs. And in Sarah's case, at the root of that conviction, is the fear that certain kinds of lived experience (what an early poem calls 'the day-to-day, that bogs the mind, voice, hands/with things you couldn't call poems') will lapse unrecorded without her. This points up, again, the basic contradiction in her work: how a considerable outlay of resources is invested in poems that do nothing more than lightly embrace the negligible. Crisp groupings of simple words – leaf, air, snow, spring, fresh – become acoustic building blocks for yoking 'things that matter and don't matter' into memorable lines.

Pause for Breath (2009), Sarah's latest collection, conceives of itself as another stay against self-importance. The title conveys a second wind ('A pause to pull socks up') but also, more interestingly, exertions of an aging body. Now 61 – she published her first book at 29 – Sarah's new poems mark time, take stock, note the hour. In one, lost vigour (or the fear of it) is reflected, and refracted, through the glimpse, from a train, of 'a derelict auto hull/in a spring-green pasture'. In another, a yawn is what happens when 'in the cave of the throat/a controlled wind/shudders and dies'. Read the right poems, and you'll find speculations on decay so rich in tone and syntax they practically beg to be spoken aloud. Sarah's real gift lies in getting the emotional proportions the way she wants them. Incidentally autobiographical, rarely confessional, her best poems estrange without defamiliarizing, respect reality while refreshing it. It's a poetry of close-ups, of observations recorded inches from the world. ('What a glitter up and down the wire/as sudden sun strikes/yesterday's raindrops!') When Sarah is writing well, her language is both necessary and sufficient. Form becomes a 'pause for breath' – a closing of the valve. 'I threw the say/of how I felt/out from me', she writes, serenely. Lines are loaded with heartache, but light to the touch. Misgivings and confusions are so immersed in an atmosphere of domesticity they have the drama of 'damp breath exhaled on glass', and are no less powerful for it. Case in point is the exquisite sonnet 'Blowing the Fluff Away':

> The sprig of unknown bloom you sent last fall
> spent the long winter drying on my wall,
> mounted on black. But it had turned to fluff

some months ago. Tonight I took it down
because I thought that I had had enough
of staring at it. Brittle, dry and brown,
it seemed to speak too plainly of a waste
of friendship, forced to flower, culled in haste.

So, after months of fearing to walk past
in case the stir should scatter it to bits,
I took it out to scatter it at last
with my own breath, and so to call us quits.
– Fooled! for the fluff was nothing but a sheath,
with tiny, perfect flowers underneath.

The language is nondescript, details almost generic ('Brittle, dry and brown'). This is diction as defiance – it dares the ordinariness of its flatness. As in 'Maintenance', her first great poem ('Sometimes the best I can do / is homemade soup, or a patch on the knee / of the baby's overalls'), Sarah displays an ear for basic sentence-sounds. The effect is air-clearing sanity, directness cut with understatement (it recalls Donald Hall's description of Jane Kenyon's verse as 'a hundred-proof glass of water'). We also have another poem held together by its own enactment: right before our eyes, the bloom-turned-fluff ripens quietly and fully into metaphor. What is arresting is how, line by line, the poem gathers emotional force without tipping the reader to the power that's building. The origin of that fluff is rooted in memories and associations kept from us. Despite the missing data, the poem is still very much what Larkin called 'an instrument of transference'. We pick up regret, guilt, maybe even self-loathing. The poem clearly harbours a secret shame ('Fooled!'), its narrator barely on speaking terms with herself. Indeed, many of Sarah's I-see-this, I-see-that poems are fed by private anguish. The stirring 'As a Storm-lopped Tree', for example, alludes to a 'terrible event' that's never named. The poems try to keep up appearances, but as with body language, they give away hints. How else to account for the subliminal oddities of this tidbit, which I quite like:

Things that wash up in winter's wake:
an old sink up-ended on a balcony,
seen through the open door –
flicker of maples leaves
in the drain hole,
the drain
draining air.

The ending has the pressure of a tweet, a tiny language-act zipping past as we read. But slow down: note the deft repetition of 'drain' and the staircase effect produced by the patterning – see how, in each line, the word drops gradually toward the left-hand margin? This is an example of how smallness, like nanotechnological code, embraces structure and symmetry. It's also an example of how smallness depends on sound, and exploits the way inflections carry emotion. How else to explain why those final four lines ('flicker of maples leaves/in the drain hole,/the drain/draining air') capture the music of loneliness and attrition? The eye that detects a 'drain/draining air' can only belong to a body that feels kinship with that up-ended old sink. This is Sarah's most appealing side, when her poetry turns readers into intuitionists, seducing us into making much of so little.

But Sarah can also make too much of her ideas. Readers will need to steel themselves against the results: strained epiphanies ('What a blank ache/is day,/its labyrinthine paths'), excruciating clichés ('Why do windows of slums flash/like jewels in the sunrise/as we pass them by?') and tedious sermons ('This is too a life./Who is to say that it is/worse than yours or mine?'). Even punctuation is affected. I can't think of a significant Canadian poet more addicted to the exclamation mark. I counted at least ten in this book, of which only one was (maybe) necessary. She can even make too little of her ideas. 'Minus 20', 'Tenacious', 'Munificent' and 'In an Evening Window' – four short descriptive lyrics which appear to aspire to a kind of Oriental simplicity – are a bit skint; too much is missing, nothing risked. This points up another peril of smallness loved not wisely but too well: it has a comfort zone. What constitutes a poem for Sarah isn't really an open question. Her taste in form, both inherited and invented, can lead to static, ceremonial shapes. It's true she's tried prose poems and long, complex lyric-sequences. But Sarah is partial to what she can control; compounds of standard English and slang (a trademark effect of many of Canada's younger poets) seem too unstable to interest her. So if I have a complaint, it's that I wish she could loosen her notions of what's permissible.

That said, a clutch of poems in this book puts the boot to that complaint. 'Lowly', 'Ho Hum' and 'Gesundheit' are deadpan, fanciful lectures on unexceptional subjects (earthworms, yawning and sneezing, respectively). Sarah's plain style meets the challenge by widening its register to include a welcome, throwaway tone. Here are the first five lines of 'Clock Song':

> Time creeps, time flies.
> Clocks keep it and tell it,
> tick it and tock it,
> stand watch on a mantel
> or hide in a pocket.

This is restraint governed by an ear that has absorbed *Mother Goose*. Each syllable ticks forward, and sound, overall, blooms. Read the lines again and again: they don't wear out their welcome (on a third reading, I had already memorized them). The rest is just as good. The poem is disciplined but never abandons its gratuitous delight in words; the whole effort sayable, even singable ('Clocks need us to wind them / and keep them true. / We depend on clocks, too, / and don't always mind them'). Sunk into the poem's euphonies is the idea of extinction. The clock song, after all, is the song of time running out. It's a melody to tap your toes to, and the jaunty tune helps make the message – we're goners – stick. Fear of death paired with love of language is not something we often see in Sarah's tool kit of effects. But she uses it here to invent a new way for her poems to sound.

Take 'Splinter'. Composed in eight-line stanzas of lapidary speed and generous impulsiveness, the poem describes a visit to the hospital to remove 'a toothpick-sized wedge / of old wood, none too clean'.

Seated 'among bleeders and breathers/through oxygen cones', the speaker is embarrassed to see herself fuss over so minor an injury. But behind the unceasing patter is a spooked mind; the poem is trying to calm itself down. 'Splinter' is a great example of what Sarah can do: take something unpromising and keep adding surprises to it until the idea swells with originality. The poem is also a rare example of Sarah's nearly getting carried away. As things are, she remains a nuts and bolts poet. She places her subject matter up front, while in the background, meanings assemble:

> all told, full five hours of fidget
> for the sake of a digit.
> Then a ten-minute procedure.
> The needle, the scalpel, the tourniquet,
> tetanus top-up, wipe-up of ooze,
> a dressing of gauze: at last a prescription.
> Day's redemption: to learn the infection
> soon would have spread to the bone,
>
> that we near lost a finger – caught in the nick! –
> for a paltry rough sliver edged under a nail.
> – But that is just telling the tale.
> A splinter, now what is a splinter?
> A broken-off bit of the mass if what's Other,
> come to invade, to pierce to the quick?
> Something to bleed around – waken us – fret us?
> So breath itself lodges in us.

This is a knock-out ending – and nothing youth could ever arrive at. The last line is remarkable not only for the way 'lodge' suggests the classic cliché of terror writing ('breath lodged in my throat') but how it recalls our very first breath as infants, that sudden in-rush of air that seals our fate. To see a splinter as the grim reaper's scythe might seem like overkill, but you don't have to be a hypochondriac to understand that we die from life. Like some insidious virus, it 'lodges in us', slowly asphyxiating us – in stages, over a span of decades – with every lungful of air. In a sense, Sarah closes with the act that starts the clock. Breath and death are, of course, perfect rhymes, though it's not a bad idea to reread that last line with the words switched, and feel the jolt. This is a magisterial poem – no dud notes, language on a winning streak. Sarah's vocabulary is so discriminating, each word wears the complex self-investigation that brought it into being. The result is a form that feels uniquely hers: disciplined, compressed, emphatic, airy.

Most of Sarah's poems are nowhere near as good as her best. This makes it distressingly hard to crow about her collections as a whole (it might be one reason why Sarah has never won a prize). It also means Sarah is a poet tailor-made for anthologies (and she is certainly represented in many of them, including the Norton). This is not without cost. Living poets associated with specific books as well as specific poems – think of Erin Mouré's *Furious* (1992) or Don McKay's *Night Field* (1991) – often have an easier time generating an air of inevitability around their careers. Books seduce us into reading, as William Logan writes, 'in sequence of an expectation'. That is, they create a compelling narrative – one that frames the great poems while allowing us to forget they are few and far between. A reputation like Sarah's, however, balancing on stand-alone achievements, can be all too easily left alone. *Pause for Breath* likely won't change that. Its strongest poems will be welcomed into the canon, while the world takes little notice of the poet who wrote them.

Sarah probably isn't too concerned. 'We will begin to reclaim poetry', she writes in her collection of essays *Little Eurekas* (2007), 'when we learn to praise poems, not poets'. How utterly appropriate, then, that one of the most popular poems in the book was first published, unsigned, in *Arc*'s Anonymous issue (*Arc* 61). 'Echoes in November' resonated strongly with readers. It was included in *The Best Canadian Poetry 2009*. It also triggered an admiring response, published in a later issue of *Arc*, by Zach Wells, who declared the poem 'cut in marble … so perfect are all its parts'.

'Echoes in November' is what you might call a kitchen sink epiphany (or an example of what D.G. Jones calls Sarah's '*poésie de cuisine*'). The speaker, unsurprisingly, is something of a homebody. She stands at the chopping board, while her mind roams, idly bringing together unlike ideas: 'things that shadow things,/that breathe or borrow/essence not their own'. The poem is a master class on how poems get written. Specifically, it's a lesson on how much goes on in a poet's head when it seems nothing is. The entire poem exists to let Sarah tee up a point of a view ('Correspondences are everywhere') in order to crush it down to the microscopic intimacy of her conclusion:

> knife in hand
> above the chopping board,
> savouring, raw, a stub
> of vegetable not destined
> for the pot,
> and faintly tasting
> at the back of the palate
> the ghost of a rose
> in the core of the carrot.

Those last two lines ('the ghost of a rose/in the core of the carrot') read as a manifesto for Sarah's own method: crisp, pure, clasp-tight, aphoristically concise. The very pith of pithiness. So much is stuffed into that sense-quickening image: the passing of time, shedding of old selves, the inevitability of death. Sarah is a one-woman-and-acoustic-guitar kind of poet, her plinking notes deepened by philosophical sonorities. But there's another association buried deep in her use of 'rose': T.S. Eliot's remarks about the 'disassociation of sensibility' – his belief that, in seventeenth-century poetry, intellectual thought broke free from the experience of feeling. Eliot argued that, unlike Donne, for whom thought was 'an experience; it modified his sensibility', Tennyson and Browning 'do not feel their thought as immediately as *the odour of a rose*' (italics mine). And then he wrote this:

> When a poet's mind is perfectly equipped for its work, it is constantly amalgamating disparate experience; the ordinary man's experience is chaotic, irregular, fragmentary. The latter falls in love, or reads Spinoza, and these two experiences have nothing to do with each other,

> or with the noise of the typewriter or the smell of cooking; in the mind of the poet these experiences are always forming new wholes.

Eliot's theory that poets are 'constantly amalgamating disparate experience' shadows Sarah's poem, which, in its final image, proves his theory by transforming the jumbled sensations of her taste-cued Proustian recall into a 'new whole'. The apparent modesty of the poem belies the intellectual architecture holding it up. We're reminded, once again, that smallness is the trick of packing a limited space with implication (Eliot's 'smell of cooking' seems to take up residence in Sarah's kitchen). Sarah budgets these clues carefully, making sure there's enough to splurge on other things, like grammar and tone. The poem's form – a skinny column of thin-sliced lines – appears as a discrete absence, scrupulously shaped but scarcely asking for attention. This is Sarah's ambition: that the subtlety of her art, and the quiet career attached to it, will be amplified by the surrounding tradition.

But smallness courts neglect. Composed in a minor key, Sarah's poems seem out of scale with so much going on now. Sarah asks to be judged on her brass tacks, but readers are after other things: imagistic ravishments, supersaturated effects, spice-warm sounds. So perhaps, for many younger poets, my praise might seem much too much about too little. This would be wrong. There's only one smallness about Sarah that exceeds its merits: her readership.

KAREN SOLIE

ONE WOULD BE hard-pressed to cite a single feather that was ruffled by the welcome given Karen Solie's debut, *Short Haul Engine* (2001). Everyone seemed to see eye to eye on the hype. This consensus – marked by scads of reviews, profiles, interviews, prize nominations and anthology appearances – was neatly summed up by Heather Spears. 'Karen Solie', she declared in *Arc*, 'is obviously on her way to becoming a major poet'.

Such surmises often end up looking silly, but even the most skeptical of us (those, say, who might bristle at a reviewer using the occasion of a first book to stretch the charm of a qualifier like 'major') couldn't help but feel that the acclaim was apt. That for all the excesses of Soliemania (did Lynn Crosbie really suggest in the *Globe & Mail* that the poet's 'stardom' was about to go 'supernova'?) Solie herself was the real deal. The proof was in poetry that was exemplary, if not altogether untypical, in its rigour, trenchancy and skill. Technically, it avoided lyric extravagance for basic-wage Canadian vernacular. Thematically, it sought out noir settings – cityscapes, seedy hotels, after-hours dives, bleak gas stations – to match that vernacular. And emotionally, it turned over that vernacular to fast-talking vamps invented to smash the norm of tranquillizingly generic female speakers. *Short Haul Engine*, in other words, didn't give readers any warm fuzzies.

Solie's 'grit and diesel' voice has since been tested by new female poets (Evie Christie and Elizabeth Bachinsky, most notably) similarly fond of talking in pithy streetwise ways. But comparisons only confirm the difference. We know what these wildcats can't do because we know what Solie can: rawboned forms, pitiless one-liners, whip-snapping wit, cool plotting and harshly humorous narratives. None – not yet – can match her flip lip.

The poetic territory *Short Haul Engine* staked out is once again on view in Solie's very fine sophomore effort, *Modern and Normal* (2005). While nothing in the book strikes me as a bold departure, the new poems show her in fighting trim, holding forth in her signature key of flinty reflection. More than ever Solie places the highest value on what works; methods that in the first book seemed chanced-upon are now used in full knowledge of their effectiveness. As a result, her poems, already remarkable for cutting to the chase, now test the very adhesion of their syntax as they dodge dull formulations ('The trouble's not the tear-down,/it's the stall of afters when our hands hang') or cleanly and swiftly secure the mood of a milieu ('Open liquor./Open road. The bars do well, blinking sleepless/in the scrub') before resuming the hairpin curves of their action.

One of the secrets of Solie's unique phrasing is its economy of scale. The poems are constructed out of bite-size vignettes held together by an argot that is musically full and exactingly flensed. As a result, her lines are brisk, direct and comfortable in the mouth. While this kind of clever-casual soliloquizing is easy to find these days (Matt Rader and Nick Thran are two examples), Solie has a surer sense of its potential than most poets. 'Pricked by a whim, we blew town/with something like intent' is not exactly plain-spoken, but Solie's skill is to make it seem as though it were, as if such phrasing could slip into conversation. But that alone wouldn't be enough to make us notice her poems. Solie's real gift lies in the way her mainstream patter connects with real-time sensibilities. She specializes in slang summing-ups that capture our cultural mood with seismographic accuracy. Take the title. By using 'modern' to refer to our present de-resonated condition – its air of aftermath, of having outlived its best occasions – and 'normal' as the ironic gloss, Solie serves up a crisp motto for a felt historical lack. How does she do it? How does she so unfailingly find zeitgeist-riding sounds? Short answer: by rejecting sentimentality. Nothing remarkable there. What is remarkable is the sophistication behind her arias of anti-sentimentality, though that requires a longer answer.

In Solie's poetry, no *mea culpa* is so painful that it can't start on the fly: 'I lied about the shortcut, the high road,/all of it'. This admission occurs early in *Modern and Normal*, and its terseness is entirely in character: Solie will come clean, but won't gab. The phrase 'all of it' curtly packages that attitude, even if it's really the line-break – and the unmistakable stress it places on 'all' – that gives those three flat words their implication. We get the sense of a mind toughly at ease with its own ambivalence, and, more significantly, of an aesthetic bored by the easy enumeration of sins. Solie's distinctive tones involve precisely these brassy speech rhythms – her's is a voice that lights up when it touches down on bedrock sounds like 'all of it'. I won't pretend to feel guilty for my behaviour, her speakers announce. And I can't be bothered to wear everything on my sleeve.

It takes a special poet to wring such complexity from monosyllables most ears would have dismissed as ephemera. In fact, Solie does amazing things with the mundane content of much that we say: the empty statements, slack yakking, conversational filler – all of which she transforms into epiphanies of compression: 'Spring ahead, fall back. It all works out'; or 'So what? I tried. So what'; or (my favourite) 'Home,/home'. Solie's great insight in *Modern and Normal* is how an identifiable attitude can be encoded in the tiniest shifts of tone. The hard-nosed reverb of these phrases recalls dozens of similar effects in *Short-Haul Engine* (when a bruised-up waitress appears in 'Alert Bay, Labour Day' Solie's reaction is swift: 'Walls here/are made of luck and the girls/walk into them').

Modern and Normal consolidates this point-blank voice, distributing it among heroines who are always ready to face facts. There's the seasoned sexual assertiveness of 'One Night Stand' ('I'm known in certain corners/as a real live wire, tireless booster/of the last one standing'), the regret-weary optimism of 'Science and the Single Girl' ('All things find a purpose/in the end, even the done-for,/done-in') and the self-reproachful self-portraitist ('Doesn't play well with others. Tries hard'). What emerges isn't a feminist position so much as a shadow side identity: undeceived, candid, cunning. When Solie gets this alter-ego moving in step with the caustic properties of her language, the results dazzle. A first-rate example is 'Cardio Room, Young Women's Christian Association':

You won't know me. Any resemblance
to the woman I was is purely
agricultural. That fluff. A pink annual
given to low-born intemperate acts
unbecoming a modern person. No more.
I'm tough. Nothing
could eat me. No profligate billy
with a hacking cough, or that old goat
and his yen for plagues, floods and burning
fun places to the ground. Not you,
either. There was a time
I rolled like dough, plumped up
to be thumped down with artless yeasty
chemistry. Dumpling. Honeybun.
I sickened some. But evolved
in a flash, like the living flak
of a nuclear mistake. In space-age fabrics
I've moved more iron than a red
blood cell, climbing and climbing
the new world's dumbest tower. I'm on
to this. Alongside the rest
I sweat it out with the smug one-party
affability of a sport utility vehicle.
Deceptively little cargo space.
Even covered in mud I look great.

Solie is a zealot of snappy comebacks. She loves the sonic energies released by curses, rants and all manner of go-to-hell palaver. Of course, it's rarely as one-note as that; Solie can wax lyrical with the best of them. But to a good extent the freshness of *Modern and Normal* comes from verbal aggression, and the way Solie uses it to conjure proxies – to create, as it were, Angry Young Women. In the above poem, Solie builds her 'modern person' (literally so, it seems) around the modern-day obsession with body image. The dream of the pin-up is being rejected in favour of a very different cover girl: uppity, disputatious and threat-issuing. (Solie's voice has some of the swagger of

Angela Carter's dismissal of Elizabeth Smart's lachrymose classic *By Grand Central Station I Sat Down and Wept* – 'By Grand Central Station I Tore Off His Balls would be more like it', Carter once growled). This is not a spiritual makeover: The speaker isn't the slightest bit interested in learning how to be a presence in the world or trying to connect with a more universal human experience. She wants to be 'tough'. The archetype of the powerless, fey poetess is being cardioed into something buff and ready. We can see it happening before our eyes. As the speaker blisters her (male?) interlocutor, the fast-changing notes break into virtuosity: 'There was a time/I rolled like dough, plumped up/to be thumped down with artless yeasty/chemistry'. The aural whimsy and adjectival capering of this simile show a poet excited by the words she uses, who sees their multiple meanings and feels their weight and texture. These are also the lines of a poet attempting to pull from Canadian speech – which too often has kept a civil tongue in its head – a different kind of music: a music of coiled-up pugnacity and knowing menace. 'You won't know me' thus becomes a disguised credo, a caveat of generational contrariness. Solie, one might say, is giving a post-Atwood, post-Crozier, post-Zwicky finger to the norm.

A fuller account of the compelling oddity of her work, with its theme of a 'modern' shape-shift, also needs to touch on her deft reversals of gender expectations. Sloughing off a sense of self with its 'resemblance/to the woman I was' requires role-playing, and Solie offers readers a sound-centred entry into a male world of brooders, loners and misanthropes – a world in which the right accent, and not just attitude, is the access-point. What we have is a kind of linguistic cross-dressing, or demotic drag. And no matter how Chandleresque the cant, Solie can speak it as well as any clan member. Indeed, Solie's tough women sound more like tough men than the men do. 'Not everything you look at/is something', or 'Glued together with rye, or blow, or glue,/we are a regular family', or 'If there was an asshole alive,/I knew him' – or this poem, called 'Watch Your Head':

> So what? I tried. So what. Retained the use of my hands,
> a Scandinavian appreciation for the well-executed
> blindside, and the rest came back gradually. I haven't

> learned a thing. Like the man who thought a drive would do
> him good; the row had been dreadful. Instead of sticking
> to the straightaway he turned left and fell in love
> with a barmaid at the Keno parlour in Morinville.
> Or the one, down seven bills to a Tompkins VLT,
> who slunk out to get the gun, returned, and with a muttered
> *stand aside*, sighting clean on the display, shot
> the fiend to shit. Who sank into a chair then, double-barrel
> on his lap, and waited out the cops and his cronies
> gathered round the wreck trailing their own criminal
> pasts, hissing *Way to go Stan. Way to go.*

Solie has the chops for this sort of jab-at-the-world syntax. That being said, we should remember that this is scarcely her 'natural' voice. It's a performance. If the poet takes obvious pleasure in her skill at getting it right it's no doubt because such virile language is so culturally determined. Solie's success thus flaunts a provocative idea: idiom – not gender – is fate. Women are fated to sound like women because of the idiom they write in. Women, you might even say, are female impersonators. By choosing a different idiom, Solie's poems choose a different fate. 'Watch Your Head' bears this out. With its theme of psychological deadlock and its image of a stymied Stan sitting beside a mown-down VLT, the poem wittily deheroicizes the macho id (embodied by that lovely desperado mutter: 'stand aside'). The voice, however, leaves no clue as to its sexual category; the pronoun 'I' is all-purpose. Yet the fourteen-liner turns on a fascinating irony: a female poet who finds inspiration in masculine capers. 'I haven't/learned a thing' Solie tells us, and then quips a case in point: 'Like the man who …' That 'like' is the audible sign of a larger ambition: to strip away all details related to a socially specified self. Or more precisely, seeing herself mirrored in a story of low-level thuggery is a bid against separatist taxonomies, a rejection of anything that threatens to ghettoize women poets into a group capable of speaking only to themselves.

As an act of creative free will, it's convincing, but I can't help think that it also accounts for her poetry's unassuageable anxieties, the unease that causes her best deadpan moments to quiver with below-the-waterline emotional activity. Solie escapes the expectations of a female poet only to step into a looking-glass universe that reflects her back to herself as an alien. And the shorthand for this are speakers who always seem to fit into the world a little funny. She seems to tacitly acknowledge as much when she confesses to a just-jilted lover in 'More Fun in the New World' that 'When I said so long/I meant that I don't understand modern manners or the solar system/or anything. That a crucial lesson/didn't take'. Behaving badly is one of poetry's most shopworn subjects. But a femme fatale – someone, that is, who not only depicts her unfeminine coldness as a consequence of a 'crucial lesson' that 'didn't take' but gives it the glamour of criminality – is a new turn for a Canadian poet. Susan Musgrave came closest in *A Man to Marry, a Man to Bury* (1970), but her gypsy-witch fantasies, with their notion of taming men through spells, is also the sort of thing Solie seems determined to reject. How else describe using low-life strivers on the wrong side of the law (or at least astride the line) to capture the female psyche at the start of the twenty-first century? It is, to say the least, ballsy.

Backed into a corner and disappearing behind cigarette smoke: this is Solie's most cherished pose. Of course, she's plenty capable of writing cynical poems that depend on something other than pulp personas (see 'Everything's Okay', 'Under the Sun', 'The Problem of Heart Failure', 'Untitled', 'Larking'). But range is something Solie clearly struggles with, as her formal reach sometimes suffers interference from her fixations. She has no end of tolerance for guttersnipes and riff-raff, and their world of empty bars, doomed trysts and dead-end streets. She is in thrall to life as it might be (she imagines) lived in that world: hopped-up and low-wattage. Each of her poems does its bit to project this woebegoneness. In fact, it's difficult not to mark, with some dismay, that she will use almost any opportunity to settle into the quick-thinking, self-mocking cheerlessness she has been praised for. If there are glum hints in the air, Solie will zero in on them.

Complaints, at first blush, seem churlish; any lines picked at random will exhibit the rich satisfactions of her repartee. 'By winter, what had passed between them/had done so, leaving evidence of the glitch winking/glib as a stripped screw'. And there you have it: the Fall writ small. The taut, abrupt elegance belongs entirely to Solie (the compression of 'glib as a stripped screw' is exquisite). Yet the achievement is won in defeat. So fearful is she of compromising her rhetorical strengths that atmosphere is imposed at the expense of thought. To believe that 'despair/is in the details' is one thing, but to write poem after poem imprisoned by such refrains – with the speakers awarded little more than the traits essential to their ennui-expressing roles – is quite another. The difficulty with *Modern and Normal* isn't that Solie is self-consciously stoical; the difficulty is that, too often, she is exactly that and nothing more. It's as if the poems were transcripts of some B-movie with plot lines cribbed from a school-of-hard-knocks catalogue. 'You Never Know' (the punchy title, unsurprisingly, is one of her tics) concludes in typical fashion:

> And then what. You've seen it all
> until everything forsworn, some gorgeous
> hitch, drifts in like a front, blows you down
> like a barn. No matter
> that your bush league crime sprees, elopements
> and artistic retreats all end in the same cheap
> Niagara Falls motel room with a case of the jumps
> and a wan motto: no one was supposed
> to get hurt. Because we do. And turn up sooner
> or later just like you, in a tip like this
> on the wrong side of supper time, a gamer,
> and the rest of your life before you. No really.

Solie's efficiency puts pressure on every word she uses, brewing a potent telegraphese: 'drifts in like a front, blows you down/like a barn', 'a case of the jumps/and a wan motto', 'on the wrong side of supper time'. In these examples we see the classic hard-boiled influence. Not quite minimalist, but scoured free of poeticisms, and never padded. Yet the lean lucidity is depthless, two-dimensional; a stereotype of anti-sentimentality. And the trouble here is the trouble throughout. Solie treats her unladylike bon mots as the organic accretions of an emotional and psychological state. It's a risky tactic, as there comes a point when, despite our delight in her flair for the lapidary quip, we begin to ask whether a genuine sensibility is on offer or just the sound of one being rehearsed.

The one-laconicism-fits-all trick is no doubt hugely tempting for Solie since it comes with some nicely grim themes (life is a futile bid to hold things together, relationships are neither pleasant nor meaningful, tenderness is the flip side of debasement, etc.). But as a result, Solie ends up saying interestingly disagreeable things that don't always have the sincerity of a mind actually reacting to the world: the feeling zones seem faked. 'Pull yourself together', advises Solie. 'Years are neither kind/nor cruel. You drag on'. I see her point, but the problem is that kind of message can be made plausible without being true. All art selects and invents evidence for its biases. But *Modern and Normal*'s bleak gestalt strikes me more as enforced-by-Solie than as a window on the world. Our own adventures are more various, more unpredictable, more intrinsically bound up in everyday difficulties and pleasures. Yet quotidian evocations are furthest removed from the gritty textures Solie prizes. And the offshoot of her obsessiveness – judging by poems like 'Pest Song', 'Pastoral', 'Lucky' and 'Seven Days' – is a stylized distortion, a governing dysphoric bias born not of experience but of stage-managed artistic choices.

Maybe Solie's nihilistic *mise en scènes* seem exactly right to some. Maybe it's just one of those moods I find hard to get into (a variant of 'that "poetic" attitude' William Logan describes in *Desperate Measures* 'that makes poetry more depressing than daily life'). Whatever the case, it would be grossly unfair to Solie to represent her methods and measures as ready-made. Her love of grunge melancholia, although extended to a second book, hasn't stopped other inspiration from grabbing hold. Technical terms ('Hard/science lay fossilled in the scree: evolution,/cosine, fault'), found poems (mined from a range of textbooks, including meteorology and algebra) and keyed-up premises (like a breathless fourteen-liner on gopher hunting) now enter Solie's creative ken. A growing penchant for fresh associative tacks is plainly (if not singingly) displayed in certain poems: the gist-nestling ambiguities of 'Larking', the kinky Gothic of 'Determinism' or the hallucinatory figurations of 'Meeting Walter Benjamin'. All three are standout pieces in which crabwise lineation and grammar create a highly personalized sense of the world.

Indeed, Marianne Moore's remark about having the courage of one's idiosyncrasies sits well on Solie, and no more so than in 'Thrasher', which, taking the North American songbird as its subject, captures the deracinated anxiety of an urban contact with nature. Feelings of disconnectedness are conveyed by technologized pastoral images (the creature's call as 'the vinyl scratch/between tracks, a splice point), offbeat words ('urks', 'scrip', 'fledge'), a fitful use of couplets and a jittery syntax that causes the writing to pick up details in flashes, out of the corner of its eye ('brown degrees/scriven by road allowance cut at right angles through shriven/weeds'). 'Thrasher' is Solie's attempt to do her thing another way; to flex her trademark mettle into a new shape. This chance-taking also extends to poems where her astringency has been switched on but carries a different psychic charge. 'Under the Sun', for example, touches a rock-bottom aesthetic candour:

> Rain is the merging of cool air with
> warm under general conditions of humidity. Try to remember
> it has nothing to do with love
> or grief.

These opening lines are terrific: their bluntness clears the air of make-believe and whimsy and, at the same time, robs the emerging poem of any alibi. If we can't regard a bit of precipitation as an occasion for sad thoughts, what's left? What indeed. So much of our poetry depends on mostly-unexamined sentimental and ideological premises, making Solie's straight-talk, and its promise of reality un-spin-doctored, a kind of anti-poetry. It's further confirmation that *Modern and Normal* represents a shift in Canadian poetry; that alongside Solie's pragmatic sketching of bars, cafés and other demimonde theatres (as in the concrete, steel and glass 'vicinities' of David O'Meara's poetry) is a new counter-transcendental mindset. Solie's game, spiritually speaking, is to play for the lowest stakes:

This is the consolation of philosophy:
it's out of our hands. The business of bars
and stores, our separate beds, the garbaged
offices of alleyways, is aging. It sighs
in the blood like salt, slows us, and is why
our hearts are heaviest on the moment of
waking: the weight we ferry, the fright,
the long vowel opening at the centre
of a consonant world that draws the hurt up,
an empty bowl

'Under the Sun' is cast, as many of Solie's poems are, in the form of a dressing-down, and the specific enemy seems the humanistic vocabularies that Canadian poets write in; the tendency – call it pathetic fallacy, anthropomorphism, what have you – to infuse cosmologies with feeling by connecting them with the sentimentally human (viz. Sue Sinclair's *Secrets of Weather and Hope*). 'Under the Sun' is drawn to ways of looking at the universe that avoid putting human beings at the centre of it, that respect the 'Private lives of insects/and the single notes that move them'. By squaring the vast geological past ('the molecular ache of land/as it cooled') against the frivolously literary ('tears'), Solie tries to expose how certain events predispose us to words like 'love' and 'grief'. The irony, of course, is that the more she insists on a scientific universe, the more personal her subtext becomes: 'We are lonely. We/are here'.

Nevertheless, Solie's insistence on describing human affairs from a great distance is one the most characteristic aspects of her chilly word choices. 'Parallax', for instance, closes on a lonely vision of a famished, never-named animal 'with alpha nose or acute eyes that know this place/as it is'. The sting of that 'as it is' – like the 'all of it' from earlier – is intended, it seems, as a rejection of lyric utterance, delivered with all the finality of a slammed door. It is as though Solie refuses to show more that she can really feel. And indeed, when we factor in the poem's ending ('There are no themes. Just this creature only what/it is, whatever that may be. I can't tell from here') we glimpse a poet who comes into her own at precisely the point her language stops cosseting the ego, the point it stops being 'nice'. A not-nice style, however, requires a cool head. The care demanded of words when they reach that suddenly-lethal point is summed up best by something I would imagine Solie is familiar with: the first two rules for handling firearms. One, treat all guns as if they're loaded. Two, never point a gun at anything you aren't willing to kill or destroy:

> The shock is that it took
> so long, this trajectory played out
> in a fizzle towards the words
> I understand. By suppertime
> on the first day of what's left, the stock
> of a small bore .22 fits smartly
> at the shoulder. Home,
> home. Suppose this is it. Loaded,
> levelled. A rote stance
> squared off to the fence
> and the trash set up there. Empties.
> Their cylindrical shadows lie
> uneasily upon the ragweed. This
> is the man-made moment. Extension
> of the arm, the eye, the mind's
> follow-through to an end
> in shards. The clap and recoil
> of continuity cracked. Air torn
> like a letter through the middle of
> before and after.

Calling this 'An Argument for Small Arms', Solie uses flattened sentence-fragments to make the case that although poetry is a tool we use to extend ourselves, its value has nothing to do with channelling pain, empathy or morality. Poetry, rather, is the perfect crystallization of a poet's skill and intention – like the shattering 'man-made moment' precision shooting makes possible: 'the mind's/follow-through to an end/in shards'. It bears mentioning that rifles – specifically .22's –

crop up throughout *Modern and Normal* (some of these poems were also previously published in a chapbook called *The Shooter's Bible*). Solie's firearm fetish calls to mind Carl Sandburg's 'Iron' ('Guns,/long, steel guns'), or Henry Reeds' 'Naming of the Parts' ('the bolt,/And the breech and the cocking-piece') or Keith Douglas's 'Vergissmeinnicht' ('The frowning barrel of his gun/overshadowing'). True to form Solie ignores the testosterone fine print of this sub-genre and instead uses her gunplay to invoke ideas of markswomanship – Canadian poetry's own 'Little Sure Shot', one might say. Certainly it seems an apt metaphor for poems that spit out their words like so many bullets, verbal sallies that always hit their mark.

A straight-shooting poetic is clearly what Solie subscribes to, and 'An Argument for Small Arms' nails down its terms: how sound is its hook; how its standard materials are two- and three-syllable words bundled into lines that are emphatically enjambed; how its forms are simple, light-boned, but rugged; how although mostly free-verse, it builds its moments around distinctive patterns that use natural pauses and phrase groupings to mask the intricacy of its cadences (so that two casual sentences like 'Loaded,/levelled. A rote stance/squared off to the fence' are in fact a fully-turned union of consonance, alliteration and internal rhyme); and how it is especially good at loading its lilts, at embedding feelings even in the feather-touch of a comma. You never have to look very far to see it. Everywhere in *Modern and Normal* Solie gives her sneer its subtlety by processing her anger into understated climaxes of diction, with the result that the most ordinary words can find themselves weaponized. A good example is 'Nice':

> *I think I'm kind of two-faced. I'm very ingratiating.*
> *It really kind of annoys me. I'm just sort of a little too*
> *nice. Everything is Oooo.* – DIANE ARBUS

Still dark, but just. The alarm
kicks on. A voice like a nice hairdo,
sprayed. *People, get ready*
for another nice one. Low 20s,
soft breeze stroking through, ridge

of high pressure settling nicely.
Songbirds swallowing, ruffling,
starting in. Does anyone curse
the winter wren, calling in Christ's name
for just one bloody minute of silence?
Of course not. They sound nice.
I pull away and he asks why I can't
be nicer to him. Well,
I have to work, I say, and wouldn't it be nice
if someone made some money today?
Very nice, he quavers, rolling
his face to the wall. A nice face.
A nice wall. We agreed on the green
down to hue and shade straight away.
That was a very nice day.

One half of a mutually bitter twosome has just piped up. We recognize her instantly: her *isolato* vowel-modulations, her acoustics of dissatisfaction – it's the voice of a young woman burdened with a checkered past: the case-history is in her cadence. Solie is very good at activating undertones, and here uses a unique technique to both express and create a lacklustre love affair. By repeating 'nice' over and over Solie demonstrates the force that can accrue when repetition progressively darkens a word's definition and, in turn, the poem's mood (Stevie Smith's 'Pretty' does something very similar). From the first stirrings of sarcasm ('voice like a nice hairdo,/sprayed') to the barely-held-back biliousness at the end, the poem speaks two ways at once. The ending is especially satisfying for its penultimate delay on 'straight away', then the final line with its rhyme ('very nice day') tiptoeing after to devastating effect. One even senses with that last 'nice' – and the Arbus quote helps signal this angle to us – Solie's goal to let her truculence hiss like acid into the world. Poetry becomes a quest to undo life, to poison its health.

There is nothing quite like this in Canadian poetry. You might think you spot resemblances, but Solie is unlike her metropolitan, clubland sisters (Lynn Crosbie, Evelyn Lau, Sheri-D Wilson) who write poems that cling defensively to certain in-group signals. Her mordant, ultra-nimble version of this lingua franca not only strikes a different nerve, but makes other poetry in that mode sound bland by contrast. For all these reasons Solie, from her standing start, looks poised for the long run. Where she'll end up is anybody's guess. But at the moment her success is our success. We have become the very readers a poet like her needs: quick on the uptake, unafraid of audible music, aroused by quirks, impatient with 'oooo'. Having gatecrashed our literary consciousness with *Short-Haul Engine*, Solie's *Modern and Normal* once again leaves decorum trailing in its wunderkind wake. 'Screw precedent', she says. Sounds good to me.

ANNE SZUMIGALSKI

CANADIAN POETRY's he-man tradition – Acorn, Layton, Newlove, Nowlan – has made us desperate for literary mothers, and until her death in 1999, Anne Szumigalski was exactly that. Editor-nurturer extraordinaire, her devotion to younger poets drew on the caretaking skills she developed in Europe before moving to Saskatoon in 1956 (English by birth, she worked with British Red Cross during the Second World War). A mainstay of Saskatchewan's literary community, her quiet, airy poems – collected in 15 books, some award-winning – made her an odd presence among her noisier, huskier contemporaries.

Her first book, *Woman Reading in Bath*, was her best. Published in 1974, when she was 52, the collection was written in swaths of unpunctuated, feathery free verse, and remains uncategorizable. Grandmothers, mothers, little girls and childhood friends had recurring roles in Blakean dream-visions where the actual and fantastical were constantly switching places. Violence, aggression, even murder were always close at hand and treated with unsettling tenderness. Szumigalski proved especially adept at conveying psycho-sexual mysteries through pared, precise images (a gift she pushes to unforgettable effect in her much-anthologized, corpse-narrating-from-the grave monologue 'Victim'). The result was the vision of a world that was cherished as much for its discomfort as for its beauty ('I want to arrange the crabseeds/So as to resemble/Some kind of disorder'). The originality Szumigalski was discovering seemed considerable.

Alas, it was an originality that, except for a brief flowering in the 1983 collection *Doctrine of Signatures*, remained untapped. The writing stayed reverent and associatively ample, but a growing addiction to drifting evocation meant that she never found a voice stable enough to help her myth-making hit, and keep, its stride. Szumigalski's poems often sat rather loosely on the page, and although she was never afraid to raise the larger questions, one rarely got the sense that she was able to fit whatever she had to say inside the space in which she had to say it.

But even if bad habits kept her talent in check, her books revealed habits of perception idiosyncratic enough to enliven even the weakest of her poems – which, as it happens, made more frequent appearances. By the time of *Voices* (given the Governor General's award in 1995), her work had largely dissolved into rapturous vapidity. This was plain when her selected work appeared in 1997, and readers, reacquainted with the superlative earlier work, realized the extent to which she had diluted the tougher, eerier dramas of her poems.

A reacquaintance is again in order with *When Earth Leaps Up* (2006). Six years after her last posthumous book, *Fear of Knives*, executor Mark Abley dusts off another clutch of uncollected material. It's a well-edited book, though I could have done with fewer moments of overacted sadness. (Szumigalski's death, Hilary Clark tells us in her preface, 'left a hole in the Saskatchewan writing community that will never be filled'.) No new masterpieces are to be found here, nor any promising departures the poet didn't live long enough to pursue.

But while there's no poem as weird and frightening as 'It Wasn't a Major Operation' or 'Shrapnel', Szumigalski's signature strengths are out in force: a brisk ruefulness; fascinating, sense-altering word choices; a pagan awe at nature. Szumigalski excelled in parables of transformation – sexual awakenings, coming of age, rites of passage. And Abley includes some here, though with Szumigalski's idea of life 'abiding in a tiny mouthful/of sharp teeth', there's a touch more fear in her tone, a touch more unpreparedness in the face of sensed menace. Many poems have that catch-as-catch-can appeal of unfinished (and now unfinishable) drafts, but occasionally details thicken into note-perfect Delphic arias:

> for your comfort
> I bring a saltglazed pot

with thornbranch growing
blossoms still furled
in the spiked stem's black nipples

This is classic Szumigalski: enjambment as a delicate bending, and the arrhythmic heartbeat of cadence. Szumigalski might well have cringed at the idea of these drafts of poems appearing in print, but the poems do everything right that her best poems did. They also do what they did wrong: hoary romanticisms, New-Ageish over-amplifications, prose poems where the form seems nothing more than a symbol-evoking indirection device.

The cut-short context of this book, however, is important to keep in mind when making any complaints, and common-sense dictates that I point to standouts such as 'When I Think of Him …', 'It's Morning', 'Rowan in May', 'Hadrian's Dream', 'Yggdrasil and Dried Fruits and Herbs – An Autumn Basket', all of which are enough to make this book a keepsake.

In this Age of Glib, *When Earth Leaps Up* is a tonic. There are no slick quick fixes in Szumigalski's poetry. What you'll find, instead, is a reaching-out for what we used to called 'wisdom' – a tactile word-touching of abstractions that manage to get deeply at the strangeness and complexity of our lives. Szumigalski added something new to Canadian poetry, and this book is as good a place as any to find out what it was.

PETER TROWER

CRACK OPEN *The Cambridge Companion to Canadian Literature* (2004) to 'Poetry' and David Staines will give you the skinny. You'll learn about ur-pioneer Susanna Moodie, post-confederation poets and Louis Dudek. You'll learn about the modernist shakeup in Montreal, West Coast poetry and Al Purdy. You'll learn about Margaret Atwood's political themes, bpNichol and the postmodern vibe of the prairies. Summaries of this sort are hard to do well, and Staines packs an impressive amount of official wisdom into eighteen pages. His stocktaking is rather low on new details, but such jobs are often defended on the half-a-loaf principle: a bare outline is better than no outline at all.

But can such a principle also be used to defend unexceptional prose and thinking starved of intellectual verve? In sentence after sentence of Staine's entry we get the sense of a bored mind running in place, leaving things exactly as it finds them. Michael Ondaatje? His poems 'suggest a breaking down of traditional boundaries between genres'. Patrick Lane? He 'investigates the male ethos' and 'draw[s] moral conclusions about mankind's inhumanity'. These ideas may still be buzz items among CanLit's commentating classes, but to an implicated reader – deep in the fray of it and eager for fresh insight – Staines comes across as a modern-day Medici of bland, much-recycled truisms. Discussing how, for example, Robert Kroetsch 'fashions a complex archeological metaphor out of autobiography' is the equivalent of having no opinion. It's the default position, and by unwaveringly embracing the safety of such positions – safe because they stick to clichés likely to be unchallenged – academics like Staines have made themselves worthless to us.

None of this would matter much, except that few moments in Canadian poetry have been hungrier for the future, its newness and potential, than the present. 'A shakedown is in the works', is how Ken Babstock put it, 'a kind of peer-directed reckoning of who's where and what's what'. With such revisionism in the air, the appearance of any serene, settled perspective is a kind of mental decadence. And so recent books by pooh-bahs like Sam Solecki and W.H. New only confirm what has already become distressingly clear: the tenured world is ill-fitted for this era of change. What does it mean to publish, as Solecki has, a pair of docile studies on overhyped poets like Michael Ondaatje (*Ragas of Longing*) and Al Purdy (*The Last Canadian Poet*) or to publish, as New has, an encyclopedic run-through of our high points (*A History of Canadian Literature*) that excludes Don Coles, Richard Outram, Eric Ormsby and Charles Bruce? It means you aren't working first-hand, that you've no interest in the grassroots energies of your subject and no nose for finding its groundbreaking moments. In the middle of the last century, Northrop Fry's insights caught, and shaped, the emerging careers of Atwood, Layton and Reaney. E.K. Brown and Desmond Pacey's books were indispensable for anyone who needed to make sense of our then-surging poetry. And today? Today the professoriat's main contribution to twenty-first century Canadian poetry has been to ignore its shifting-and-developing complexity. The reassessments increasingly on display in *CNQ* or *Arc* hold no thrill for Staines & Co. They see literature as still-life, not sea-change. This is why a hard-mouthed, independent, belletristic criticism – what R.P. Blackmur dubbed 'the formal discourse of an amateur' – is more vital than ever. We need to return our poetry to a condition of singularity and strangeness, and success depends on full-time 'amateurs' willing to brandish the idiosyncrasies, even perversities, of their biases. From their mettlesome reviews it's clear poets like Jason Guriel, Michael Lista, Shane Neilson and Zach Wells have made this project the very engine of their criticism.

If an underdog is what these knuckly Grub Streeters need, a poet in perpetual endgame against the status quo, they could scarcely do better than Peter Trower. It doesn't hurt, either, that in an era of staid and sedentary existences, Trower's got a great story. Born 1930 in England, he loses his test-pilot father to a plane crash and moves to Vancouver at age ten with mother and brother. Eight years later, needing cash, he drops out of school and signs up at a logging camp. For two decades he risks life and limb along the province's heavily timbered fjords, rising from whistlepunk (a signalman, often the youngest on a crew) to rigging slinger (second-in-command, he picked out the logs to set chokers on). In the face of conditions so punishing you'd think they would have asphyxiated any writerly ambition, poems begin pouring forth in the 1950s. After his first book appears in 1969, he calls it quits to pursue a 'dream of songs and stories'. What greets him next is easy enough to guess. Some poets have a knack for delivering their product in an especially mesmeric way. Their work leaps out of the pack, gets people talking, finds a sort of fame. Trower, alas, was not one of those poets. Now entering its third decade, his career is still off to a slow start. This despite the tireless devotion of two publishers – Harbour and Ekstasis – who together have given him thirteen books, including three novels.

Yet things are improving, if slightly. British Columbia's George Woodcock Lifetime Achievement Award in 2002 was the first hint of a turnaround (previous winners are Phyllis Webb, Audrey Thomas and P.K. Page), and in 2005 the CAA prize, in delightful unexpectedness, hoisted him high on its shoulders. Trower has, to be sure, a fiercely loyal cadre of West Coast fans, but he's pretty much unknown to general readers of Canadian poetry, and is absurdly underrated by those who pretend to know the subject well (he doesn't make Staines and New's cut; and you can bet Solecki isn't devoting his next treatise to him). Yet these prizes are, I think, the good tidings of a larger shift. We are witnessing the opening of a fissure in the complacency with which we have habitually regarded literary neglect. And *Haunted Hills & Hanging Valleys* (2004) is a bellwether of this new mood.

Trower's selected – all 157 unskippable pages of it – is also the first of his books to take seriously the quiet puzzlement he has triggered. Namely, is he a talent spurned or a figure too minor to fuss over? While this selected doesn't make the question go away, it performs, on behalf of his fans, the salutary function of making it a fair fight. And the credit for this, oddly enough, belongs less with the poems, which are indeed impressive, than with the exceptional eye that vetted their inclusion. At a time when readying a book for publication means nothing more than circling a few typos and begging for blurbs, *Haunted Hills & Hanging Valleys* testifies to the difference a good editor can make. Silas White's uncompromising sorting-out has powerfully focused the tendencies of Trower's career. The poems do exactly what they need to: take a big, reputation-defining leap into the contemporary scene, showing us the Trower everyone has missed.

And who, then, is this new-fangled Trower? Some previous reviews, such as Zach Well's incisive piece on *The Danforth* site, have hinted at the three reasons for his distinctiveness, as does Don McKay in the excellent foreword he contributes to the collection. The first thing that becomes clear is that he is one of the few poets of his generation to channel the flow of sumptuary colloquial English that courses from Chaucer to Clare through Hopkins and Hardy to Frost. This is one of the central traditions of English poetry, but it is rarer to find in Canadian literature than you might think (plain-style peers like Al Purdy and Patrick Lane have drawn on its phrasal and syntactic effects only intermittently). Trower embraces a natural diction, a talking voice; he writes a poetry primarily made in the mouth and abundant in sophisticated, phonemic arrangements ('Back slams the windfall/but this time/there is just enough slack/to unhook the choker'). This leads to the second reason for Trower's importance: the worn-fresh fluencies of his prosody have kept pace with, if not outraced, the trendier experiments that began alongside him. The leading poetry circle of the time – UBC's Tish group, founded in 1961 – was dedicated to the expressionist, 'open field' ideals of Black Mountain poets; ideals that, as he admitted in an interview, Trower set little store by:

> The big thing at the time was this stuff with no imagery that was just broken-up prose. I never could stand the goddamn stuff but it was all the rage back then. These days, some of those guys are friends of mine but then there was a schism. I sided with the guys who preferred the streets to the groves of academia. We were the outlaw poets.

One wonders if such a sneering, street-level rejection of the era's biggest literary trend made it easier to pigeonhole Trower's populist tendencies. Yet when you consider that colleagues like Milton Acorn, Alden Nowlen, Al Purdy and Patrick Lane were, at the time, running a very successful 'outlaw' franchise – defined by the way their verse strafed its targets with plain-as-dirt words – Trower's neglect becomes all the more intriguing. Despite close friendships with many of these poets and despite first-rate credentials (he sprang directly from the blue-collar experience he wrote about, but he cut out the intellectualizing middleman and went straight for the stark details), Trower was handed the short straw. Why? Were chasers, donkey pitchers, guthammers, caulk boots and crummies so far outside our poetry's ken that they appeared irretrievably provincial? Did he acquire a reputation for being unlettered by writing about the unlettered – the boasters, bullshitters and ne'er-do-wells he toiled alongside? The same species of men appeared in Acorn's poems, yet the acclaim that met Acorn eluded Trower.

Unable to build a convincing association with the pleb-poets whose popularity might have absorbed the stigma of his so-called coarseness, he was left out to dry. Reviewers were free to define his hard-nosed qualities according to a different class-system: he was seen as prone to obvious rhymes, trite diction and clumsy thoughts – and all this early enough in the game for the insults to stick. Had the same poems been credited to Purdy they surely would have seemed more plausible. Instead, poetical but never poetic enough, Trower's everyman guise egged readers to typecast him as an artless 'child of nature'. Literary neglect is, of course, a complex phenomenon, and the problems of reception run deep and in many directions. Yet an enduring sense of Trower's 'primitiveness' seems a good reason why doubts about him linger. We enjoy thinking of Acorn, Purdy and Lane as the Greeks to Canadian poetry's Rome: sensual, earthbound and authentic. Trower, however, stands with the Goths at the gate: wild, undisciplined and cacophonous.

Given the perception of him as clodhopping, it's not surprising we've lagged in recognizing Trower for what he is: a poet capable of remarkable beauty. The irony here is that to read him is to pursue the poetry's own primary action. It is a 'dropping out of school' into a world registered by newly-awakened senses. His best poems appeal in three ways. First, as live reportage, as spontaneous, open-minded noticings. Not only with regards to nature – a martin as 'a streamlined package of brown wariness', waves that 'lathered and leapt/lurched and crashed' – but also on the specific business of forest plundering: dead trees as 'hollow fire-gutted cedar shells/spiking up among the felled timber'; a faller who 'carries the powersaw casually like a suitcase'; or the 'rotten right-of-way-timber' and how 'no matter which way we undercut them/they keep dropping crooked and counter'. (Only a good poet would hear how 'crooked and counter' locks up the line.) Straight-talking and heavily reliant on aural effects, these poems are best defined as philistinism in love with precision. Second, there is something manically absorptive about them, the greed with which they soak up mood and detail. At times, he seems almost mineralized, half-transformed into the material of his labour ('In these aisles/in this trenched incredible quiet/I am one below summer/burning in the neutral wood').

Trower loves his job, its exposed-to-the-elements slog and shoptalk. He feels the wisdom of such a life on the pulses. The real test, therefore, is whether his craggy voice can touch readers who have never logged, who have never lived in the male-locked society it evokes. It can – powerfully. And therein lies Trower's third, and best distinction. He manages, in a different way from other poets, to dissolve the distance between poem and reader. It looks effortless, though it can't be. The following stanzas, taken from 'A Testament of Hills', have the stand-easy slanginess of a poet talking right at you:

It was riding those doodlebug planes
up craggy inlets –
bouncing through the airpockets
in gutgrabbing skips and hops
to land with queasy relief,
caulk boots and a duffle bag
at some forlornshack camp.

It was block breaking
with a spar-tree half raised –
the tree smashing back into the swamp –
part of the block whistling by your head
like angry shrapnel
and in your mouth, the rusty taste of death
for the first time.

It was trying to unhook floating logs
with greenhorn fingers
in the churning bullpen
of an A-frame show –
the hard-nosed engineer
bursting with laughter
each time you hit the shivering drink.

It was sometimes the inviting eyes
of a faller's wife
dangerous with discontent and townhunger,
bored with isolation and her new husband's
rough and seldom hands,
enticing reluctant chokerboys
into scared-stiff affairs.

If the action-footage here sounds more folk song than modernist (and bear in mind that, for Trower, Pound 'died in his own intellectual garbage' and Eliot succumbed to 'dryrot') it's because its chanting tempo implies a listener. Slick the poem is not. But accessible it certainly is, and the better for it. 'A Testament of Hills' originally appeared in Trower's second collection called *Between the Sky and the Splinters* published in 1974. The same year, incidently, that Tom Wayman assembled *Beaton Abbot's Got the Contract,* Canada's first small anthology of what he dubbed 'work poetry' written from 'the insider's perspective'. Trower didn't make it into the book, but an 'insider's perspective' is exactly what he brings to his poetry. His portrayals of backbreaking, often brutish forest sojourns are hyperkinetic in ways that can't be faked. This is all the more remarkable given the coarse palate he draws on for his visual effects. Purdy and Lane attempted similar effects, of course, but Trower's abrasiveness cleaves to a descriptive idiom that, while not *sui generis*, belongs uniquely to him ('part of the block whistling by your head/like angry shrapnel/and in your mouth, the rusty taste of death/for the first time').

But more than just capturing the adrenalin of grunt work, Trower's poems are also brusquely tender. The unillusioned straightforwardness of the 'faller's wife/dangerous with discontent' is just one example; his poetry is abrim with hundreds of similarly sad, human moments. Trower's achievement flows from his refusal to retreat into a turtle shell of indifference. For all his stoic machismo, he strives for the simplest, most sensation-rich terms to pin down the hardscrabble reality of coastal camps. He wants to include everything, especially the language fussier poets snub ('gutgrabbing', 'bursting with laughter', 'scared-stiff'). Our poetry has long cherished the local, but I can think of few Canadian poets who have identified themselves so strongly with a specific place; and none who have tried to preserve, in colloquially airborne speech, the goings-on of such a deprived and depriving working-class world, and the half-journeyed days of its citizens.

Low-life odysseys have always been a factor in the tall tales that loggers included in their verse. A spinoff of alehouse ballads, the logger poem turned hard luck stories into something brisk and wry. It was not preoccupied with style. It had no notions of how 'good' poetry should sound. You sung it merely to keep evenings lively around a shanty stove. And as North American oral traditions go, it's old. The earliest known example, a short jingle called 'Lines Upon the Death of Two Young Men', appeared in a Maine newspaper in 1815. But logging dates back even further. Timber began to be stripped in the 1600s, in New England, to create charcoal for iron-smelting. It's easy to imagine that even for those who took part in the bygone days of this industry, before its big westward push, isolation was rife and recitation a sanity-saving necessity. Early sailors were tested in similar ways by their gruelling open-ocean trips, which explains why a sailing chorus provided the template for the great nineteenth-century anthem 'The Lumberman's Alphabet'. It begins: 'A is for axes that you may all know;/And B is for boys that make them all go;/C is for choppers so early begun/And D is for danger we often stand in'.

As it happens, this quatrain neatly packages the salient details – axes, boys, danger – of Trower's oeuvre. Indeed, you might say he has assembled his own alphabetary to the 'gyppos' that crowded BC's waterways and inlets. Of course, the hugely popular Robert Swanson – also from Vancouver, and a protegé of Yukon poet Robert Service – deserves mention as a precursor. Writing during the 1940s and '50s, his logging poems are still admired on both sides of the border. But as Trower has respectfully pointed out, Swanson's minstrelsy created a 'storybook place' of hard work and hard-won wisdom. While such sentimentalized heroism defines a great deal of the bunkhouse repertoire, Trower's own poetry stops short of any eyes-raised worship of this 'woods kingdom'. It plainly sees the 'drawbacks' (i.e., the 'bugs, hellish weather and wall-to-wall danger') and proposes a competing aesthetic, one where larger-than-life and lament are intimate with each other, and the claim of neither is compromised. A capital example is 'Early Shift':

At 4:30 am
by the ghostly gas station
a piece of silver paper
wind-scratching across the asphalt
is a noisy insect for the nerves.

I wait, unwillingly awake
with only a gutcan, a cigarette
and random thoughts for company.
The cops are all asleep with their guns.
The town lies ripe for the taking.

But I haven't a burglar's belly.
I'll help steal trees instead
from a hill that's warming up for me now.
By noon that bitch'll be hot enough
to make the devil sweat blood.

Across the last stars
three puny cloud-threads crawl.
Not a whisper of rain in those timid drifters.
They'll scatter like scared dogs
when the haymaker comes up.

It's time. Inescapably the crummy
trails its headlights
through the locked village
come to shanghai me once more
to a clockwork mountain.

These lines belong to a poet disabused of his frontier bravado but still obsessed with logging as a store of adventure and anecdote. He's a poet who writes by ear ('By noon that bitch'll be hot enough / to make the devil sweat blood') and thus is too erratic a technician to settle for traditional thumping rhythms. He prizes rigging crew dialect ('early shift', 'gutcan', 'crummy') but also needs a music less hidebound, less chauvinistic. He needs a music that can convey the bite of circumstance as well as smash through the patina of mass-produced style. He needs a music that can, as it were, 'feel' his feelings.

Because what's clear from 'Early Shift' – which functions as an EEG, an image-coded graph of a mind holding its breath right before the plunge into occupational drudgery – is that Trower is a far more ambivalent breed of troubadour than Swanson. Prey to qualms, his poems always scrutinize urges other logging poets embrace without reservation. Legends about the mighty, muscled, bellicose ur-logger Paul Bunyan – how at three-weeks old he rolled around so much in his sleep he knocked down five square miles of standing timber, or how he dug a few ponds for drinking water that we now call the Great Lakes – give a sense of logging poetry's penchant for outsize storytelling. Trower's no drooping lily, but he was coping with a very different story, one whose discontents fell slightly outside the signature themes of exceptional courage and victory against impossible odds (anyone 'unwillingly awake / with only a gutcan, a cigarette /

and random thoughts for company' isn't interested in singalongs). What choice was left except to take apart the logger poem and put it back together as a vessel that could accommodate his bafflement, anger and desolation? Even those of us unfamiliar with the stereotype Trower is rewriting will register at once that a norm has been jiggered. After all, it's in the music: the teeth-gritting way 'a piece of silver paper/wind-scratching across the asphalt' becomes 'a noisy insect for the nerves', or how words like 'shangai' and 'clockwork' are stamped with the sullenness of a self-divided consciousness.

Poems like 'Early Shift' (others include 'The Last Spar-Tree on Elphinstone Mountain', 'Booby Trap', 'Day to Day Blues', 'Hell's Gate' and 'Cinderwind') mark a shift in logger poetry away from workmanlike craftsmanship toward expressive unconventionality. Trower exchanges verbal airbrushing for a direct gaze at unpleasantness. Free of literary obligations, there's nothing to stop him from reading the forest as an almanac of vengefulness, where 'the season takes aim on us' and 'the woods hiss disappointment' after each narrow escape. Trower's unsettling close-ups (where even 'slugs move like severed yellow fingers') are thus a means of registering feeling as well as a way of seeing. In such a hostile environment he hears his own protest echoed everywhere ('saws will yammer their nagging dirge') and even weather darkens in sympathetic meteorological glower ('In the sinister season/the mountains pull down the rain'). The task of accurate description, you might even say, forced Trower inwards; logging, and its lethal landscape, became a spiritual staging-ground for fatal reckonings of the self.

Yet Trower seems, at times, sincerely worried about his bias for logging's *danse macabre*: 'What would my English uncles have said –/ those staid upstanding good and proper men', he asks. We'll never know, though Canadian poetry's 'good and proper men' have certainly had their revenge. Two generations of reviewers and academics have missed the innovatory aspects of Trower's work – the sophistication simmering under the sturdy, unpretending surface of its depiction – and have used his regional subject matter as proof of his genre status as a 'logging poet'. And what pigeonholing left for dead, misguided enthusiasm finished off. Ungenerous as it is to say, Trower aficionados have often taken delight in his booze-bottle-broad crudity. A genius of the genius loci is thus Bukowskied into a roughneck ruralist. Howard White, a fellow BC poet, has gone so far as to accuse hero-worshipping 'urban poets' of wanting to create an 'impossible fiction' about the working class, and loggers specifically. In 'These Here Poets' he complains about how:

> Canada Council gives em ten thousand bucks
> to write about what it's like
> to be a workingman
> cost you half a day's pay to buy it
> and here's all your own words
> all phonied up to sound like
> some fucking Okie or something

White has a point. We've all come across these 'phonied up' poems. And lately, with so many of our poets showboating a bias for ruggedness, it's hard not to feel Canadian poetry is being overrun by professional toughies. This is nothing new, of course. The working-class has been creatively revered ever since Virgil's *Georgics*. The difference is that today Joe ordinary is so fetishized for his authenticity that any poet who celebrates him regards himself as having touched the hem of a great profoundity. This is why we feel easy with Trower. By combining the two – labourer and lyricist – he embodies the nobility of common sense; he is artlessness incarnate. We forget, however, that there's nothing instinctive about true accessibility. We forget that comprehensible idioms are not intuited but painstakingly forged. Casual, colloquial poets like Tom Daw, Al Pittman and barfly-wunderkind Daniel Jones have been vexed by similar 'impossible fictions'. Each poet helped encourage the clichés (i.e., earthy, unspoiled by sophistication, hotly emotional) by which he was later dismissed. Les Murray has called these clichés literature's 'inbuilt habits of scorn', and their prevalence has made the displayed naivety of Trower's poems a low-hanging fruit for readers (be it plucked in praise or rebuke).

Fact is, Trower is 'merely' a logger-poet only in the sense that Frost is 'merely' a farmer-poet. Logging may have given him a subject, but Trower's poetry, like any significant poetry, is distinguished by its style, by its exceptional arrangement of sounds and meanings. This style, as I've argued, emerged from the need to reinstate the realism of hardships softened by sentimental vocabulary. But more crucially, it's also the expression of an ear smitten with the unloveliness of those hardships. What helps the rough-stuff descriptions in *Haunted Hills & Hanging Valleys* rise above lumpen-prole writing, in other words, is that they're dedicated attempts at getting new sounds down on paper. You might even say that by acting out his fascination for jaw-cracking vernacular, Trower produced the autobiography of an aesthetic. As a young man, he arrived at 'the jungle' and listened to its native speech (slackassed, mancatcher, moolah, poor stiff). As an artist he took to this language like an inner land, and migrated into it:

> One slackassed spring
> I picked up a hiring-slip from a man-catcher in a bar
> told him I'd fly up the following day
> guy was so tickled he fronted me twenty bucks.
>
> I had more good intentions than a Sally Ann street preacher
> but with all that moolah, I ran a little amok
> found a lot of beer a bottle a broad
> missed the goddamn plane.
>
> Well, I kicked myself a bit over that one
> played the duck for the mancatcher
> felt like sixteen kinds of a drunken fool
> till I read the evening paper.
>
> Seems like half a bloody mountain
> had slid down the camp I was bound for
> bulldozed the cookshack into the sea
> buried the rest of it, killed five men.
>
> One of those poor stiffs could have been me!
> That was about the only time

drinking ever handed me more
than a sore head and a bad reputation.

This – called 'A Ticket to Ramsey Hill' and published in 1986 in *The Slidingback Hills* – is a lovely effort at putting readers in touch with the briskly colloquial sentence-sounds Trower was hearing around him. If you had cause, I suppose you could dismiss the poem as crude yokelism. 'With all that moolah, I ran a little amok' reads like kitchen-sink English. In fact, it *is* kitchen-sink English. Trower's coup was simply to create a voice from such low diction, to let its monosyllabic noise loose in moments of quick, precise, vivid phrasing. The effect – an impulsively paced, extemporaneous fluency – is remarkable, as is the robust character that emerges from the unpretentious wordplay. Each word pulses with the speaker's sense of his own particular, complicated personality; uncannily so when he grins at himself at the end ('One of those poor stiffs could have been me!').

For all its coherences of syntax and stanza, it would be easy to overlook the poem's structure. Form, here, vanishes into the sonic sum of its parts, leaving an elusive, but tactile sense of someone talking aloud. Trower has a special talent for making his audio effects credible – how he gives the wryness of 'tickled' its perfect decibel level – but when one's successes are this rough and homemade they risk going unnoticed. Idiomatic grace notes like 'one slackassed spring' and 'felt like sixteen kinds of a drunken fool' are so instantly readable they lull us into ignoring the accent being registered on our ear; and how, with subtle plain speech pressures, that accent compels us to care about the speaker. There are more poems like this in *Haunted Hills & Hanging Valleys* – 'The Slidingback Hills', 'Goosequill Snags', 'The Animals', 'The Guests', 'Day to Day Blues' – and they are worth paying attention to. Trower likes percussion, brazenness, volatility; his poetry has been, in part, an attempt to find a style that can absorb those qualities. But through deft reseedings of slang, his half-sad, half-stoic voice can ripen into something altogether more unsettling. 'Industrial Poem', for example, begins bluntly. But how disarming its laid-back tone; how large the shadow its vicious story casts into the reader's mind:

That night, Slim Abernathy
pushed the wrong button and wrapped his best friend
three times around a driveshaft
in directions bones won't bend.

They shut her down and eased him out
broken most ways a man can break
yet he clung to his ruin for twenty-four hours
like a man to a life-raft for his death's sake.

They'd hardly hurried him away from there
as we stood around shockdrunk, incapable of help
when they cranked those expensive wheels up again,
started rolling out more goddamn pulp.

'Hamburger for lunch tonight, boys!'
joked a foreman to the crew.
I wish he'd smelled our hate but never even flinched
as the red-flecked sheets came through.

If you were around in 1978, you might have come across this poem in *Ragged Horizons*, the only one of Trower's books published by McClelland & Stewart. Funny to think of him briefly invading the literary centre with a major Toronto press. And indeed, this sort of outsider prickliness is precisely what invigorates Trower's poetry. His career embodies a conflict that W.J. Keith, in his 1985 *Canadian Literature in English*, identified as 'genteel versus vulgar' – a 'creative clash' Keith traces back to Susanna Moodie's *Roughing It in the Bush*. Powerful provincial sympathies colour Trower's perspective when it comes to form. The belief in intuitive expertise is central to his poetics. And there's no more absorbing example of this than the offhandedly enjambed, irregularly near-rhymed quatrains that hold together 'Industrial Poem'. In his gloss of the poem for *Arc*, Zach Wells classified it as a dressed-down ballad. I agree. The versification may look frayed, split off from any orderly pattern, but it certainly lays bare a balladeer's sense of anomie. It's the sort of voice – rueful, bitter, blazing with raw biases – that can erupt when rules of decorum are turned upside down. 'I write totally from real life. I don't build words from words', said Trower in an interview. The ending, with its dash of gore and appalling humour, is a superb summing-up of Trower's aesthetic dissent, his dismissal of literary self-importance. Do readers need to be told those 'red-flecked sheets' are Trower's own poems? Can the point be any clearer? Unlike poets, men have jobs that are dangerous and have real consequences, and, unlike poems, the mistakes they make can't be undone in the next draft. This is surely the nerviest, most unsentimental *ars poetica* in Canadian letters since Acorn put on his overcoat to type a bitter little poem.

Logging camps aren't Trower's only subject. East Vancouver factories, beer halls and flophouses have also inspired similarly jagged, unguarded, electric poems. It's clear however that, throughout it all, Trower has stayed with what he knows. His poems are at their best with people very much like himself and experiences very much like his own. His veneration of 'real life' leads to language that gives off considerable emotional heat. Trower likes the rushed-upon effect; he likes rashness. But he sometimes seems to lose interest and hurries his lines, which leaves his poems feeling fast-forwarded rather than honed.

For this reason it's probably unwise to praise Trower without also confessing that his work is kinked with all sorts of problems. His language is vivid but sometimes psychologically flat; energetic but sometimes too undifferentiated and raw. Lines are jinxed by bad wording and loose-logic; many endorse the notion that only if your pronouncements are dire enough are you viewing the world accurately. Many struggle to find a stable tone, moving between brisk statements and overcooked lyricism. Trowers can be both bewilderingly creative and bewilderingly inconsistent. There are fascinating poems that simply don't work, where the aggregate of his strategies never finds its shape. His chunky hyphenless word-clusters – Joycean fusions like 'endofnowhere' – get tiresome. This also goes for the alliteration he tends to deploy as an all-purpose anti-boredom device, sprinkling it over poems to give them a quick-fix emphasis, a synthetic pep. His love of the coursely calculated effect sometimes makes him prey to tremblingly earnest moments. Anecdotes turn writerly and sentimental, characters become caricatures.

The irony, of course, is that Trower's bad poems draw on the same fireworks as his good ones. What makes one gesture blaze with charisma can make another theatrically fizzle. Trower is indifferent to the difference, and this constructional caprice has allowed him to stay his own man. He has no interest in the fashionable sound-off-the-wall quirkiness, the odd juxtapositions. Nowhere do we feel today's ironic, no-big-deal approach to poem-making. Clumsy, yes. Heavy-handed, sure. (And why not? After all, 'any poet', Randall Jarrell wrote, 'has written enough bad poetry to scare away anybody'). But for all his errors in judgement, Trower's relation to his subject rarely feels opportunistic. His fervency is real, and never invented for the sake of a 'poem'. Unfortunately, it has also helped peg him as a poet from whom no great difficulties are expected, and thus unfit for masterdom.

But what does greatness mean, really? Aren't we tired of the Mega-Statement poets, the A+ achievements, the careerist strivings after Big Topics? Distinction-making is a vital part of criticism, but doesn't it behove us to look for ambition where it 'shouldn't' exist? For someone stuck on the obscurer reaches of our poetry, Trower's sudden popularity tells us a great deal about the level of frustration that exists with official taste. If Trower is now at the centre of a new debate, if he is helping stoke the first stirrings of an alternative conception of the Canadian canon, it's partly because of the hard-fought singularity of his work. This would be fine, insofar as it meant he was appreciated as a unique voice (which I think he is), but less fine if it meant that in his stocky, shy stout-heartedness he was branded a regional curiosity (which he isn't). *Haunted Hills & Hanging Valleys* furnishes our first serious look at Trower's style and sensibility, so it's no surprise that the cover features hills thickly scrimmed in fog, dark vistas to be delved into. Please do.

MODERN CANADIAN POETRY: AN ANTHOLOGY

ANTHOLOGIES ARE ALTERNATE WORLDS. They create, through distortions of arrangement, verse universes that unfold differently from the one readers already know. No better recent example of this exists than *Modern Canadian Poets* (2010), released by British publisher Carcanet Press and edited by Canadian poet-critics Todd Swift and Evan Jones.

Swift and Jones believe the reason for our poetry's poor exportability is a nationalist fervour that elbows aside first-rate – if not world-class – Canadian poets whose only sin is their interest in British and American models. This thesis led to an intriguing thought experiment: what would a Canadian poetry canon that actually welcomed such internationalism look like? The answer, if *Modern Canadian Poets* is any indication, will give Canadianists heartburn. Atwood, Ondaatje and Purdy are out. Also chucked are Lane, Bowering, Kroetsch and McKay. Instead, the dream team is headed by – wait for it – Alfred Bailey, John Glassco, Anne Wilkinson, Douglas LePan and Daryl Hine.

Huh? Precisely. The anthology tries to crack an old dream: assemble a 'beachhead of poetry' compelling enough to melt the indifference of the larger English-language audience. The editors wanted 'individuals as opposed to schools, leaders as opposed to adherents'; poets, in other words, who flashed with 'hybrid, cosmopolitan, linguistic genius'. The fact that so few Canadian readers will recognize these poets is, in a sense, the point.

I can think of no equivalent for what Swift and Jones have attempted: to rebuild a national canon from scratch using the obscurest of figures. Is it subversive? Well, factor in that Carcanet is one of the UK's leading poetry presses, that the last foreign-published Canadian poetry anthology appeared half a century ago, and that many British poets will take their first cues about Canadian poetry from this book – then you get a sense of the exhilarating sneak attack Swift and Jones have perpetrated on our image abroad.

These two men are not alone in breaking ranks with the CanLit bloc: they belong to a generation that has sided with the neglected, maligned and unfairly out-of-print. Let's call these implacable young critics the 'rebooters'. Amanda Jernigan, for example, has been instrumental in plucking Richard Outram from a premature limbo. Zach Wells has championed Kenneth Leslie, Peter Trower and Peter Van Toorn. For Evan Jones, it's Daryl Hines. Jason Gurial has made a compelling case for George Johnston. And Anita Lahey – who, as editor of *Arc* poetry magazine dedicated an entire 2007 issue to 'Canada's Forgotten and Neglected Poets' – keeps the flame for Elizabeth Roberts.

Each of these rebooters is digging up what has been buried, rooting for a second option. They confront notions of what belongs in our literary heritage through a process of backtracking. Cultural consensus, they remind us, is a special effect sparked from the right conditions coming together – conditions that can be revisited and, if we're lucky, challenged. Deep down, rebooters believe the poetry world as it 'is' rests on very thin ontological ice.

The hope of a rebooter, however, isn't simply that their chosen poet will be saved from forgetting, but that a previously discredited set of pleasure-principles will be salvaged as well: technical mastery, sophistication, eloquence. What rebooters, by implication, dismiss isn't 'Canadian poetry' but the programmative version fashioned from it. Prodding us to think about what failed to happen, therefore, the rebooter helpfully exposes literature for what it is: a vast multiverse in which one reality briefly wins out. A 'canon', in other words, is what emerges when the branching possibilities narrow down to specific winners (Al Purdy) while the have-nots (Ron Everson) crowd the dead ends, representing plausible-but-never-realized universes. Universes that, often, are many parsecs more sparkling, madcap and mischievous than the one currently inflicted on us.

Anthologies like *Modern Canadian Poetry* are vital in keeping our beliefs off balance. They are vents for the sense of contingency that oxygenizes every era with doubts. By marshalling an otherwise random bunch of poets and pointing them in a new direction, rebooters Swift and Evans have created an imaginary zone of real facts to unpin our shared recognitions. In one of Borges' great stories, a group of shadowy conspirators invent a counter-reality called Tlön only to watch it invade the real world. We can only hope.

STEAMPUNK ZONE

In our mashup-mad era, we yearn for unpigeonholeability. We don't want to be different. We want to be weird. We want to be total category-killers. As a result, it's hard to find a poet – free-versifier and formalist alike – who doesn't believe at heart that he or she is far too heterodox to be trapped in existing definitions of traditional and experimental. Contemporary poetry now comprises a vast invented form: the godknowswhat.

That the selections in *Best Canadian Poetry in English 2012* echo and reprise this yearning should come as no surprise. From Rachel Lebowitz's unnerving, nursery rhyme-inflected prose cycle ('Cottonpolis') to Robert Earl Stewart's smoky, image-loaded stream of consciousness ('A Wind-Aided Fire'), this book is a mixed bag. It's the outcome, one might say, of a collective decision taken by Canadian poets to dart in all directions at once. To be sure, I plucked these poems from print and online journals with no bias except to find verse that provided a fresh entry into reality; that offered something, some equivalence between sound and feeling, I didn't already know, or couldn't find elsewhere. Good poets are stylists, and I hunted for styles whose distinctive qualities generated memorable insights. Yet, when assembled, many of the one-of-a-kind elements I admired – which each seemed unexpected, an emergency measure – turned out to share the same triggers. It made me uneasy. Don't misunderstand: these are wickedly good poems. But the task of finding them has forced me to reflect on the high price of writing under the influence of what F.R. Leavis would have called our 'poetical modes'.

On my desk, sit three squat anthologies from three countries: *Identity Parade* edited by Roddy Lumsden, published in the UK; *American Hybrid*, edited by David St. John and Cole Swenson, published in the US; and *Open Field* edited by Canadian Sina Queyras. All appeared within the last seven years. To read them, close on the heels of one another, is to be left agape at the current scale of Anglo-American verse. The books add up to 1200 pages, nearly one-thousand poems and comprise almost two-hundred poets from three countries. And that's only as far as these three tomes will let us see: there's a good deal more out there. One recalls Ian Hamilton's observation, back in 1994, that English poetry 'can no longer be thought of in the singular'. The shift, he argued, was from poetry to poetries. The fissioning has since escalated until, at present, English-language poets all seem to speak in tongues. Everywhere we're overrun by franchises of self-defined difference. To a certain extent, this is bardoltry as usual. Good poets have always tried to stand apart from their literary age. But today that individualism, to be accordingly recognized, needs to pay fealty to a period that has scrambled easy classifications. And what does such a period demand of our poems? Boundary-crossing, genre-splicing, exploratory flings between once-irreconcilable techniques. There may no longer be a generally endorsed sense of what constitutes poetry, but almost everyone agrees on what a poet needs to do in order not to be left behind. Thanks to the internet, even national identity is growing increasingly irrelevant as cultural trends continue to be erased by a global synching-up of motives. *Identity Parade* surveys the 'pluralist' generation of British and Irish poetry, *American Hybrid* showcases American models of 'hybridization' and *Open Field* nets Canadians who reveal a 'particular blend of formal and innovative work'. English-speaking poets may be separated by a border and an ocean, but the zeitgeist has assigned each of us the same thesis.

Canadian poetry seems ideally suited to this era. Its masterworks, such as Irving Layton's 'A Tall Man Executes a Jig' or A.M. Klein's 'A Portrait of the Poet as Landscape', have always been marked by a glorious miscegenation of influences; or, to use Peter Van Toorn's words from his 1985 book *Mountain Tea*, 'there's always a carnival voice /

calling you inside to see the choice / of goods usually hawked at the honeyed / gates of paradise'. Heeding this carnival voice has turned the recent scene into a teeming bazaar, where younger poets proudly wear the bright, patchwork clothes of their cosmopolitan nurturing. But something else defines this group. They are the first generation for whom the battle lines of mainstream versus avant-garde (what an earlier time dubbed 'cooked' and 'raw') have outlived their usefulness. The intense need to set free a shifting sense of self has helped produce the unusual range of devices in this book: intricate puns, up-to-the-minute slang, scat-singing wordplay, many-sided metaphors. These devices are brandished by poets who have not only come out the other side of the poetry wars, but aspire to heal the divisions in their poems. We see this in the cerebral, cubist elegance of Lisa Robertson's 'Scene' or the flagrantly self-conscious, gear-switching rhymes of Shane Rhodes' 'The Paperweight' or the ludic largess of Adam Dickinson's 'Call to Arms'. These poets belong to a circle that aggressively resist schools, unsettles assumptions and crossbreeds near-infinite varieties of form, from rhyme-rich free verse to mishmashes of lyric and found texts.

Two recent debuts can serve as examples. In *Crabwise to the Hounds* (2008), Jeramy Dodds specializes in densely metaphoric accounts (surrealist tall tales? Gothic head trips?) that would look right at home in experimental lit mags like *The Capilano Review* or *Rampike*. But the book also flashes some serious formalist cred, with Ormsbyesque passages that nestle enthusiastically into their internal rhymes, assonances and alliterations ('Capillaries are winter maples scrubbing the mist' or 'Shipwrights shoulder-pole / bedrolls and Swede-saws / through a cellophane of rain'). Which is it? Which faction does Dodds belong to? Who knows. It's how poets like him confound that commands our attention. Linda Besner also fails to fit. Her poetry marries a maniacal love for oddity with a loathing for recycled language. One standout in *The Id Kid* (2011) is 'Villeneuve Villanelle' in which Besner, who lived in polyglot Montreal for many years, draws on Canada's double heritage of French and English to devise an argot that evades ordinary prose syntax. In the process, she orchestrates an entirely original soundscape:

A van, verily, *une livraison, l'avenir arrived d'ailleurs*, a day
avowed comely, *lueur d'avril* bespoke, bespilled – *ça brille.*
L'imprévu s'avance impervious; appears apace, *s'est envolé.*

A novice driver, *évidemment.* One *virage rapide*, and all *bouleversé*,
an avalanche of navel oranges *devant la fruiterie.*
A future in delivery, *vraiment.* Moreover, this arrival – *le camion, la journée* –

grand évenement for the vagrants pocketing oranges *à volonté*,
poursuivi by the vainglorious vendor, *à petit avail. Ainsi*,
unforeseen advances; *une apparition imperméable* that *vite* blows away.

Une idée, maybe, of ivied-over avenues *à suivre*, asway
with lilas, novelistic verandas. *Rossignols*. Lily-of-the-valley.
En accouchant, l'espoir. Arriving, *d'ailleurs*, a truck, a day *en verité*,

a vaudeville on *la rue* Villeneuve: thrown oranges, oranges *lancées*;
flown oranges, *oranges volées*. Runnelling nuance *d'après ceci*:
une proposition inattendue; ghost in a raincoat, *échappé.*

Abundance, rolling. *Une voie* beloved *d'agrumes*, ravished *d'abeilles.*
And *attendant aux feux*, unbeknownst to driver, fruitman, *sans-abris*:
a van, verily. *Une livraison, l'avenir* arrived *d'ailleurs* – a day
imprévu s'avance impervious. Appears apace; then *envolé.*

One could argue, with justification, that Besner is simply reinventing a traditional form. But the poem also struck the *soi-disant* experimental poet Sina Queryas, who wondered on her blog if 'the way this poem is built might be similar to the way a conceptual poem is built'. Queryas' question exposes the grey zone many brash arrivers – Michael Lista, Joshua Trotter, Leigh Kotsilidis among them – now thrive in. It's a steampunk zone: populated with lavishly anachronistic, retro-futuristic inventions – all creolized, vibrant and often intricate. Steampunk was popularized by speculative works of fiction like William Gibson's *The Difference Engine* (1990) and Neal Stephenson's *The Diamond Age*. In those books, gadgets of the future are grafted onto Victorian sensibilities and vice versa. (Imagine Longfellow augmented by Bluetooth or nanobots in coal clouds.) Our younger poets practise a similar 'path not taken' creativity, defined by salvage and customization, neither backward nor progressive. If Canadian poetry were a sci-fi novel, it would take place in 1900 London with robots, goggle-donning hackers, airships, gear-driven computers and zombie hordes.

None of this has led to anything you'd call a revolution, though their poems – with their unpredictability, braininess, wisecracks and backtalk – are glimpses of the exhilarating upside-world Canadian poetry might find itself in when completely free of colonial concerns. This current crop of poets doesn't seem to suffer anxiety about what they do, what's allowable, what tone to take. No one loses any sleep over a reader's confusion. They believe poetry has the power, if not the obligation, to exceed interpretation, and their poems always hunt for larger intellectual frameworks to join (check out the endnotes in their books, which every season grow longer and more esoteric). We once prized homegrown styles cut off from the world. Today the rule is 'only connect'. No association is too odd or unlikely. Ideas exist in a state of high-spirited hyperlinkability.

As a result, more is going on in Canadian poetry than ever before – more sonnets, sestinas, flarf cycles, centos, erasure poems, plunderverse, uncreative writing, concrete. There is also a lot of what no one likes to admit: fatigue. Who can keep up? And for those who try, how does one make sense of it all? Maybe a better way to address this comes from (of all places) the catalogue bumf for Jacob McArthur Mooney's 2005 debut *The New Layman's Almanac*. As a poet, Mooney is fascinated by questions of decipherability ('Not the word but the inflec-/tion it presents'), and his poems mull over the results of various kind of reckonings ('1+1–1=1'). The publicity kit picks up on this. 'As a collection', we're told, 'its primary question is: What are the rules?' This is an excellent question. Much better than claiming there are no rules or insisting we break the rules. This is because 'What are the rules?' assumes the existence of a game. (It doesn't hurt that it sounds like something uttered by some poor sod – a friend of a friend, roped in at the last minute – as he's being handed a pile of poker chips.) As it happens, there are basically two kinds of games. Those with rules you need to know before you play them, and those with rules that can only be discovered as you play them. In his indispensable book *Questions of Possibility*, David Caplan argues that 'the plurality of alternatives that contemporary poets encounter' has destabilized our sense of 'acceptable options'. A circumstance, Caplan says, that 'makes the poets' formal choices nearly impossible to anticipate'. In other words: forget what you know. We've been invited to a game held together by a set of rules that are self-devised, unique, complex and subject to instant change.

Isn't this, in a sense, what I've always wanted? Yes. It's been our destiny ever since the mongrel brilliance of E.J. Pratt's gigantic, fast-paced verse-narratives began appearing one hundred years ago. So why am I glum? Because while our poetry is now home to ravishingly odd confections, and while many of these poems bring me under their spell, they never quite make the sale. I'm a pushover for anything 'counter, original, spare, strange', as Hopkins put it. I read such poems for matters of style, of sound. I read to understand why I like what I do, why some poems seem to me more memorable than others. I read, ultimately, to take this knowledge into my own poems. But after a point, after celebrating the explosion of poetic techniques, I have to ask myself: what are all those techniques *for*, exactly? Jonathan Ball's Borgesian *Clockfire* (2010) was an exceptionally interesting book: 77 impossible-to-stage plays ('The audience enters the theatre. One at a time. As they enter, they are slaughtered. The curtain hangs in mid-air'). Yet a part of me fears this is poetry in the same way short-selling is considered legal: by the skin of its teeth. W.H. Auden once described his dream reader as someone who cherished 'curious prosodic fauna like bacchics and choriambs'. But bacchics and choriambs are worthless unless they're intrinsic to the perception that seeks them out; unless they're essential for minting a specific kind of meaning – a sharpness of feeling, an urgency – that those devices, and only those devices, make possible. *Clockfire* is Ball's version of Auden's bacchics and choriambs. The book is its own nonce form, and as such, a steampunk act of conceptual savvy; a cool idea, well-executed. But is it the by-product of a poet getting into deep trouble? The function of a mind grappling at genuinely felt expression? Am I the only one who found himself impressed, then distressed that I could grasp a great deal about the poems, except why they were written?

I don't mean to pick on Ball, who is one of our most talented younger poets, but to use his fascinating book to make a larger point: that there's difference between a game and a poem. Both should be played with as much skill as possible, but a game is played for its own sake, while a poem, and our pleasure in its gambits, depends on the recognition it is saying something true about life. A poem, essentially, is a game with a single price of admission: that its rules aren't cut off from the sadness, exultation or distress that pushed the poet to fashion those rules in the first place. I've reconciled myself to the fact that we've moved past poetry as the zero-sum sport Frost called 'prowess – something to achieve, something to win or lose'. Yet we seem pretty far from the only other option likely to generate memorable work: the clue-gathering Auden called the 'game of knowledge, a bringing to consciousness, by naming them, of emotions and their hidden relationships'.

A poem, according to Auden's formulation, comes to a head. It's a breakthrough into clarity that draws together the maximum information available. This requires us to believe words aren't just what they do, but what they mean; that form isn't just an R&D staging area – will popping in this stanzaic shape make the poem more acoustically untypical? – but embodies a sense of responsibility for the effects being created in other minds. Gregory Betts' *The Others Raised in Me* (2010) is a collection of 150 poems that cuts and remixes words found in Shakespeare's Sonnet 150. Matthew Tierney's *The Ides* uses software to record twenty seconds of audio from the radio, which he then transcribes onto an Excel spreadsheet and tags according to various criteria. In each case, the results have been fascinating. But what untrendy mystery, what human plight, hope or grief have these projects brought to consciousness? Yes, I get it: the goal, in part, is to escape the trap of the already-done. But even so, what are the stakes? Why should we care? Is all that steampunking being applied to profound ends or merely skin-deep? To be sure, what appears to drive Betts and Tierney is anything but trivial: to rebuild the foundations of the lyric from scratch, to submit their nonpareil concoctions as counterprogramming for the Canadian canon. And yet that strikes me as the easy part; made obvious by the scores of poets doing it. Such poetry is frequently over-deliberate; a didactic version of originality, one that keeps insisting on its novelty. Much of it testifies, at best, to the presence of a creative habit, but not the intensity of art. Diction and syntax are paired up in distractingly pleasant, half-lucid marriages which rarely achieve the organization and intention required for poetry. Umberto Eco has called this drug 'suggestive verbalism' and too many Canadian poets are hooked on it. The real game of writing poetry remains the part that rests entirely on a lucky break: the creation of a singular, stand-alone word structure that satisfies emotionally and intellectually while signalling itself as an artifice.

Have our poets been that lucky? Absolutely. I love the backbone Asa Boxer puts into his hunches: he produces uncannily precise images that grow out of his intuitions about sound. If you find yourself unexpectedly moved by Amanda Jernigan lines it's largely due to the way she has streamlined her statements but doubled their aural weight: everything is sadder because the words are crisper. I marvel over how Nyla Matuk can dress abstractions in sensualized details and how her surrealistic thinking moves crabwise; cross-referring, branching out. What ultimately lingers aren't her insights – which land cleanly and memorably – but the thought-process whose zigs and zags are their own reward. Or Karen Solie, whose brainy verse-patterns decode emotions to a chill clarity. The result: black humour, a discreetly rich pessimism and a mind in constant, fascinated dialogue with its own disappointments. Bruce Taylor has patented a new genre: the meditative cliffhanger. His poems take the shape of an idea or mood clarifying itself in stages, leaving readers on tenterhooks to find out where he'll go next. Hairpin enjambment – every line taking a sharp left turn – is the most recognizable suspense-building feature, giving the poems a jaggedly uneven look. Visually, this advertises his quick reflexes, but also a living sense of form: Taylor adds new lines to pull new ideas in, allowing him to continuously refresh what he is thinking. As a result, his poems never feel like they are created top-down, from a concept, but bottom-up, one word at a time.

But, just as often, Canadian poets don't play the odds as much as stack the deck. As more of them keep one eye on the lyric tradition and one eye on whatever comes next, they increasingly try to force a breakthrough by splitting the difference. The result can be too perfect, as if it were the winner of a contest to compose the ideal hybrid poem. Adam Dickinson has a project called *Anatomic: Semiotic Bodies, Chemical Environments* for which he plans to subject himself to exhaustive chemical testing. Why does he intend to do this? 'By making a map of the toxicological and symbiotic circumstances of my body', he says, 'I want to then use this information to create methodologies for producing poems'. Whether Dickinson's 'methodologies' will produce good poems remains to be seen, but so unimpeachably does his super-experiment ape the terms of what we now expect from our poems, the venture lives in its own hybridized universe. Indeed, the dominance of the steampunk aesthetic, the easy availability of its procedures, has led to a growing uncertainty about how to discuss such linguistic lab work, or even whether anything meaningful can be said at all. The entrepreneurial spree of poets patenting new forms, and the feeling of optimism and copiousness that accompanies it, overwhelms taste. When every poet happens to be writing exactly the kind of poem he or she set out to write, and every poem embodies exactly its theoretical intent, it becomes harder to say which poems are good, and why; how one kind of recombining and estranging differs from another; what books are truly counter, original, spare, strange.

In practical terms, the situation has left reviewers, editors and anthologists scrambling to describe poems in ways they hope will pique the curiosity of readers. That means, too often, sentences are variations on 'so-and-so's poetry exists in the middle ground between tradition and innovation'. Period styles in poetry in other words, beget period styles in poetics. In our case, criticism becomes a kind of catechism, a reiteration of steampunk principles. Take Jeff Latosik who describes Dodds as 'One half the muscular lyricism of a Ken Babstock or Karen Solie and one half the unfettered linguistic play of a Christian Bök or Margaret Christakos'. Or Rhodes' publisher NeWest who says he 'combines moving lyrical poetry with experimental verve'. Indeed, when even an excellent critic like Zach Wells is compelled to characterize Trotter's poetry as 'mix[ing] the anti-matter of postmodern language games and shifty subjectivity with the matter of traditional structures and lyric poignancy,' you realize no one is immune. Such explication, however well meant, is so far removed from what the poetry is actually doing that it becomes a way of concealing a vacancy in our thinking. The area between tradition and innovation is an intellectual fiction: you cannot go there to write poems. It doesn't exist. What *does* exist is the thousands of ways poets compose with and against the formulas available in English. You cannot, a priori, negotiate a trade-off between round avant peg and square trad hole. One *can* invent a voice that catches the friction between carefully crafted structure and spontaneous departure. Indeed, the pervasiveness of terms like 'hybrid', 'plurality' and 'elliptical' – or what Ron Silliman calls 'third-wave poetics' and Jay Millar calls 'retro avant garde' and Queyras calls the 'avant lyric' – marks a new conventional wisdom that is part conviction, part guff, part make-believe. And as intellectual thresholds are reduced to practically zero, we are fast approaching a kind of free economy: it costs nothing to blog about these things. God knows it means nothing.

There's a lovely image in William Gibson's novel *Count Zero* (1986) of a sentient computer deep in an abandoned space station, creating beautiful Cornell boxes out of junk. The boxes make it into the hands of admiring art dealers on Earth who are unaware of their provenance. In the same way, Canadian poets generate, as if on automatic, wonderful contrivances from disparate materials. These are poets who care about their poetry and work hard at it. Like watchmakers, they build machines out of the minutest parts; unlike watches, these machines are full of beguiling generosity for errant incidents. But too often we are faced with an artificial intelligence, simulated for believability, not an actual style. Style is what happens when originality becomes indistinguishable from the poem itself. It's a way of mingling the unfamiliar 'new' and the still-compelling 'old' so that we can no longer separate them. Style is therefore the result of a voice so grounded in its subject, the effect is not a self-regarding newness but a newness absorbed into the poem, a newness ripening into something effortlessly manifold and available. Such poems may not be the sort fusionists like, but they are the sort real poets write.

III

NEXT DOOR CAFÉ

We were bored, so we stayed. The days knocked deep
into other days. A glacialness set in, and life kept pace
with the dried fruit in the jar. Brushed steel gave back
our pissed-off bits, our doubled selves so drained of disguise
we forgot where it was we were hoping to go, holed up
all summer in a corner so dark you'd half expect bison
chalked on a cave-face every time we cadged a light.
It was the kind of place where morning fell for everyone
but harder for some, where bad decisions were lived
counter-clockwise, and endlessly refitted to finish up flush,
where afternoons were a gradual squander of sobriety,
shot glasses lamped with whisky on cue and empties
were the crags of a quandary drunkenness clung to.
Tables where, outside the shrieking reach of the talkers,
can't-sleeps stayed and night-shifters cooled heels
attended by soul-tools: cellphone, lighter, cigarette.
Nights of middle-aged men enduring middle-aged men
in their cups, buying rounds, half-cusped on high stools.
Sun-up found a few run aground, upshouldered hulls,
while our own lives were an endless keel-scrape where
the pluperfect errand was the errand always deferred.
A kind of time travel, I guess. We sat back and watched
the future screen its clichés of us: those besuited
and briefcased, with their died-and-gone-to-heaven whistle
when handed a pint; those done-to-a-turn divorcees
in duffle coat and boots (wine-sipping casualties of the wife wars);
those who, smashed, stand too suddenly slewing into you,
and those who, if you join, you join uninvited.

THE KNOCK KNOCK OF UNREGARDED HOURS

NEXT DOOR CAFÉ is an actual bar in Parc Extension, a formerly Greek north-end Montreal neighbourhood. Home to many of the city's poorest, 'Parc Ex' was a crime-ridden no-go zone until the late eighties. But over the last decade, its streets have been bustling with new immigrants (Sri Lankans, Sikhs, Pakistani) and young renters (students, hipster couples, young families) pushed northward by skyrocketing rents in über-gentrified Mile End. My wife and I were part of this Plateau exodus, and moved into the area in 2003. Soon after, Jennifer began bartending part-time at Next Door Café, a testosterone-rich drinking hole where old and new – lifelong Parc-Exers and Mile-End expats – rubbed shoulders.

Next Door Café was a *carpe noctem* kind of place. I don't mean it came alive after dark, but that nighttime was when the regulars drifted in. It was an astonishing pileup of undesirables: near-derelicts, loners, bullshit artists, showboaters, blue-collar professionals and whack jobs. Their stories – as relayed to me by Jennifer, in the early morning after one of her shifts as we walked back home – were stock tall tales, the kind that tee up a confrontation with cop, or wife or boss, and feature the killer comeback. They were the kind of stories told by men who long ago were forced to settle for who they were but came to the bar to fictionalize better stats (humiliations endured: 0). These were men who wanted to establish a rep for no retreat, who wanted to be on record for owning a gumption always ready to move up a gear. Though you also knew they were men who woke up to the knock knock of unregarded hours, and lay there – dry-mouthed, perspiring

– seized by an up-late, can't sleep, whose there, name-writ-on-water kind of feeling.

I hope the poem captures some of their shtick and sadness. Mixed into my effort were also memories of my own barfly days. Younger, my friends and I loved nothing better than to hole up in some off-trail establishment. Far from being antidotes to loneliness, or houses of company and community, bars seemed to us the saddest places on earth. Of course, we had absolutely no business being there. We were well-fed, mother-pampered Italian boys, with good homes and large families. We didn't have a clue what it meant to be down on your luck. Those bars gave us a crash course. Unsurprisingly, we became obsessed by their rough-patch mood, the heartbreak hanging in the air, the sense that life was now too late for wish-fulfillments or third-act redemptions. The experience – surrounded by heads bent over drink or tilted up in quiet talk – was a lot like sitting in a Sunday pew. The solitude enforced by the sum of all those second thoughts heightened my senses to everything around me: the low light, the TV screen, the sounds of ice clinking, the glasses being placed beside on the plank of polished wood (it was, on reflection, the beginnings of the prepoem creative 'zone' poets enter when excited by events). Unlike church, however, the ritualism was devoted to the breakdown of the body and destruction of the spirit. How apt that, in some US states, pub owners once doubled as undertakers.

'Next Door Café' sprung from those dead bodies, men idling in a borderland existence between one condition and the next. It led directly to the poem's style: compressed, noun-heavy, with cautious, slightly energy-sapped enjambments. What rescues the languidness of those lines, in my opinion, is the way the language stands and looks. The descriptions seem to me to have a compound-eyed quality: they try to see around and behind the various male codes on display. And while the poem is ultimately about unprogress, inertia, the failure to learn from mistakes ('where bad decisions were lived/counter-clockwise, and endlessly refitted to finish up flush'), the poem also appears to be tracking an insight. By degrees, and through repeated sounds and words, the speaker is figuring something out. We see that in the gallery of alternative selves being tried on for fit. It's poetry as method-acting: the speaker's inner life condensed and generalised into sundry portraits of guyhood. The poem could be read as a kind of a mini-*Bildungsroman* that tries to square up the many sides of the speaker's personality. The voice, as some have told me, is difficult to situate, which I guess underscores the most difficult trick of all: to pose as yourself.

As for the poet, here's what he figured out: a poem will often bear witness to predicaments for which it can offer no consolation. That realization only surfaced when I wrote the last line and could go no further – though I doubt it's the sort of 'click shut' ending Yeats had in mind.

ACKNOWLEDGEMENTS

Thank you to the editors of the following magazines, anthologies and books where these essays and reviews were previously published, sometimes in very different versions. ¶ 'Lazy Bastardism: A Notebook', *Poetry*, January 2010. ¶ 'Margaret Atwood', *Arc Poetry Magazine*, Winter 2008. ¶ 'Margaret Avison', *Canadian Poetry*, no. 59, Fall/Winter 2006. ¶ 'Earle Birney', *The Globe & Mail*, 12 December 2006. ¶ 'J.D. Black', *The Montreal Review of Books*, Spring 2007. ¶ 'James Denoon', *Arc Poetry Magazine*, Summer 2007. ¶ 'John Glassco', *John Glassco and the Other Montreal: Selected Poems* (Frog Hollow Press, 2011). ¶ 'Michael Harris', *Language Acts: Anglo-Quebec Poetry, 1976 to the 21st Century*, eds. Jason Camlot & Todd Swift (Vehicule Press, 2007). ¶ 'Adam Kirsch', *Poetry*, May 2008. ¶ 'James Langer', *The Globe & Mail*, 18 June 2009. ¶ 'Irving Layton', *Quill & Quire*, March 2006. ¶ 'Medbh McGuckian', *Poetry*, November 2008. ¶ 'Don McKay', *Books in Canada*, May-June 2007. ¶ 'A.F. Moritz', *Books in Canada*, December 2004. ¶ 'bpNichol', *Maisonneuve Magazine*, Spring 2011. ¶ 'Eric Ormsby', *Canadian Notes & Queries*, no. 68, 2005. ¶ 'David O'Meara', *Arc Poetry Magazine*, Summer 2009. ¶ 'Jay Parini & Tom Paulin', *The Globe & Mail*, 28 June 2008. ¶ 'Robyn Sarah', *Arc Poetry Magazine*, Winter 2010. ¶ 'Karen Solie', *Canadian Notes & Queries*, no. 71, 2007. ¶ 'Anne Szumigalski', *The Globe & Mail*, 26 August 2006. ¶ 'Peter Trower', *Books in Canada*, September 2005. ¶ 'Modern Canadian Poetry', *Quill & Quire*, April 2011. ¶ 'The Steam Punk Zone', *The Best Canadian Poetry 2012*, eds. Carmine Starnino & Molly Peacock (Tightrope Books, 2012). ¶ 'The Knock Knock of Unregarded Hours', *Approaches to Poetry: The Pre-Poem Moment*, ed. Shane Neilson (Frog Hollow Press, 2009).

This book is set in a digital revival of a typeface designed by the printer John Baskerville and cut in steel by John Handy in the 1750s.

ABCDEFGHIJKLMNOPQURSTVWXYZ
ABCDEFGHIJKLMNOPQURSTVWXYZ
abcdefghijklmnopqurstvwxyz & 1234567890
ABCDEFGHIJKLMNOPQURSTVWXYZ
abcdefghijklmnopqurstvwxyz & 1234567890

John Baskerville (1706–75) turned to printing in midlife after a successful career as a writing master and a Japaner of household goods in Birmingham, England. Finding the available printing methods and materials lackluster, Baskerville simply followed his own tastes, designing his own types and modifying his presses, inks, papers and technique to his liking. The results were stunning. Although he printed books for Cambridge University for a while, Baskerville's innovations were largely dismissed by his countrymen and his publishing ventures were not profitable. English readers simply preferred the rough, laid paper and the wonky warmth of William Caslon's Baroque-flavoured typefaces to Baskerville's smooth, white paper, crisp Neoclassical letters and intensely black ink.

This prejudice may have had more to do with the fact that Baskerville was an iconoclast and an outsider than with the particular results of his innovations. The American printer and diplomat Benjamin Franklin, after listening to a Londoner pontificate on how Baskerville's terrible printing was 'blinding all the readers of the nation', produced an unlabelled type specimen and asked the fellow to instruct him on Baskerville's failings. The guest obliged, pointing out 'disproportions' and 'errors' in the type with a tone of authority. In fact, he only succeeded in demonstrating his own ignorance. The specimen Franklin showed him displayed William Caslon's types. 'I spared him that time the confusion of being told that these were the types he had been reading all his life', Franklin wrote to Baskerville. 'He never discovered the painful disproportion in them, till he thought they were yours.'

It wasn't until the early twentieth century, when revivals were cut for Monotype and Linotype typecasting systems, that Baskerville's types earned their proper due. Elizabeth Bishop once wrote that she felt Monotype Baskerville was her preferred typeface for poetry books. Printed letterpress, Baskerville indeed holds its own. One of the most soundly designed books of Canadian poetry I own is set in Baskerville (E.J. Pratt's *Collected Poems,* designed by Frank Davies in 1958). But the flat, modern offset-printed page has not been as sympathetic a medium for the fine hairlines of Baskerville's letters, and on screens his type fairs even worse, at least for continuous reading. If it is to be successfully used today, some revision will perhaps be necessary, guided by a sensitivity to the characteristics of the media which mirrors Baskerville's own willingness to tinker until he'd achieved the desired effect. The digital version of Baskerville used in this book has been slightly modified to that end; the experiment continues. – A.S.

 Gaspereau Press acknowledges the support of the Canada Council for the Arts and the Nova Scotia Department of Communities, Culture & Heritage.

Typeset in Baskerville by Andrew Steeves & printed offset and bound under the direction of Gary Dunfield at Gaspereau Press, Kentville, Nova Scotia.

1 3 5 7 6 4 2

Library and Archives Canada Cataloguing in Publication

Starnino, Carmine
Lazy bastardism / Carmine Starnino.

ISBN 978-1-55447-118-8

1. Canadian poetry (English) – 21st century – History and criticism. I. Title.

PS8155.1.S73 2012 C811'.609 C2012-905456-9

GASPEREAU PRESS LIMITED ¶ GARY DUNFIELD & ANDREW STEEVES ¶ PRINTERS & PUBLISHERS
47 Church Avenue, Kentville, Nova Scotia, B4N 2M7
Literary Outfitters & Cultural Wilderness Guides
www.gaspereau.com